Grassroots Economies

Anthropology, Culture and Society

Series Editors:
Jamie Cross, University of Edinburgh,
Christina Garsten, Stockholm University
and
Joshua O. Reno, Binghamton University

Recent titles:

The Limits to Citizen Power:
Participatory Democracy and the
Entanglements of the State
VICTOR ALBERT

The Heritage Machine:
Fetishism and Domination
in Maragateria, Spain
PABLO ALONSO GONZÁLEZ

Vicious Games:
Capitalism and Gambling
REBECCA CASSIDY

Anthropologies of Value
EDITED BY LUIS FERNANDO ANGOSTO-FERRANDEZ
AND GEIR HENNING PRESTERUDSTUEN

Ethnicity and Nationalism:
Anthropological Perspectives
Third Edition
THOMAS HYLLAND ERIKSEN

Fredrik Barth:
An Intellectual Biography
THOMAS HYLLAND ERIKSEN

Small Places, Large Issues:
An Introduction to Social
and Cultural Anthropology
Fourth Edition
THOMAS HYLLAND ERIKSEN

What is Anthropology?
Second Edition
THOMAS HYLLAND ERIKSEN

Deepening Divides:
How Territorial Borders and Social
Boundaries Delineate Our World
EDITED BY DIDIER FASSIN

At the Heart of the State:
The Moral World of Institutions
DIDIER FASSIN, ET AL.

Anthropology and Development:
Challenges for the Twenty-first Century
KATY GARDNER AND DAVID LEWIS

Children of the Welfare State:
Civilising Practices in Schools,
Childcare and Families
LAURA GILLIAM AND EVA GULLØV

Private Oceans:
The Enclosure and Marketisation
of the Seas
FIONA MCCORMACK

The Rise of Nerd Politics:
Digital Activism and Political Change
JOHN POSTILL

Base Encounters:
The US Armed Forces in South Korea
ELISABETH SCHOBER

Ground Down by Growth:
Tribe, Caste, Class and Inequality in
Twenty-First-Century India
ALPA SHAH, JENS LERCHE, ET AL

When Protest Becomes Crime:
Politics and Law in Liberal Democracies
CAROLIJN TERWINDT

Race and Ethnicity in Latin America
Second Edition
PETER WADE

Grassroots Economies

Living with Austerity in Southern Europe

Edited by Susana Narotzky

First published 2020 by Pluto Press
345 Archway Road, London N6 5AA

www.plutobooks.com

Copyright © Susana Narotzky 2020

The right of the individual contributors to be identified as the authors of this work has been asserted by them in accordance with the Copyright, Designs and Patents Act 1988.

British Library Cataloguing in Publication Data
A catalogue record for this book is available from the British Library

ISBN 978 0 7453 4022 7 Hardback
ISBN 978 0 7453 4023 4 Paperback
ISBN 978 1 7868 0577 5 PDF eBook
ISBN 978 1 7868 0579 9 Kindle eBook
ISBN 978 1 7868 0578 2 EPUB eBook

This book is printed on paper suitable for recycling and made from fully managed and sustained forest sources. Logging, pulping and manufacturing processes are expected to conform to the environmental standards of the country of origin.

Typeset by Stanford DTP Services, Northampton, England

Simultaneously printed in the United Kingdom and United States of America

Contents

List of Abbreviations   vii
Series Preface   viii
Acknowledgements   ix

1. Introduction: Grassroots Economics in Europe   1
   Susana Narotzky

PART I: MAKING A LIVING

2. Bondage Unemployment and Intra-class Tensions in Greek Energy Restructuring   25
   Theodora Vetta

3. Work, Wage and Subsidy: Making a Living Between Regulation and Informalization   50
   Antonio Maria Pusceddu

4. Criminalizing Livelihoods: "Illegal Vegetables" and the Return to the Home   73
   Carmen Leidereiter

5. Austerity, Social Values and Value: The Social Economy and Entrepreneurship in Catalonia   92
   Patricia Homs

PART II: SOCIAL REPRODUCTION

6. Austerity Welfare and the Moral Significance of Needs in Portugal   113
   Patrícia Matos

7. Family, Housing as an Asset, and the Production of Welfare   131
   Jaime Palomera

8. Social Reproduction in Times of Crisis: Inter-Generational Tensions in Southern Europe   143
   Susana Narotzky and Antonio Maria Pusceddu

PART III: EXPERIENCING AND EMBODYING AUSTERITY

9. The Entrepreneur's Other: Small Entrepreneurial Identity and the Collapse of Life Structures in the "Third Italy" 173
   Giacomo Loperfido

10. The Body Politics of Austerity in Portugal and Spain: Women, Dispossession and Agency 192
    Diana Sarkis and Patricia Matos

11. Austerity from Below: Class, Temporality and Scale in Grassroots Analyses of Crisis 214
    Diana Sarkis and Stamatis Amarianakis

Notes on Contributors 239
Index 242

Abbreviations

ASEP (Supreme Council for Civil Personnel Selection)
COBAS (Confederazione dei Comitati di Base)
DEI (Public Power Corporation)
EEC (European Economic Community)
ECB (European Central Bank)
PCP (Portuguese Communist Party)
RETA (Régimen Especial de Trabajadores Autónomos)
RIPESS (Intercontinental Network for the Promotion of Social Solidarity Economy)
TAIPED (Hellenic Republic Asset Development Fund)
XES (Solidarity Economy Network of Catalonia)

Series Preface

As people around the world confront the inequality and injustice of new forms of oppression, as well as the impacts of human life on planetary ecosystems, this book series asks what anthropology can contribute to the crises and challenges of the twenty-first century. Our goal is to establish a distinctive anthropological contribution to debates and discussions that are often dominated by politics and economics. What is sorely lacking, and what anthropological methods can provide, is an appreciation of the human condition.

We publish works that draw inspiration from traditions of ethnographic research and anthropological analysis to address power and social change while keeping the struggles and stories of human beings' center stage. We welcome books that set out to make anthropology matter, bringing classic anthropological concerns with exchange, difference, belief, kinship and the material world into engagement with contemporary environmental change, capitalist economies and forms of inequality. We publish work from all traditions of anthropology, combining theoretical debate with empirical evidence to demonstrate the unique contribution anthropology can make to understanding the contemporary world.

Jamie Cross, Christina Garsten and Joshua O. Reno

Acknowledgements

All the participants in this volume were part of the European Research Council Advanced Grant project *Grassroots Economics: Meaning, Project and Practice in the Pursuit of Livelihood* (GRECO). The generous support of this grant enabled us to undertake a yearlong fieldwork as well as to spend some three years analyzing, debating and contrasting our findings with each other and with many colleagues. These multiple encounters at workshops and conferences helped us develop our ideas during this period and we thank them all for their insights. Naming all those whose help went into producing this volume is impossible as the list is extremely long. A generous ICREA Acadèmia Award from the Generalitat de Catalunya provided Susana Narotzky much needed research time for which she is extremely thankful.

Our extended fieldwork could not have been conducted without the generosity of the people who opened their homes, minds and hearts to us, and shared with us their everyday lives and their analyses of why and how things had changed in recent years. We owe to them more than we can ever express in words, but we still want to record here our incommensurable gratitude.

Some colleagues have been involved in a continuous way with our intellectual endeavor and to them we owe a tremendous debt of gratitude. First and foremost are the members of our scientific board of advisors, who followed our project closely over five years: Dina Vaiou, Antónia Lima, Enzo Mingione and Josep-Antoni Ybarra, we couldn't have done it without your help and support! We extend our thanks also to Simone Ghezzi, who became an informal member of the board.

We are thankful to the colleagues who accepted our invitation to participate in the theoretical workshops that launched our project: Florence Weber, Agnès Tricoche, Susana Matos Viegas, Frances Pine, Pierrette Hondagneu-Sotelo, Isabelle Guérin, Tania Murray Li, Jane Collins and Sharryn Kasmir. We owe a special thanks to Niko Besnier and Anita Hardon who invited us to co-organize teaching workshops at the University of Amsterdam early on in the project. Thanks are due to Chris Gregory and Karen Sykes for their Moral Economy workshop at the University of

Manchester, which was a milestone; to Chris Hann and Don Kalb for the many instances in which they have invited us to share our ideas with their teams at the Max Planck Institute for Social Anthropology in Halle and at Utrecht University, and Bergen University; and to Deborah James at the London School of Economics for also including us in various workshops on debt and advice.

Our gratitude also goes to the co-organizers of the *Ten Years of Crisis* conference in Lisbon, Ana Luísa Micaelo, Antónia Lima and João de Pina Cabral, as well as to all the participants who traveled sometimes great distances, and provided so much intellectual excitement, in particular we thank Dimitrios Theodossopoulos, Lourdes Benería, Federico Neiburg, Anna Perrin-Heredia, Evthymios Papataxarchis, Jane Collins, Frances Pine, Abel Polese and Sílvia Bofill who acted as discussants. Likewise we are grateful to all those that participated in the final *Grassroots Economics* conference at the International Institute for the Sociology of Law in Oñati, Gipuzkoa, and in particular to Vincenzo Ferrari who kindly offered the venue and Malen Gordoa Mendizábal who made it happen with her perfect organization and the help of Carles Baños. We want to particularly thank those that took on the commitment to act as discussants: Diane Elson, Costis Hadjimichalis, Enrica Morlicchio, Jaume Franquesa, Enzo Mingione, Victoria Goddard, Jeff Maskovsky, Sharryn Kasmir, Cris Shore, Deborah James, Antónia Lima, Gustav Peebles and Devi Sacchetto.

We also thank some friends and colleagues that have been very present along the way, in no particular order: Aliki Angelidou, Dimitra Kofti, Theo Rakopoulos, Phaedra Douzina-Bakalaki, Jane and Peter Schneider, Ayse Çaglar, Monica Heller, Alexandre Duchêne, Benoît de l'Estoile, Jeanette Edwards, Elisabeth Schober, Sari Pietikäinen, Sarah Green, Penelope Harvey, Keir Martin, Ida Susser, Nina Glick Shiller and Gavin Smith. We are aware that those who have participated in many of our intellectual debates cannot all be named, but we hope they know how grateful we are for their insights and critiques.

A special mention is due to Olga Lafazani, who joined our project and was a crucial member of our team, but found herself increasingly drawn towards activism during the refugee crisis to which she has devoted much of her life. She has been a great colleague whose incisive critique we have missed but she opted for much-needed action. We thank her heartily for all she has done.

We also want to thank Takeo David Hymans for helping us with language editing, always a difficult task that he has undertaken with professionalism and care, and we are equally grateful towards all those who have made the book materially possible at Pluto Press especially David Castle and Robert Webb.

Finally, we wish to express our deepest gratitude to our partners, families and friends who provided crucial support and care all along the project. This book is, in more ways than one, a collective endeavor.

1

Introduction: Grassroots Economics in Europe

Susana Narotzky

This book proposes a bottom-up approach to studying the impact of economic crises and structural adjustment policies on the livelihoods of working people across Europe. Over the past decade southern European countries—particularly Portugal, Italy, Greece and Spain—have been at the forefront of these economic dynamics. Named and shamed as the "PIGS", and used as scapegoats for the disastrous effects of European Monetary Union by showing what befalls countries when they do not comply with the Maastricht Treaty, the PIGS' alleged failures have fueled talk of replacing European "convergence" with a multi-speed Europe centered around a group of responsible "core" nations. Meanwhile, in southern Europe, prospects for well-being and upward social mobility, or even stable employment, have grown increasingly elusive since 2008. As a result of structural adjustment measures, a long recession, and continued unemployment and precarity, the middle-class horizons that once defined working class projects of social mobility have disappeared. For many, downward mobility for the next generation is experienced daily.

Not a few leaders in northern Europe have resorted to cultural stereotypes to describe the economic failings of their southern counterparts, ascribing negative traits to entire countries and their citizens, as part of a process aimed at producing national collective guilt. In so doing, they have naturalized the social and political economic relationships that produce inequality within and between regions, which many perceive to be unjust. Although economists and policymakers have furnished analyses and advised on political action to end the economic crisis, it has often resulted in greater precarity and inequality, producing social unrest including nationalistic and xenophobic reactions. In no small measure, this is because the "technical" models that inform these policies reveal little grounded knowledge about how real people make economic decisions in everyday life—within particular social and cultural environments and locally specific, historically produced institutional frameworks, embedded in multiple regimes of value.

This volume proposes an anthropological perspective that considers real life possibilities and strategies for making a living as well as models of the economy used to frame and understand larger economic processes and to guide everyday action. We consider the logical connections that ordinary people make by reflecting on their own experiences, against the backdrop of state policies and expert discourses that saturate the social field. Observation of people's everyday practices and bottom-up understandings of economic constraints and opportunities will deepen our understanding of how ordinary people make economic decisions.

Through comparative ethnography in Portugal, Italy, Greece and Spain, we show how concrete and place-bound economic practices are articulated through meanings, values and ideologies tied to unequal processes of production and distribution, both locally and globally. Economic practices are relational: they build on different institutional frameworks and involve multiple scales of value, creating complex and often ambiguous or contradictory meaning-environments in which people cooperate or compete. In our analysis, we show how value conflicts develop in practice and how they produce tangible effects in the wider economy.

Findings from our southern European field sites reveal how official regulatory practices can produce or restrict livelihood opportunities, as well as affecting the relative power of authoritative discourses on the value of regulation and grassroots counter-arguments that oppose, reinterpret or create other channels of legitimacy. A word of caution is first needed here, as we understand "grassroots" in a slightly different way from much recent usage. One of Merriam-Webster's entries for "grassroots" describes *"the basic level of society* or of an organization especially *as viewed in relation to higher or more centralized positions of power."* We adopt this broad definition rather than the more common focus on organized mobilization ("grassroots movements") that tends to equate the grassroots with social movements to improve society. The aim of our work is not to pre-judge the practices and discourses of ordinary people, but to observe and analyze them. The distinction we intend to draw at the outset—as a heuristic tool—is between "grassroots economies" (the practices of ordinary people to make a living) and "grassroots economics" (the logical connections developed by ordinary people to explain such economic processes).

Ultimately, our work addresses the widely experienced breakdown of social reproduction and struggles to overcome it, both at the immediate, everyday, personal level and on the wider scale of systemic understandings of continuity. The chapters articulate ethnographic cases embedded in historical, political and economic relationships with theoretical debates of various kinds. These include, among many others, the reappraisal of classical concepts such as "small commodity production" within the neoliberal push towards small and micro enterprises and self-entrepreneurship; the critique of "southern" welfare models that rely on institutionalized kinship support as they are challenged in contexts of austerity; and the conceptual value of the formal–informal distinction as opposed to its regulatory value regarding actual practices of labor devaluation and fiscal avoidance.

We address the latest, uneven transformations of capitalism from the point of view of ordinary people's everyday lives, models, priorities and personal or collective (in)capacities to act or stand still. We will see how industrial restructuring, globalization, financialization, and competitive and rent-seeking processes are co-determined at different scales by complex interactions between unequal agents, framed by moral arguments configured through valuation struggles. Rather than supporting a general theory of neoliberal capitalism, our ethnographic research in southern Europe points to the increasingly illiberal organization of capitalism.

This book is a creative combination of the edited collection and the monograph, and results from a collective process of developing, sharing, analyzing and theoretically engaging with our ethnographic material both during and after fieldwork. The authors have therefore become *co-authors* through continuous debate during the various phases of research and analysis. Most have visited each other's field sites and gained first-hand, guided insight into the livelihood experiences, conflicts and logics that only long-term fieldwork can unveil. The book is an anthropological monograph of a collective kind. Unlike edited collections, the comparative method is inbuilt, enabling theoretical discussion without forgoing the concrete realities and processes we seek to explain. The authors attend to the "global sense of place" (Massey 1994) within everyday interactions; spatial diversities and similarities are considered from within historical processes of unequal and combined development at different scales— regional, national, European, global—that inflect local expressions of neoliberal practice.

Uneven Accumulation and Privilege

Unevenness has a history, one that describes the development of capitalism as a particular constellation of connections and disconnections (see Makki 2015 for a review of the literature). Ray Hudson (2016) in "Rising Powers and the Drivers of Uneven Global Development" traces the historico-spatial transformations captured by the literature on uneven development as follows. The "old industrial development literature" of the 1960s and early 1970s stressed center/periphery relations (Wallerstein 2004) and the development of underdevelopment (Frank 1967) in which the industrial center imported raw materials and labor and exported finished goods, thereby siphoning off surplus value and blocking development—a trend resisted by import substitution industrialization and tariffs often linked to post-colonial national development policies. This was followed in the late 1970s and 1980s by the "new industrial development literature" (Fröbel et al. 1980; Arrighi 1994; Silver 2003) which traced changing forms of unevenness linked to the deregulation of markets and the undermining of labor movements in core countries, most notably the movement of productive capital in search of lower labor costs (often aided by repressive political regimes and lax environmental regulations). As a result, deindustrialization and unemployment overwhelmed the traditional core countries (UK, US, western Europe) (Hudson and Sadler 1989) while extractive industries and land grabs in the "peripheries" expanded previous forms of dispossession (Li 2011; Borras et al. 2012). Although the global north/south metaphor came to replace that of the center/periphery, exports of raw materials and foreign investments became increasingly complex, including south/south and south/north flows of capital and resources.

The third shift in the uneven development literature, which Hudson locates in the late 1990s and 2000s, focused attention on multinational corporations moving from direct production to brand management and the capturing of monopoly rents (Harvey 1982, 1974) through intellectual property rights, virtual commercialization platforms (Amazon, Uber, AirBnB, etc.) and financial products (Henni 2012; Standing 2016). This move was accompanied by the financialization of corporate, state and ordinary people's incomes, the greater role of tax breaks, offshore tax havens, enclaves and export processing zones and the blurring of legality and illegality in the everyday operations of worldwide capitalism at different scales (Gill and Kasmir 2016; Lapavitsas 2009; Neveling 2014). In terms of production, long supply chains, outsourcing and subcontracting often fed on unregulated or indentured forms of labor (Breman and van der Linden 2014). In the financial and fiscal domains, corruption, generalized bribery, tax avoidance or evasion, tolerance of money laundering and transfer pricing became widespread. While research and development, information and communication technologies, value-added services, and designer and luxury goods would revitalize western economies, the growing absolute surplus population worldwide, including in the old core countries, was pushed towards illegal (criminal or fiscally opaque) forms of livelihood: drug dealing, prostitution, smuggling, counterfeit production, street vending, subsistence and petty production. These were often tied to the legal economy through money laundering (Duffield 1998) or financial instruments such as micro-credit (Guérin et al. 2014).

The main idea behind the concept of "uneven and combined" capitalist development is that capitalist relations in their different forms are grounded, mutually constitutive and comprehensible only as wholes (Smith 2016; Makki 2015). Here, I wish to apply this insight to the concrete combinations of the main abstract forms of surplus extraction: monopoly and competition. Monopoly depends on the political power needed to enforce differences and carve out protected spaces, whilst competition relies on the political power needed to level the playing field for economic actors and enforce freedom of circulation.

Competition is the basic ideological argument of policies that reduce protective regulation and subsidies: the rolling back of the state should diminish costs and improve productivity, which are the keys to increasing global market share in an open, competitive environment. However, "competitive" policies mostly apply to the vulnerable, namely to labor, the self-employed and small firms. Although large firms also compete, their power allows them to lobby and corrupt policy-makers into regulating all sorts of privileges including "business friendly" environments (tax breaks, state contracts, land rezoning, bailouts) as well as the imposition of product "standards," a form of regulation that erects barriers for potential competitors. The privileges of corporate firms include effective toleration of legal loopholes that enable siphoning off profits without paying taxes. This means that, on the one hand, small firms and labor are increasingly forced into a "despotic" market of unfettered competition. On the other hand, large corporations enter the market from positions of privilege that enable them to secure market share on grounds other than competition. Generally speaking, reaping monopoly rents is the aim of all capitalist firms as they seek to control the market by pushing competitors aside and becoming price-makers by whatever means possible. Finally, the growth of the finance, insurance and real estate sectors in present-day capitalism, together with the exponential increase of e-commerce and internet service-providing platforms, is responsible for the rise of rent-profit (access) as opposed to surplus-value profit (productive) within practices of capital accumulation.

What we call capitalism has always combined the ideology and practice of competition with the objective of reaping monopoly rents and limiting competition through political leverage. As different kinds of actors struggle to set the rules of the game, we see the role of the state in co-producing the playing field. In general, actors with greater power will obtain more privileges and be less affected by competition. This is true for firms but also for labor, as powerful unions and professional guilds evidence through the creation of internal or protected labor markets.

Why is this relevant now? Neoliberal ideology espouses the idea of individual and corporate freedom from state interference as the objective of pure capitalism. But what we are witnessing today is a move towards an illiberal form of capitalism in which the state is a major player in the regulation of privilege. Rather than providing equal opportunities by redistributing assets through public services, governments and supra-national institutions are creating privileges for big corporations and wealthy individuals, thereby negating both the liberal ideology of equality and the postulate of freedom from state intervention. Indeed, austerity regimes encourage the creation of status groups and brokerage networks at different scales that promote inequality and dependency, often through the use of violence (Gill and Kasmir 2016). This is certainly the case on the fringes where the absolute surplus population tries to eke out a living.

Two consequences are crucial: (1) competitive global market frameworks are selectively enforced on powerless actors while monopoly privileges are instituted for the powerful; and (2) actors are shifting from struggles around exploitation—i.e. capital/labor (class) struggles—to struggles for or against privileges in attempts to redefine boundaries of inclusion and exclusion in accessing resources.

In Europe, less powerful actors experience this increasingly illiberal capitalism as a betrayal of the liberal promise of equal opportunity fostered through the prevention of privilege and public spending on basic services. In Portugal, Spain and Greece, such were the clear promises of the transition to democracy and integration into the European Economic

Community (EEC). As these promises have been broken, we have witnessed how laboring people make two contradictory claims to the state: (1) the elimination of the privileges of powerful economic actors (e.g. of the banks, "the rich" and corrupt politicians); and (2) the protection of "citizenship rents"—i.e. their own privilege as citizens—by excluding immigrants from entitlements and by closing national borders. While these demands are generally supported by different groups of social actors, they can overlap in particular conjunctures.

Many other forms of "micro-privilege" are also sought to make a living. For example, personal networks (mostly family and friends) provide resources analogous to rents as their access is protected; petty tax avoidance expresses resistance to the rent (often perceived as a form of tribute) captured by the state, likening it to a tax break; and political leverage through local brokers helps enable access to various kinds of public (information, preference of access to subsidies or advice) and private (illegal markets) resources. These practices—which often signal a retreat from collective mobilization although they occasionally develop into mutual aid associations—are simultaneously forms of re-embedding the economy and of using non-contractual obligations to access resources premised on personal status and social position rather than universal rights. The ambiguity and tension between "taking advantage" of kinship or friendship relations and developing reciprocal forms of support in a context of decreasing market opportunities is ubiquitous. As the trend towards monopoly increases within present-day capitalism, resistance appears to be shifting away from collective mobilization for the expansion of equal rights towards individual or segmented attempts to capture micro-privilege pools to get by. This is also a form of depoliticization, as such struggles become both fragmented and personalized. Against this inward-looking strategy, activists who oppose privilege and stress the recuperation of "the commons" focus on equal access to public services as a struggle to maintain the rights of citizenship (Collins 2017) or as the core of future systemic change (de Angelis 2007).

Scales of Regulation

Portugal, Italy, Greece and Spain share relatively recent pasts of prolonged dictatorship. They also suffered civil wars that highlighted the internal divisions of the nation-state's citizens, mostly on the grounds of class and political project (Pavone 2014). In contrast to Italy, which became and remained a democracy following the Second World War, Portugal, Greece and Spain experienced "transitions" in the mid-1970s to become liberal democracies integrated into the European project. Joining the European Economic Community meant different things to different constituencies. For policymakers in these countries, the EEC offered an enlarged market and the possibility to further pursue industrial restructuring targeting productivity increases while obtaining funds to retrain and relocate redundant workers, develop infrastructure and a functioning welfare state. For workers, many of whom had been labor migrants to the industrial and urban centers of France and Germany, joining the EEC promised the consolidation of democratic and labor rights and better livelihoods. For all, it meant convergence with northern Europe.

Industrial restructuring in the 1980s resulted in massive unemployment which was only tempered by European structural funds. While the structural transformations of this period witnessed growing labor conflicts, governments argued that liberalization and enhanced productivity and competitiveness would deliver widespread well-being through access to a larger pool of consumer goods. While some of these promises materialized through the disbursement of EEC structural cohesion funds, in the minds of many workers and firm owners, the 1980s remain the "crisis years"—a prominent structure of feeling in all four countries under study. In regions where the development of "industrial districts" absorbed the impact of the closure of large industries, such as the Italian Veneto, the "crisis years" came later—in the 1990s—when competition from central-eastern Europe and pressure from globalization became overwhelming following the GATT Uruguay rounds and China's entry into the World Trade Organization in 2001. To date, however, the use of anti-dumping provisions targeting raw materials and labor intensive manufactures such as textiles and footwear, as well as the imposition of standards on imports, have directly or indirectly resulted in the re-imposition of barriers to imports into the EU from mostly Asian economies (Davis 2009; Prevost et al. 2011).

In any case, scales of regulation increasingly overlap as tariffs and standards are designed by supra-national entities but are left to be translated into norms and enforced at the national and local levels. Shalini Randeria (2007) speaks of the "cunning state" that operates in this kind of legal plurality, one in which the state presents itself as unaccountable towards its citizens but also upstream towards international institutions. Cunning states "are in a position to negotiate the terms on which they share sovereignty in certain fields of policy-making while retaining control over others. They deny power only to deploy it in order to evade responsibility" (Randeria 2007: 6). This is an important reminder that sovereignty is distributed at multiple scales and among different instantiations of the state (Abrams 1988; Gupta 1995) but is also acted upon by agents at multiple scales (Das and Poole 2004). The European variant of the 2008 financial crisis has often been seen as an attack on national sovereignty by undemocratic supra-national institutions such as the EU (Hadjimichalis 2017) or the imposition of a particular national economic project such as German ordoliberalism (Matthijs 2016; Blyth 2013). While such analyses underline both regional unevenness and scales of power, they tend to essentialize the locus of the state in its active or passive regulatory role as well as its agents' positions in the complex geometries of rulemaking and enforcement.

Inspired in the German ordo-liberal tradition, the Maastricht Treaty (Council of the European Communities 1992) consolidated a policy based on fiscal stability, controlling inflation, the deregulation of labor and export-led growth for the European Union. European Monetary Union was followed by the introduction of the single currency, and the barring of the European Central Bank (ECB) from becoming a lender of last resort, produced a series of imbalances that escaped the control of both the European Commission and the ECB as well as of national states and regions (Blyth 2013; Hadjimichalis 2017; Lapavitsas et al. 2010). In the short-term, monetary union lowered the traditionally high costs of borrowing in the southern peripheries for treasury bonds as well as for inter-bank credit. Easy credit from financial institutions fueled housing bubbles (Alexandri and Janoschka 2017; López and Rodríguez 2011) and consumption, all of which led to high levels of private debt. The boom years of the turn of the century were also due to the deregulation of capital markets, land re-zoning and immigration providing pools of cheap, often unregulated labor mostly in construction, agriculture and domestic services. Financial derivatives and securities added fuel to the fire (Li Puma and Lee 2004). Following the collapse of Lehman Brothers in the USA, the inter-bank credit market dried up. The domino effect of non-performing loans left financial institutions undercapitalized, leading to bailouts or nationalizations that created or increased public deficits (Blyth 2013). Only Greece (and to a lesser extent Italy) had significant public debt at the time, mostly due to pre-crisis welfare expenditure, budget mismanagement and a weak taxation system (Nikiforos et al. 2015; Lapavitsas et al. 2010).

All of this is well known, as are the austerity measures imposed by the "Troika"—the International Monetary Fund, the European Commission and the European Central Bank—in the Memorandums of Understanding that accompanied the bailout loans. They can be summed up as an injunction to governments to cut spending and raise taxes, strengthen competitiveness through labor devaluation and raise income through the privatization of public goods. The moralization of the financial crisis produced a nationalization of responsibility that tended to create a corporative understanding of guilt, amplified by the media and national and northern European policymakers (Schaüble, Merkel, Dijsselbloem) (Streek 2013; Fourcade 2013; Matthijs and McNamara 2015).

Citizens, households, working people and small entrepreneurs, however, did not passively accept regulatory orders imposed from above. Their non-compliance with legal regulations and their alternative understandings of what constitutes legitimate activity amounted to an everyday kind of struggle. What enables the "viability" of petty businesses in the tourist service industry, for example—the avoidance of taxation and non-payment of social security contributions—has fiscal consequences at the larger political economic scale of the national budget's redistributive capacities. At the same time, non-compliance can be seen as a form of popular resistance to the mandated transfer of financial institutions' private debt into public debt subsequently converted into household debt through increased (especially indirect and housing) taxation. Ordinary people have also made cunning use of the new regulatory opportunities (for example tax breaks on purchasing homes, low interest rates, housing developments in re-zoned land) following calculations of well-being often related to the social reproduction, security and well-being of the family. We can think of these frameworks for decision-making as alternative regulatory orders that are nevertheless intimately connected to policy regulation.

This book explores such entanglements by focusing on the everyday practices and understandings of ordinary people in Portugal, Italy, Greece and Spain during the years of austerity that followed the 2008 financial crisis. The scales of regulation include households, personal networks, and local, national and supra-national institutions as we observe how different social actors have navigated the ambiguities of legal frameworks and legitimate practices. The book thus pursues the bottom-up study of grassroots economies (i.e. how people make a living) and grassroots economics (i.e. how they explain the logics of the economic processes of which they are part). The abstract explanatory frameworks invoked by ordinary people, which often incorporate elements from the media and from activists of different persuasions, are always inflected by their own experiences and by particular accounts of the past. The chapters in this book present numerous instances where expert explanations come into conflict with people's own experiences, something that we interpret as struggles over evidence (Narotzky 2019).

Reinventing Oneself

The 2008 financial crisis accelerated the shift towards "new" forms of labor. Unemployment rates above 20 percent—topping 40 percent for younger cohorts—have had lasting effects on the labor market and on people's aspirations, projects and identities. Paid and unpaid work, workfare schemes, temporary jobs, small entrepreneurship, and social and solidarity cooperatives overlap with kinship obligations, citizenship entitlements to subsidies and benefits, ideological projects and contractual relations. While the kinds of social recognition entailed by these different forms of earning a living vary widely, they are not clearly bounded categories as the chapters in this book will show.

Especially in industrial and agricultural settings, the loss of an economy based on production is seen as a material and moral loss—of stability, of citizenship entitlements attached to employment, and of an ethos of hard work and reward attached to effort. Precarious livelihoods often hinder deriving identity from work, as toil is divorced from valued positions in society. Where they do constitute a mode of identification, they are devalued and often problematic. The material devaluation of workers through instability and wage reductions thus results in moral devaluation, in feelings of inadequacy (in terms of skills and the fulfilment of family obligations) and shame. But the opposite is also true as mostly workers in the private sector (often themselves unemployed) see the austerity-driven wage cuts and redundancies for public sector workers as largely justified on the grounds that civil servants' wages are responsible for the public deficit, a discourse disseminated through the media.

Across our cases, we find the injunction to "re-invent" oneself as an entrepreneur—a classic neoliberal trope—either welcomed as an opportunity or accepted as a necessity. Entrepreneurial programs proposed by the neoliberal state are at times attuned to the ethos of hard work and the achievement of autonomy through the market—as opposed to depending on state benefits or on wage employment—echoing the small commodity production imaginary (in agriculture, manufacturing and commerce) of "being my own boss" and accessing "freedom." We find its translation in the entrepreneurial imaginary of small and medium enterprise family firm owners, small farmers, the self-employed and members of social cooperatives, even when many are part of sub-contracting chains and dependent on credit and labor from family members, subsidies from local, national or EU funds and loans from commercial banks (Narotzky 2016). For young people targeted by EU start-up funding, becoming an entrepreneur is often embraced as a creative form of self-valorization where talent and imagination will provide a meaningful way to earn a living. Others feel that they are pushed by stringent fiscal regulations and surveillance to become entrepreneurs—businesspeople—against their will, when they only want to make a living. Such is the case for many self-employed workers at the end of manufacturing subcontracting chains, who are at pains to think of themselves as entrepreneurs (Leidereiter in this volume).

In the austerity environment of unemployment, precarity and the credit crunch, many entrepreneurial ventures are either in deep crisis (Loperfido in this volume) or in fact involve volatile and often illegal forms of seeking rent as a livelihood income. People use their family homes as assets when they rent rooms to tourists or students, or when young adults return to the parental home so they can rent out their own. People also use their homes as collateral to obtain credit for their entrepreneurial projects (Palomera this volume; Vetta and Palomera 2020 forthcoming).

But there is another way in which rents are becoming pervasive in the austerity environment: privileged access to resources that can be described as "micro-rents" linked to personal networks of family, friends, state agents or to residential hierarchies. These micro-rents can take the form of privileged access to employment, housing, income, care, seed capital and benefits. What they have in common with ordinary "rents" is that they are based on a "privilege" that marks boundaries of exclusion and inclusion, and that the resources they channel often appear as "unearned" rather than the result of "hard work." Often the state is perceived as having produced privileged groups of working people, for example civil servants and pensioners who can reap rents from their access to this category (Vetta this volume; Narotzky and Pusceddu this volume). Resourcefulness takes many forms and, often, far from realizing the entrepreneurial imaginary of freedom and autonomy, re-inventing oneself reconfigures existing forms of dependence.

Depoliticization

Contrary to the accounts of solidarity grassroots movements that have emerged in the wake of the terrible breakdown of social reproduction after the financial crisis (Rakopoulos 2014, 2015; Cabot 2016), we have witnessed only scattered experiments of alternative, non-market solidarities (Homs this volume). Solidarity has mostly been tied to the Church, the state, the family and especially women (Sarkis and Matos, Loperfido, Pusceddu, Leidereiter this volume; Sarkis 2018). Forms of mutual help rely on different ideological discourses, expectations and entitlements that result in different moral valuations, practices and material transfers. Charities, state benefits, third sector organizations, self-organizing groups and family networks imply different reconfigurations of self-worth as well as feelings of dependency and autonomy, entailing the renegotiation of the boundaries between claims and entitlements, rights and needs (Narotzky and Pusceddu this volume). Arguments and evidence for making claims over resources result in solidarity practices that produce conflict and differentiation around deservingness, inclusion and exclusion.

This has consequences for mobilization. While labor movements have traditionally focused on the relation between workers and the firm in terms of returns to labor and capital (wages vs. profit) and on working conditions, present-day mobilization focuses more broadly on social reproduction. In Spain, massive demonstrations such as the Dignity Marches of 2015 claimed the right to "bread, work, and a roof." Although work remains a central demand often tied not only to income but to self-respect, food and housing are also highlighted as entitlements. Other massive demonstrations during the 2011–13 period were launched in defense of public services such as healthcare and education, and more recently, public pensions (Narotzky 2016), revealing that responsibility for livelihood is seen to rest on political rather than economic actors. The emphasis on privilege that accompanies many analyses also points to eminent political responsibility; at stake is a particular understanding of the substance of citizenship and of the state's role in caring for and upholding the right to life.

We have not found these mobilizations everywhere. Where they have emerged, they often target specific grievances. Instead, we have largely seen widespread acceptance of austerity and the continuous dispossession of the means of livelihood—a form of fatalism coupled with adaptive strategies to make ends meet and angry discourses about an "economic war" waged by northern countries, attacks by political and economic elites on working people, or the deprivation of social rights (Sarkis and Amarianakis this volume; Knight 2015). While people's analyses are influenced by media and political discourses, these propose heterogeneous—often incompatible—explanations of the political economic causes of the fiscal deficit and of its solutions, which include, among others, opposition to at least some austerity measures, better redistribution, legal protection against foreclosure, radical exiting from the eurozone, economic protectionism or anti-immigrant policies. Embedded in people's experiences, all of these discourses offer causal explanations and speculation about what the correct policies should be.

Where we find recognition of common distress—as amongst precarious workers, welfare recipients, bankrupt small family firms and retired pensioners—the general capacity of scaling up to their structural systemic position of commonality and becoming a collective agent is lacking. We get recognition without the ability to organize affiliation and movement. In areas where industrial unions—now discredited as elitist and corrupt—had been strong, we find references to past struggles that were successful. But often, they appear unrelated to the current experience of precarity or to the state's responsibility in implementing austerity (Vetta, Leidereiter, Pusceddu this volume). Anger couples with shame and with immediate struggles to make a living, which are often a mix of both sharing and protecting resources from others' claims (Breman 1976).

The discourse of austerity is presented by EU neoliberal elites as an opportunity for southern European countries to finally "do their homework" and "catch up." In turn, governments in southern Europe present controlling the deficit, deregulating labor protections, privatizing public services and becoming more competitive as a collective responsibility, something that the competitive northern countries have done long ago. We have seen how regulation can be used as a coercive weapon, especially when implemented in a selective and discretionary manner creating diffused fear (Leidereiter this volume; Narotzky and Smith 2006). The menace of destitution and the failure of social reproduction for the younger generation is acute, creating an atmosphere of revolt against injustice but also amenable to negotiation and resilience.

Gramsci (1987) argued that the exercise of government requires both coercion and consent. But what kind of consent has enabled the prolonged and ongoing period of austerity? Matos and Pusceddu (forthcoming) show how the task of rendering austerity "common sense" rests on the narrative of sovereign debt as a collective responsibility and austerity as necessary for national survival, a national emergency. At the same time, the injunction towards structural adjustment is presented as an external constraint necessary for sustaining EU membership. The nation state then appears as a mediator in its role of creating consent for austerity: it depoliticizes its policies, rendering them common sense and an opportunity to converge with northern Europe. At the same time, the state loses its legitimacy as a protector and provider of public services through the lived experience of how austerity fuels downward mobility and widening inequality. Everywhere we find similar arguments presented by policymakers and diffused through the media, as well as an ambivalence over the mismatch between lived experience and official discourse. As Matos (this volume) points out, transferring many of the tasks of redistribution to charities can be read as a depoliticization of citizenship rights by recasting them in terms of primordial needs and adjudicating them through a ranking of material and moral deservingness.

Different forms of surplus extraction, exploitation and accumulation rest on different moral economies constituted as the hegemonic "good" and variously challenged by subaltern groups. Historically, we have seen shifts in the languages of contention (Roseberry 1994) that challenge dispossession and exploitation. While moral arguments of worth alternate with economic arguments, both are political expressions of conflict and struggle that address social inequality. To analyze processes of political mobilization and depoliticization, we need to conceptually retain the articulation between political and moral economy as people live and experience their lives within complex processes of valuation that comprise moral, material and social power differentials. We also need to analyze these entanglements and articulations of differential social values for their ability to maintain or transform the conditions of possibility for making a living and leading a life worth living. Finally, we need to analyze how different groups of social actors claim access to resources using idioms of moral or political entitlements when addressing political institutions, market actors and other socially characterized groups.

Social Worth: Valuing People, Relationships and Work

Starting in the early 1980s, industrial restructuring has shattered the expectations of stability and well-being of many workers in Europe's industrial regions. Sub-contracting chains, firm relocation to lower wage regions, financialization and selective infrastructure development have all conspired to differentiate anew spaces, places and the people that inhabit them. The financial crisis of 2008 once again transformed the valuation systems that constituted people's social worth. How would recognition and respect be forthcoming for those without formal work in situations of increased dependency, and burdened by debt? To what extent was capital accumulation related to rendering certain people and places worthless (Li 2009)? How were younger generations supposed to live? For many, precarity and uncertainty are the lived experiences of inequality wherein one's identity and worth are consistently devalued.

Growing unemployment and precarity have transformed subjectivities in the most intimate of ways, as people have become forced to rely on personal or institutional forms of dependence discredited by the ideology of autonomy and self-reliance. This systematic humiliation has produced a struggle to change the valuation frameworks according to which a life acquires value and meaning (Narotzky and Besnier 2014; Skeggs and Loveday 2012). Valuation is the process that creates social systems of categorization that describe and evaluate social life, the former through the differentiation and naming of entities and the latter through their ordering and ranking. Valuation struggles are not only fought around "evaluation" (the process of ranking) but also over the framing system itself (what is defined as relevant). Most of the cases that we present in this book are struggles around the categories for valuing human worth.

The breakdown of expectations and feelings of abandonment by the state fuel anger, self-deprecation and despair, but also a growing acceptance of trade-offs that generate some income in exchange for a loss of power, autonomy, dignity or health. The reconfiguration of households towards extended family patterns around resources provided by senior generations (pensions, homes), the acceptance of unhealthy and exploitive practices at work, the claiming of social benefits and involuntary emigration—all are common strategies to make a living, predicated on a revaluation of the worth of people engaging in these relations. Ordinary people in this ongoing "crisis" often see themselves as the victims of powerful individuals or abstract forces that seek to destroy their wills, bodies and lives. As public services shrink under austerity (foremost among them healthcare and education), the unequal worth of people is there for all to see. Death becomes a metaphor and inner-city ruins its material expression as people proclaim, "the town is dying." But death is also a reality as morbidity and mortality rise with the material effects of discrimination. The only aspiration left for young people is "to have a life"—to escape the death omen surrounding them in their social and material environment.

Wealth that can be accounted for in market terms is one of the main ways of pegging a form of value on individuals (often extended to their families). This wealth may come from different sources that will nuance its meaning in terms of personal social value: wages are different from assets as valued in the market and from rents, for example. The stability of this wealth, the possibility to make it grow or transfer it to the next generation (through investments and savings) will affect its owners' worth and future family prospects. Various forms of insurance against loss of income (mostly through home ownership) express the aim of individuals to maintain their personal worth and protect it from various kinds of risks (mostly inflation). Economic wealth has to be translated into social worth to become valuable; it does this through consumption, reciprocity transfers and political leverage. Moreover, the economic practices of individuals produce (moral) rankings that define their "reputation," as when over-consumption or allegedly imprudent household finances result in decried over-indebted individuals and households. One of the most salient effects of this latest crisis is that forms of wealth that had been saved (homeownership) and invested in the younger generations (education) as a form of personal valorization have been endangered or otherwise lost. Simultaneously, the expectation of earning an income and the dignity tied to work have evaporated, closing off many of the avenues to becoming a respected person (autonomy, marriage).

In addition, the value attached to wealth depends on its form and the social relations through which it is channeled. People (individuals, households, collectivities) are valued differently according to whether they access in-kind goods or services through personal networks and affective relations (care practices), or access public goods, services and welfare transfers through state institutions. They will be categorized according to different valuation systems if their income is formally "visible" and regulated by the state, or if it falls through the cracks of regulation. Indeed, people's income-based worth engages them in different ways with the state through taxation and redistribution, and produces particular forms of entitlement and exclusion. Citizens' rapport with the state and assessments of their fellow humans' worth renders them differentially vulnerable to employers, loan sharks and other market agents.

In sum, many of the central struggles of present-day capitalism, in southern Europe and elsewhere, are experienced and waged as struggles of valuation and revaluation (de Angelis 2007; Collins 2017; Harvey 2012; Bear 2015)—as conflicts around categorization systems that produce different *kinds* of valuables, things and persons amenable (or resistant) to capture by the processes of capitalist value accumulation. The chapters in this book can all be read as instances of valuation struggles of an everyday kind, whether we find women in a market insisting on the legitimacy of their trade (Leidereiter this volume) or workers in mines trying to define and belong to the appropriate category to be hired (Vetta this volume). The chapters are organized into three sections—Making a Living, Social Reproduction and Experiencing and Embodying Austerity—which each analyze the practices and understandings of working people under austerity and the valuation frameworks that are produced and challenged through this process. The section on "making a living" focuses on the tensions and conflicts that arise in the search for material resources, and on how fragmented or cohesive identities emerge around diverse regulatory instances. Here, official definitions and regulations of income-providing opportunities configure livelihood practices with different values that people might tolerate, rework or contest. The section on "social reproduction" focuses on the articulation of the intimate, everyday reproduction of social life framed in social units such as domestic networks, with the reproduction of an encompassing and differentiated social system, a society. Here, experts, state agents and benefit recipients all contribute to the making of diverse moral frameworks that configure idioms of deservingness and fairness, and justify entitlements, inclusive and exclusionary practices. The final section on "experiencing and embodying austerity" looks at the gendered effects of increased livelihood vulnerability on minds and bodies, and at attempts to find a logical explanation for what has happened. The search for meaning is informed by present and past experience, by memories of collective conflict and endurance, by mainstream media and expert narratives, and attempts to project trajectories into an imaginable future.

Each chapter presents valuation struggles from a different angle, whether skills and employment, the value of older people's retirement pensions, or the value of the laboring body are the issue of contention. Taken together, the chapters in this volume present a portrait of people's unrelenting agency towards establishing a better future in material and symbolic terms, in terms of resources and respect. In the process, some of these efforts are captured directly or indirectly in the value accumulation circuits of capital. Others, however, appear to remain weapons of resistance.

References

Abrams, Ph. 1988 [1977]. "Notes On the Difficulty of Studying the State." *Journal of Historical Sociology* 1(1): 58–89.

Alexandri, G. and M. Janoschka. 2018. "Who Loses and Who Wins in a Housing Crisis? Lessons from Spain and Greece for a Nuanced Understanding of Dispossession." *Housing Policy Debate* 28(1): 117–34.

Arrighi, G. 1994. *The Long Twentieth Century: Money, Power and the Origins of Our Times*. London: Verso.

Bear, L. 2015. *Navigating Austerity. Currents of Debt along a South Asian River*. Stanford: Stanford University Press.

Blyth, M. 2013. *Austerity: The History of a Dangerous Idea*. Oxford: Oxford University Press.

Borras, S.M. Jr., J.C. Franco, S. Gómez, C. Kay and M. Spoor. 2012. "Land Grabbing in Latin America and the Caribbean." *Journal of Peasant Studies* 39(3–4): 845–72.

Breman, J. 1976. "A Dualistic Labour System? A Critique of the "Informal Sector" Concept: III: Labour Force and Class Formation." *Economic and Political Weekly* 11(50): 1939–44.

Breman, J. and M. van der Linden. 2014. "Informalizing the Economy: The Return of the Social Question at a Global Level." *Development and Change* 45(5): 920–40.

Cabot, H. 2016. "'Contagious' Solidarity: Reconfiguring Care and Citizenship in Greece's Social Clinics." *Social Anthropology* 24(2): 152–66.

Collins, J.L. 2017. *The Politics of Value. Three Movements to Change How We Think about the Economy*. Chicago: University of Chicago Press.

Council of the European Communities. 1992. *Treaty on European Union*. Luxembourg.

Das, V. and D. Poole, eds. 2004. *Anthropology in the Margins of the State*. Santa Fe: School of American Research Press.

Davis, L. 2009. "Ten Years of Anti-Dumping in the EU: Economic and Political Targeting." *ECIPE Working Paper nº2*. Brussels: European Center for International Political Economy.

de Angelis, M. 2007. *The Beginning of History. Values Struggles and Global Capital*. London: Pluto Press.

Duffield, M. 1998. "Post-Modern Conflict: Warlords, Post-Adjustment States and Private Protection." *Civil Wars* 1(1): 65–102.

Fourcade, M. 2013. "The Economy as Morality Play, and Implications for the Eurozone Crisis." *Moral Categories in the Financial Crisis*, MaxPo Discussion Paper 13/1.

Frank, A.G. 1967. *Capitalism and Underdevelopment in Latin America*. New York: Monthly Review Press.

Fröbel, F., J. Heinrich and O. Kreye. 1980. *The New International Division of Labour*. Cambridge: Cambridge University Press.

Gill, L. and S. Kasmir. 2016. "History, Politics, Space, Labor: On Unevenness as an Anthropological Concept." *Dialectical Anthropology* 40(2): 87–102.

Gramsci, A. 1987 [1929–35]. *Selections from the Prison Notebooks.* New York: International Publishers.
Guérin, I., S. Morvant-Roux and M. Villarreal, eds. 2014. *Microfinance, Debt and Over-Indebtedness. Juggling with Money.* London: Routledge.
Gupta, A. 1995. "Blurred Boundaries: The Discourse of Corruption, The Culture of Politics, and the Imagined State." *American Ethnologist* 22(2): 375–402.
Hadjimichalis, C. 2017. *Crisis Spaces. Structures, Struggles and Solidarity in Southern Europe.* London: Routledge.
Harvey, D. 1974. "Class-Monopoly Rent, Finance Capital and the Urban Revolution." *Regional Studies* 8(3–4): 239–55.
Harvey, D. 1982. *The Limits to Capital.* Oxford: Basil Blackwell.
Harvey, D. 2012. *Rebel Cities. From the Right to the City to the Urban Revolution.* London: Verso.
Henni, A. 2012. *Le capitalisme de rente. De la société du travail industriel à la société des rentiers.* Paris: L'Harmattan.
Hudson, R. 2016. "Rising Powers and the Drivers of Uneven Global Development." *Area Development and Policy* 1(3): 279–94.
Hudson, R. and D. Sadler. 1989. *The International Steel Industry: Restructuring, State Policies and Localities.* London: Routledge.
Knight, D.M. 2015. *History, Time, and Economic Crisis in Central Greece.* New York: Palgrave Macmillan.
Lapavitsas, C. 2009. "Financialised Capitalism: Crisis and Financial Expropriation." *Historical Materialism* 17: 114–48.
Lapavitsas, C., A. Kaltenbrunner, D. Lindo, J. Michell, J.P. Painceira, E. Pires, J. Powell, A. Stenfors and N. Teles. 2010. "Eurozone Crisis: Beggar Thyself and thy Neighbour." *Journal of Balkan and Near Eastern Studies* 12(4): 321–73.
Li Puma, E. and B. Lee. 2004. *Financial Derivatives and the Globalization of Risk.* Durham: Duke University Press.
Li, T.M. 2009. To Make Live or Let Die? Rural Dispossession and the Protection of Surplus Populations." *Antipode* 41(S1): 66–93.
Li, T. M. 2011. "Centering Labor in the Land Grab Debate." *Journal of Peasant Studies* 38(2): 281–98.
López, I. and E. Rodríguez. 2011. "The Spanish Model." *New Left Review* 69: 5–29.
Makki, F. 2015. "Reframing Development Theory: The Significance of the Idea of Uneven and Combined Development." *Theory and Society* 44(5): 471–97.
Massey, D. 1994. *Space, Place and Gender.* Cambridge: Polity.
Matos, P. and A. Pusceddu. (forthcoming). "Austerity, The State and Common Sense in Europe: A Comparative Perspective on Italy and Portugal." *Anthropological Theory.*
Matthijs, M. 2016. "Powerful Rules Governing the Euro: The Perverse Logic of German Ideas." *Journal of European Public Policy* 23(3): 375–91.
Matthijs, M. and K. McNamara. 2015. "The Euro Crisis' Theory Effect: Northern Saints, Southern Sinners, and the Demise of the Eurobond." *Journal of European Integration* 37(2): 229–45.
Narotzky, S. 2016. "Between Inequality and Injustice: Dignity as a Motive for Mobilization During the Crisis." *History and Anthropology* 27(1): 74–92.

Narotzky, S. 2019. "Austerity Lives in Southern Europe: Experience, Knowledge, Evidence and Social Facts." *American Anthropologist* 121(1): 187–93.

Narotzky, S. and N. Besnier. 2014. "Crisis, Value, Hope: Rethinking the Economy." *Current Anthropology* 55(S9): 4–16.

Narotzky, S. and G. Smith. 2006. *Immediate Struggles. People, Power and Place in Rural Spain*. Berkeley: University of California Press.

Neveling, P. 2014. "Three Shades of Embeddedness, State Capitalism as the Informal Economy, Emic Notions of the Anti-Market, and Counterfeit Garments in the Mauritian Export Processing Zone." In D.C. Wood, ed. *Production, Consumption, Business and the Economy: Structural Ideals and Moral Realities*. Bingley, UK: Emerald Group Publishing.

Nikiforos, M., D. Papadimitriou and G. Zezza. 2015. "The Greek Public Debt Problem." *Nova Economia* 25: 777–875.

Pavone, C. 2014. *A Civil War: A History of the Italian Resistance*. London: Verso.

Prevost, D., L. Choukroune, R. Creemers and J-F. Huchet. 2011. *EU-China Trade Relations*. Directorate-General for External Policies of the Union. Brussels: European Parliament.

Rakopoulos, T. 2014. The Crisis Seen from Below, Within, and Against: From Solidarity Economy to Food Distribution Cooperatives In Greece. *Dialectical Anthropology* 38(2): 189–207.

Rakopoulos, T. 2015. Solidarity's tensions: informality, sociality, and the Greek Crisis. *Social Analysis* 59(3): 85–104.

Randeria, S. 2007. "The State of Globalization: Legal Plurality, Overlapping Sovereignties and Ambiguous Alliances Between Civil Society and yhe Cunning State in India." *Theory, Culture and Society* 24(1): 1–33.

Roseberry, W. 1994. "Hegemony and the Language of Contention." In G.M. Joseph and D. Nugent, eds. *Everyday Forms of State Formation: Revolution and the Negotiation of Rule in Modern Mexico*. Durham: Duke University Press.

Sarkis, D. 2018. "'Muerta a trabajar': consideraciones feministas sobre la crisis (de la reproducción social) en Vélez-Málaga (España)." *Revista Andaluza de Antropología* 14: 89–107.

Silver, B. 2003. *Forces of Labor: Workers' Movements and Globalization Since 1870*. Cambridge: Cambridge University Press.

Skeggs, B. and V. Loveday. 2012. "Struggles for Value: Value Practices, Injustice, Judgment, Affect and the Idea of Class." *British Journal of Sociology* 63(3): 472–90.

Smith, G. 2016. "Against Social Democratic Angst About Revolution: From Failed Citizens to Critical Praxis." *Dialectical Anthropology* 40: 221–39.

Standing, G. 2016. *The Corruption of Capitalism: Why Rentiers Thrive and Work Does Not Pay*. London: Biteback.

Streek, W. 2013. The Construction of a Moral Duty for The Greek People to Repay Their National Debt." *Moral Categories in the Financial Crisis*, MaxPo Discussion Paper 13/1.

Vetta, T. and J. Palomera (2020 forthcoming). "Concrete stories: Financialization and Inequality in the Construction Chain." *Antipode* 52(3).

Wallerstein, I. 2004. *World-Systems Analysis: An Introduction*. Durham: Duke University Press.

PART I

MAKING A LIVING

2

Bondage Unemployment and Intra-class Tensions in Greek Energy Restructuring

Theodora Vetta

Introduction

"Mama DEI is gone," many of my interlocutors in the mountain town of Kozani in northern Greece ironically lamented. They were referring to the announced further privatization of the semi-public electricity company DEI [Public Power Corporation S.A], whose coal mines and power plants stretched over 160 square kilometers of former agricultural land, just 14 km from their homes.

The restructuring of the country's largest industry—one that covered more than 90 percent of final consumers and until very recently represented 80 percent of domestic energy production—was part of the memoranda Greece signed with the International Monetary Fund, the European Union and the European Central Bank accompanying the bailout agreements of 2010, 2012 and 2015. It was part of a much broader privatization of state-owned assets, including the ports of Piraeus and Thessaloniki, 14 regional airports, the former Athenian airport for peri-urban development, small islands, the leading gambling company OPAP, land for renewable energy projects, the railway, 210 touristic enterprises, marinas and 72,000 titles of real estate (Hadjimichalis 2014a, 2014b). Indeed, Greece in the past decade has been at the center of European political debates as the possibility of GREXIT spread anxiety and fear of unpredictable domino effects that could threaten the very existence of the European single currency. Amidst strikes, violently repressed popular revolts and a controversial referendum in 2015, a series of harsh austerity measures were legislated to "sanitize" what was thought to lie at the roots of the new Greek tragedy: the profligate state. While more structural understandings of the "crisis" located it at the heart of capitalist accumulation, financialization and uneven geographic development (Hadjimichalis 2017; Lapavitsas 2012; Maniatis and Passas 2013; Mavroudeas 2014), mainstream technocrats, media and members of the ruling Greek and European political class asserted that it was the Greek state and people who were living beyond their means. Avoiding the GREXIT scenario thus meant entering a regime of strict international supervision whose jurisdiction reached far beyond monetary regulation into the realm of biopolitics (Athanasiou 2012).

Although the lives and prospects of the vast majority of people—some of them more vulnerable than others—were violently disrupted, the analytical lens of rupture may be misleading as the "crisis" did not signal the beginning of a new policy model. The narrative of national salvation in fact morally legitimized the acceleration of older neoliberal reforms, now realized through "fast-track" legislation, societal despair and media terror (Mylonas 2014, 2017). This chapter focuses on labor devaluation as the other side of the coin of public dispossession. Based on ethnographic fieldwork undertaken in Kozani in 2015 and 2016, I show that a more tacit and silent privatization was already underway within the energy sector, not only through subcontracting—a common feature of industrial restructuring—but through the growing precariousness of public contracts. Austerity intensified already existing inequalities and dependencies between and among permanent and precarious staff in DEI mines and power plants and along the company's subcontracting chains. Workers were increasingly tied to calculative logics of self-formation and to what I call "bondage unemployment," a peculiar circular labor regime whereby unemployment became a prerequisite for employment. This model not only blurred the boundaries between public and private, but informed the moral significance of these categories within a wider political debate on "exiting the crisis" and imagining the future. The idiom of Mama DEI encapsulates the state's Janus face: the tensions around care and control. The lack of any solidarity-with-DEI actions (even in a place as dependent on the company as Kozani) and the failure of DEI workers to challenge further privatization and reclaim electricity as a public good point to the complex ways in which labor's "disorganization" (Kasmir and Carbonella 2014) navigate this public/private friction.

Mapping the Field

The Public Power Corporation (DEI) was founded in 1950 with the explicit goal of creating a national energy system of production and distribution "for the public interest." Although the British Power and Traction Finance Company first brought electricity to Athens in 1889—thus paralleling developments in New York, London and Berlin—in the wake of the Second World War Greece had among the lowest rates of electrification in Europe and showed scant signs of industrialization. The energy sector, an arena of quasi-colonial competition (Psimmenos 1999), was based on imported coal and oil and was run by a scattered ensemble of private and municipal companies. DEI's first national plan (1950–55) was made and supervised by the American company EBASCO Services and funded by the Marshall Plan and Italian World War Two compensation. The guiding economic model of the time counseled the shift to the exploitation of domestic resources based on locally produced cheap energy. Initial plans for developing a nuclear industry never materialized and DEI eventually turned to the exploitation of abundant coal and surface water resources through thermoelectric and hydroelectric plants. As a state monopoly, it acquired the exclusive right to produce and transport electricity and, from 1956 to the end of the 1960s, nationalized 415 energy companies, created a national grid electrifying the countryside and fueled the Greek version of the postwar economic miracle (Samiou 1998).

DEI's spectacular expansion began in the mid-1970s when, following the oil crisis and problems of energy sufficiency, the company began to explore the lignite deposits of Western Macedonia, where I did my fieldwork in 2015–16. The existence of lignite in Ptolemaida in Kozani district was already known in the late 1930s. But even before then, villagers—mainly Greco-Turkish War refugees who had arrived in the region following the exchange of populations with Turkey in 1922 and who had previous mining experience—were digging small tunnels in their yards to extract coal either for domestic use or for the local market. After 1959, DEI gradually bought the mining companies that had operated in the region since 1925—Paulidi, then Liptol—producing briquettes, nitrogen fertilizers, semicircles and electricity. The expansion of the mines and the development of power plants transformed Kozani—a poor, marginalized mountainous area subsisting on agriculture and herding—into a major industrial center,[1] branded as the "energy heart of Greece." By 2008, Greece had become the second largest producer of lignite in the EU (after Germany) and the fourth worldwide. Lignite has been celebrated as the "national fuel"—"our own black gold" (Kavouridis 2008).

The privatization of DEI was not a new development. It had been tied to the EU integration imperatives since Greece's accession in 1981 and was a prerequisite for "harmonizing" Greece within the EU's common energy framework (European Commission 2015). EU energy policy can be summarized along two axes: (1) the decarbonization of the economy and transition to so-called "clean" renewable energy following concerns about climate change (Paris Agreement signed in 2015) and the entry of finance capital into this market (European Commission 2016); and (2) the creation of a common energy market that addresses the problems of energy sufficiency and dependency on oil and gas from outside the EU (European Commission 2014). This model presupposes the liberalization of energy production and trade as well as the dissolution of vertical public companies in the name of market efficiency. It also enforces the financialization of the energy sector as energy and various derivatives and certificates such as CO_2 credits are traded in regional exchanges. The energy stock exchange system homogenizes prices and links supply and demand through bilateral trade agreements with binding supply.

Within this framework, DEI became a publicly traded company in 2001 and was split into separate companies for production, transport and distribution. The state held 51.1 percent of the shares and controlled the company's management. Private energy providers entered both the wholesale and retail market while global and local leading players, often in consortiums, invested in energy production from gas and renewables. But this was considered insufficient to tackle the so-called monopoly in the energy sector, with the European Court of Justice since 2008 issuing a number of rulings convicting Greece of impeding the establishment of a free market by granting DEI privileged access to cheap lignite.[2] In 2014, following the bailout memoranda, 17 percent of DEI was transferred to the newly formed entity Hellenic Republic Asset Development Fund (TAIPED), responsible for the privatization of public assets. In 2018, the remaining 34 percent of shares passed to the so-called "public hyper-fund," the Hellenic Corporation of Assets and Participations S.A. Finally, following a series of failed privatizations, the Syriza-AnEl government passed a law in April 2018 allowing the sale of 40 percent of its lignite production (mines and power plants) and promising a 50 percent reduction in DEI's retail clients. Nevertheless, the first international tender in January 2019 proved fruitless, with investors, fearing the rising costs of decarbonization, lobbying to include DEI's more profitable hydroelectric plants in the offer.

As a result of these developments, in the last 15 years DEI has pursued a strict strategy of disinvestment. The company was restricted from enlarging or diversifying its portfolio, showing that the restructuring of the energy sector was not primarily about protecting the environment. More importantly for our purposes, production and the company's cash turnover were growing until the crisis, while the number of regular workers was being reduced.

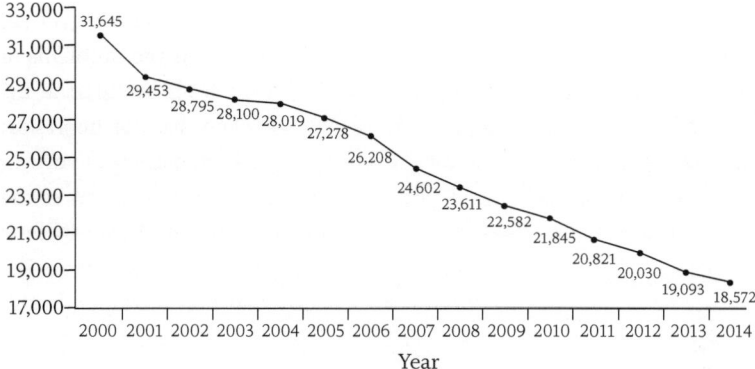

Figure 2.1 Number of regular workers in the Public Power Corporation (DEI) Group. Source: www.dei.gr

Between 1993 and 2015, DEI transformed the production process by not hiring any regular staff with stable working contracts in the Lignite Center of West Macedonia. Instead, the company outsourced growing parts of production (extraction, maintenance, transport, cleaning, etc.) to private subcontractors. These included medium-sized construction companies from the region and metropolitan centers as well as larger firms in global consortia recruited for bigger projects such as the construction of the new power plant Ptolemaida V. Contractors typically had their own subcontractors that used more technically inefficient and dangerous methods, and hired workers under hyper-exploitative terms (Vetta and Palomera 2020 forthcoming). Although subcontractors initially entered production as auxiliary bodies, it is estimated that today they perform more than 50 percent of the extraction work, rendering idle part of DEI's colossal mining machinery. At the same time, major labor gaps were covered by DEI directly hiring precarious workers (not through intermediaries), mainly on the basis of fixed eight-month contracts. Indicatively, the number of regular workers fell from 9,000 in 1997 to 6,000 in 2006 to 4,000 in 2012. While the number of workers with eight-month contracts fell from 1,500 in 2006 to 1,000 in 2012, the number of workers in subcontracting firms kept rising to reach approximately 1,500 in 2016.

This production scheme could only function through the institutionalization and hierarchization of labor divisions and the subsequent exploitation of deep intra-class inequalities. The hiring of regular and precarious workers, subcontractors and subcontractor workers led to very different work experiences, rights and opportunities, access to resources and political representation. Indeed, anthropologists studying industrial settings have documented how such categories of regular/casual workers are operationalized and the impact they have on labor's political response (Gill 2016; Hann and Parry 2018; Beynon, Hudson and Sadler 1994; Kasmir 2014; Lazar 2017; Mollona 2009; Narotzky and Goddard 2017). Scholars have problematized the cost-efficiency rhetoric for casualization and focused on questions of power and discipline, highlighting how gender, generation, race, caste, ethnicity and kinship cut across labor divisions. Sometimes, these divisions are so sharp that they create bounded, rigid groups (Parry 2013). At other times, they create such fluid or porous formations that the dichotomy becomes elusive or at least problematic (Kofti 2016, 2018).

In any case, this seemingly dual labor market cannot be taken for granted. As Carbonella and Kasmir (2014: 11), following Federici, argue, "the making and remaking of such divisions is the lifeblood of labor accumulation. Each wave of dispossession makes or remakes particular working classes again; old divisions are deployed and new ones institutionalized." After all, precarity is far from a novel labor condition or solely the product of recent capitalist restructuring. Globally and historically, stable secure employment of the Fordist type was the exception rather than the rule (Breman 2013; Baca 2004). Greece was never an industrial Fordist economy to begin with; its social formation was sustained by the pluriactivity of working class households while limited industrialization mostly concerned capital-intensive heavy industries and tiny—usually family—firms at the end of global subcontracting chains, giving rise to the thesis of industrialization without proletarianization.[3] Nevertheless, the symbolic epitome of livelihood stability—and maybe the Greek version of the middle-class dream—has been public sector employment, the promise and realization of which has at several moments in history been used as a redistributive tool to attain political consent (Dertilis 2016 [2004]; Lyrintzis 1984; Sotiropoulos 2004; Tsoukalas 1986). It is the direct casualization of this wider public domain that interests me here, with the blurring of the public and private in the realm of social experience and representation enriching our understanding of class inequalities and projects.

Casual Labor

Thomas was 33 years old, born and raised in Kozani, divorced, and a father of a two-year-old child. During my fieldwork he was employed, on and off, on temporary eight-month contracts at the nearby Kardia power plant. These short-term contracts were not related to the temporary nature of the work; they were covering long-term needs and for this reason were recurrently procured. By law, each contract had to be followed by at least four months of unemployment, the so-called public sector's impediment. This was a standard rule for casual public sector employment, theoretically meant to cover seasonal or urgent tasks. Even one extra day of work would imply that labor needs were constant, thus granting the worker the right to become a so-called "permanent" [regular worker, μόνιμος]. As the industry requires 24/7 operation, Thomas worked on rotating shifts at a spreader machine in the lignite deposits department, transferring coal from conveyor belts to the stockyard in order to fuel the thermal burner. Anyone who has visited an open mine and power plant can imagine the extreme labor conditions, the constant deafening noise and vibration exposure from the enormous machines, the suffocating atmosphere of dust and coal coupled with the region's harsh climate with temperatures in the long winter plummeting to -10°C. As expected, the rate of health problems (respiratory diseases, cancers, strokes) was high in the whole region. So was the number of labor accidents due to the old and badly maintained heavy equipment, meager safety measures and control, and the intensification of responsibilities due to personnel reduction. Despite the labor legislation covering all economic sectors, energy miners (both regular and casual) did not enjoy the normal five day/40 hour scheme. Due to understaffing, there were four groups of shifts instead of five, meaning that workers would work six or seven days before having rest. In addition, the extra hour needed for transport in the mine was not considered and paid as extra time. This hour was divided into two parts (43 minutes + 17 minutes), the former paid in money as a "shift benefit" and the latter accumulated and transformed into a so-called "red-repos" [day off]. Overall, everyday toil implied everyday risk for a small hourly wage.

According to DEI, labor costs were reduced by over 2,800,000,000 euros between 2010 and 2015, or by more than 700,000,000 euros per year.[4] Permanent staff had their monthly salaries capped at 2,700 euros, and their average salary cut by 37 percent. But cuts were not equally distributed within the company since they largely involved cutting benefits, extra hours and shifts, all part of the income mix of workers in production rather than distribution or administration. Austerity measures thus fed into already existing divisions between production, administration and management within DEI. These were additionally articulated in territorial terms, as witnessed in the discourse of "dirty northerner coal-miners" (in Kozani) versus "clean southerner bureaucrats" (in Athens) that surfaced when the "northerners" felt ignored or disrespected.

For the contracted staff, the changes were more dramatic. Before the 2012 memorandum with the Troika, Thomas received around 1,200 euros per month, depending on the extra hours he worked on weekends, nights and holidays. As an assistant technician with a modest position in the hierarchy, Thomas could earn up to 1,500 euros a month (including benefits). When we met in 2015, he had already upgraded his license to that of a fore-technician. However, his basic salary was now 600 euros. The hourly wage for a worker with less than three years of experience was 28.50 euros (gross) for those younger than 25, and 31 euros for those older than 25. Following the 2012 memorandum, the system of monetizing work experience based on a three-year scale was abolished; many benefits were cut, and overtime work was limited due to declining production (for boosting renewable energy into the grid).

At best, Thomas could now hope for a monthly wage of 800 euros, or about half of what he previously received in a less skilled position. Unable to meet his financial and familial obligations, he rented his inherited flat and returned to his parents' house. His unemployed ex-wife, with their child, did the same thing. So did Thomas' younger sister when she was unable to meet her professional and motherhood obligations in Thessaloniki, returning to her parents' flat with her newborn child. Such mobility patterns were common for this generation, revealing the centrality of family care, property and pensions for social reproduction in the current crisis period (Narotzky 2016). Thomas' livelihood and the livelihoods of those close to him were entangled in a web of dependencies that had expanded with the crisis—not without tensions and conflicts that would each day test and stretch these bonds to the limit.

Thomas had begun working for DEI in 2005. He finished technical school with expertise in plumbing and cooling systems and returned to school for another year to specialize as a mechanical technician. He then began upgrading his license, from technician to head-technician to foreman. The new license implied work experience and written and oral exams as well as a 300 euros fee. By the time he started working, the housing boom had already peaked; since he had neither capital nor any "entrepreneurial spirit," as he ironically said, he started applying for technical positions at the municipality and the municipal water-heating company. His father, now a pensioner, used to work at the municipal treasury. Alongside his network of contacts who could potentially help his son, he believed in secure public sector employment. Even if Thomas dreamt of studying at the university, there was no family budget or expectation for this. Following a gendered family plan common in Kozani, it was the daughters of the family, like Thomas' two sisters, who went on to higher education; the sons should seek a permanent position at DEI.

But this aspiration among men was not always the case, as older people recalled DEI representatives coming to their villages to recruit workers. In the 1950s and 60s, mining was not as mechanized, and the pay was far less than what people could earn in agriculture or petty commerce. Many more people opted for seasonal migration to work on large infrastructure projects in the Middle East. But since the 1980s, a combination of strong unions, political favoritism, and a particular post-dictatorial historical conjuncture of redistribution in favor of labor had transformed the picture, with DEItzis shedding their previous image as poor *karvouniaris* (a pejorative for coal miners) to becoming status-bearing employees, ideal grooms for the region's unmarried daughters. The high salaries and lump sum payments at retirement, the good insurance and health coverage, and the high replacement rates of pensions were considered acceptable trade-offs for risky, unhealthy labor, particularly in a poor district such as Kozani. At the same time, it created deep inequalities in the local labor market that gradually came to be articulated as the "privileges" of a labor aristocracy and not as earned entitlements. These inequalities were discursively revitalized and politically rearticulated under an austerity regime that legislated labor's devaluation and privatization, with DEI workers and their unions morally stigmatized as a non-democratic "guild" protecting their expensive members.

Grievances about privileges and fairness were no less pronounced among the casual staff as inequalities between them and the "permanent" staff were tremendous in terms of pay, representation, power and risks. The categories of regular and casual, however, were not as rigid as they may initially seem. Relations of kinship, political affiliation and, most importantly, ties of common origin—from expropriated or soon-to-be expropriated villages—cut across the regular/casual dichotomy, creating a range of obligations and dependencies enmeshed in suffocating power relations of simultaneous control and protection. At the same time, the categories of regular and casual were not particularly fluid. Casual workers aspired to one day be included among regular personnel but could no longer transform their contracts. Before 2001, there were objective conditions (such as the duration of renewed contracts) for regularizing employment. Furthermore, as the company's management was not really autonomous but appointed by the government, there were several instances of politically regularizing staff (*μονιμοποίηση*, becoming permanent) in exchange for PASOK and New Democracy votes, for example during the pre-election period of 1993 when the New Democracy government regularized the contracts of more than 6,500 casual workers. Such precedents created high expectations that never materialized for Thomas' generation. Two developments brought such possibilities to a halt. First, there was the 2001 constitutional prohibition (following EU directive 1999/70 on fixed-term labor) on transforming casual into regular contracts in the wider public sector, as DEI in 2001 became a private shareholding company that should function according to market principles. Second, the state (which at the time still held 51 percent of the shares) placed the entire recruitment process under the auspices of the Supreme Council for Civil Personnel Selection (ASEP) to guarantee objectivity, transparency and meritocracy in the selection of personnel. These developments were quite contradictory and, as we shall see, created much confusion regarding DEI's property regime and the entitlements and expectations that derived from it: if DEI was to function according to the market, why was there a need for a standard public sector recruitment process? But if DEI was still a public company, why erase workers' entitlements?

Bondage Unemployment

ASEP was introduced in the public sector in 1994 (law 2190/1994) and its scope expanded in 2009. The selection of successful candidates was based on a complex credit system whereby a mix of educational, social and health criteria were placed in a hierarchy and quantified into points [*μόρια*]. Those who gathered the most points were recruited first until all positions were filled. For DEI's standard eight-month contract, the calculation was as follows.[5]

1. Points for each technical degree equal the grade of the degree multiplied by 40. Someone who has finished a technical school with the

lowest grade (5) nets 200 points. The excellent grade of 10 nets 400 points.
2. Each month of relevant-to-the-position work experience nets 7 points (up to a maximum of 60 months).
3. Each month of unemployment (up to a maximum of 12 months) nets 75 points. (The first 4 months—the public impediment period—gets 200 points). Training courses offered by the unemployment agency (OAED) also count as months of unemployment.
4. Candidates with three children get 150 points, plus 50 points for any extra child. The same stands if the candidate him/herself was a child of such a large family.
5. If the candidate's children are minors, the first two receive 30 points each. Any extra children receive 50 points.
6. Single parents get 50 points for each child. The same applies if the candidate was a child from a single-parent family.
7. Candidates with 30 percent incapacity get 150 points. Larger percentages are multiplied by 3 (e.g. 60 percent incapacity translates to 180 points). If the candidate's parents, children, siblings or spouse have 50 percent or higher incapacity, the percentage is multiplied by 2.

The standardization and expansion of this system to all professional specializations and the casualization of public sector employment fueled a frenzy of accumulating skills, sometimes completely irrelevant to the needs of the particular job opening. This was not limited to DEI workers. Just a few hundred meters from the Kardia power plant, archeologists on eight-month contracts were excavating land that would be expropriated for expansion of the mines. Almost all had impressive credentials, confirming household budget surveys that find education to be high on household priority lists, even in times of crisis (Grigorakis 2014). The alleged Greek obsession with education notwithstanding, one must dig into the employability system in place to understand this abundance of superfluous credentials: for precarious white collar workers, including teachers, municipal workers and archeologists, a MA degree nets 200 points, a second MA 60 points, and a MA outside the position's expertise 30 points. Each foreign language (depending on the level) nets 30–70 points, a second bachelor's degree 150 points, and a PhD, 400 points. The scarcity of positions and the ranking of quantifiable CVs have enhanced a particular calculative logic and constant self-formation (cf. Papagaroufali 2013).

Last but not least, the state introduced the so-called "home-grown rule" (*εντοπιότητα* meaning nativeness) for certain job openings, ranking candidates according to their residential proximity to the working place. This employment criterion was an attempt to fight unemployment in the countryside and to prevent further internal migration to the bigger cities. Yet, the decision to include it in some calls but not in others provoked heated debates and confusion. Within DEI, regular job competitions did not apply the home-grown rule, except for positions in the islands considered remote borderland areas. For casual jobs in the mines and power plants, however, residential location mattered and was conceived as a redistributive mechanism for compensating environmentally affected communities. Four zones—concentric circles around the production area—made up a scale of priority for all recruitments. Zones A and B included villages that had already been expropriated or relocated since the 1970s and those that were to be relocated in the near future due to the expansion of mining. Zone C corresponded to the nearby municipality of Ptolemaida, while Zone D covered the municipality of Kozani, 14 km from the mine. Finally, Zone E included the rest of national territory. When recruiting workers, residential proximity was not translated into points like education, health or civil status, but acquired priority over other criteria. If DEI for example needed 100 casual workers, recruitment would start from Zone A, then B, then C and D, regardless of the points accrued by each candidate. Candidates from Zone A fulfilling the basic requirements were always ranked higher than candidates from Zone B, regardless of whether the latter had more points.

According to my interlocutors, the home-grown priority was not an important issue before the crisis, as casual contracts were abundant both in DEI and other public technical services. In recent years, however, DEI's annual procurements were reduced from three to just one. At the same time, the collapse of construction witnessed a flood of technically qualified workers entering the energy sector, creating a large surplus labor force. Practically, this meant that after the priority given to residents from the so-called lignite villages (Zones A and B), very few positions were available for the rest. Ultimately, the particular employability system, the scarcity of work and the abundant labor supply created a vicious circle wherein workers would at best work for eight months followed by another six to eight months of unemployment. Thomas and many of his colleagues who belonged to Zone D (Kozani residents) described this situation as entrapment. They not only had to live with insecurity and drastically reduced incomes; they were also doomed to unemployment if they wanted a chance to obtain the next casual contract.

> Why am I trapped? I am trapped by the system, because now that my eight-month term is over, I will get to do my public sector's impediment [be unemployed] for the next four months. However, if, by the time there is a new vacancy, I am already working elsewhere, I will lose my unemployment advantage, since one needs seven to eight months [of unemployment] to collect the necessary points to become eligible again. You see? If I want to find another job in the meantime, it has to be undeclared. If the money is not "black," I lose my chance of getting hired the next time [since other jobs outside DEI don't give points for previous service]. So, what is there to do? I'm in limbo. Should I go find another job? Should I stay unemployed, doing nothing? I mean, even now, having 70 months of working experience as I do, the competition is already fierce… as practically everyone has both a head technician's license and adequate experience. People are simply waiting to be called to work.

Indeed, a peculiar system of bondage unemployment was taking root as unemployment was a vital precondition for "staying in the game" for a future contract. Getting the necessary points meant either pushing workers into hyper-exploitative irregular labor markets and debt or putting extra strain on kinship support networks as unemployment benefits lasted for only four months and were reduced by 22 percent in 2012, reaching the almost symbolic monthly amount of 360 euros. This second scenario was common as the once-flourishing black market had withered. In the past, it was relatively easy to get a non-declared job in a coffee place or in construction or maintenance; one could always count on some kind of income for at least the four months of the obligatory labor-break until the time came for a new casual contract. But in 2015–16, "the state was desperate for cash." Taxation became the main instrument to socialize public debt and immense efforts were put into collecting taxes and fighting tax evasion through labor inspections. Even small subcontracting firms in the "labor jungle" of the mine and power plants now always offered some kind of formal contract, even if it had no relation to actual working hours or the profession. For example, firms that in the past would have hired informally would now hire full-time technicians but formally register them as part-time cleaners. As a result, many workers were stuck in this limbo between wage and wagelessness, depression and anticipation. For many, privatization did not represent an ideal plan, but it did offer hope for change. "Too late for a career shift," Thomas cynically joked. "If nothing changes, either you suck it up, or pack your things for Switzerland."

Intra-class Conflicts

Asking casual workers whether unions took action on their behalf was like releasing the storm winds from Aeolus' bag. Without exception, all of the precarious staff I met (as well as many permanent staff) passionately expressed their dissatisfaction with and distrust of the unions. The widespread stigma of the so-called *ergatopatera* (workers' father) in society—a caricature of the professional, lazy unionist-bureaucrat who thirsts for his "chair" (position-power)—was even more pronounced among precarious workers, whose disillusion was often transformed into anger and even hate. While the trajectory of trade unionism in Greece is beyond the scope of this chapter, the prevailing image of the higher echelons of the movement over the past two decades—what critics from the left have labelled "governmental unionism"—includes undemocratic structures, electoral fraud, consensual strategies (despite the pronounced testosterone), partocracy and corruption (Mavridis 2000; Tsakiris 2004; Zamparloukou 1997). It was not until very recently that precarious workers were allowed to become union members. But even when they acquired the right to vote, they could not be elected for any kind of position.

The immense gap in representation fueled already existing inequalities between permanent and precarious staff. The inequalities were not simply financial, although receiving half (or less) of a colleague's salary was already upsetting. Casual workers were de facto placed under the authority of permanent ones, usually had more difficult tasks and were more accountable and controlled. Allegations that permanent staff were constantly evading work were omnipresent in everyday conversations. As Grigoris, a casual worker in the South mine, repeated, "things work out here on automatic mode, depending on the good will of each of us." He meant that there was no real control and, above all, sanctions for the regulars as DEI was still functioning like a state-owned company: "the whole public sector works like this, once you enter [as a regular] you can have peace of mind and you will eventually find ways to do things as you like. Nobody wants troubles/conflicts (*φασαρίες*) and there is no real boss to tell you what to do or fire you."

Accusations of waste and appropriation of public property fueled widespread discontent Anna (32) and Renos (30), both casual IT workers in the administration unit, were in favor of privatization as they thought it necessary for meritocracy—merit here understood as education, hard work but also moral integrity:

> There is so much rot in DEI, better to privatize it so only those who deserve it can stay... Here in administration, many maybe work four out of eight hours, and still they get 2,000 euros. They play cards on their PC and there is always a victim colleague to do the entire job. But they are greedy and miserable too. If you want to infuriate a DEItzis, just cut five euros form their salary. It's enough, they are gonna fuck everything. They dare to complain now because they got used to living on feathers [a comfortable life]. All this crying and misery, "I have kids, I have loans." You are telling me this when I get 600 [euros per month]?? Fuck you! But even before, they were fighting among themselves for the free milk [that the company distributes]; the toilet paper is finished after just one hour! They take everything home, whatever they find, as if it belongs to them... The chief of staff now asked for a car, cause you know, he doesn't want to put wear and tear on his own by coming here every day. And on top, he brings receipt for gas! He leaves work to go to Kozani, to the bank, to the municipality, all for his own personal business and he wants us to also pay for his gas!

Both insisted that there is no mechanism for control, let alone sanctions for such behavior, since the "big party" was happening at the concessions section with the private contractors. "For the personnel," said Renos, "there is an evaluation that is typical for the public sector. But as elsewhere, it's a joke. People grade each other, and even if they don't like some, they still don't want to get into fights. So why bother?"

Such discontent came from younger permanent staff as well. There were clear hierarchies drawn along generational lines as many older workers, after years of climbing the ladder, had much higher wages and occupied positions of surveillance/control (*εργοδηγοί*), with their established support networks within the company granting them different kinds of perks. The educational level of precarious or permanent younger staff was often much higher than that of the older generation who had been hired in the era of so-called triumphant political favoritism and a rising demand for labor (the mid-1970s to the mid-1990s) without the qualifications and transparent recruitment mechanisms required today. In any case, temporary contracts were not restricted to low-skilled labor but included all specializations ranging from unqualified workers to engineers. The decision of many regular workers not to retire when they reached the otherwise standard legal threshold—because their pensions would be much lower than their salaries—was another source of animosity.[6] As an informant once told me, and many would agree, "in the tough times we live in, how dare they stay and steal the jobs of the younger generation, of their own children? Shame on them." Staying was translated as arrogance and moral provocation, whereas the very fact that they had such a choice was seen as yet another public sector privilege.

Of course, as things are never black and white, there were also instances of solidarity and support. Permanent staff, out of compassion, would often approve precarious workers' extra hours or Saturday shifts (although these were never realized). "I feel sorry for them and I try to help if I can. Their salaries are so low that it's hard for them to get by." Another common secret was attributing responsibility to DEI for labor accidents to "save the poor wretch [φουκαράς]" from fines and extra costs. For example, when reporting accidents caused by driver negligence, reports drafted by permanent staff often referred to problems with the road, absolving the driver. This practice was particularly common when it concerned small subcontractors and their workers: "look at these poor people, they are all indebted up to their ears… if I give them a fine, I know I'm killing a family. So, they escape with a warning and I put the costs on the company." These companies were usually at the very end of the subcontracting chain where the boundaries between family and firm were blurry, if they existed at all. Many were kept afloat through bank credit, most often in the form of mortgages or consumption loans, having the family property as a guarantee (Vetta and Palomera, 2020 forthcoming). For this reason, bankruptcy was rarely an option since it implied the liquidation of family assets. More often than not, firm owners would seek protection under the household indebtedness law (Vetta, forthcoming) or enter into informal debt with their contractors, deepening their already unequal relationships. While these situations were all widely known, compassion is also an act of power, implying patronizing attitudes, fostering dependency and reproducing structural inequalities in the sphere of production. The moral collapse of unions in the eyes of both permanent and precarious workers left the most vulnerable workers at the mercy of volatile patterns of solidarity that created further obligations, power asymmetries and even humiliation.

Last but not least, conflicts were not restricted to those between permanent and precarious workers. In fact, the most heated debates were among the precarious workers themselves, largely revolving around the leading criteria for employability: residential proximity to the mines and power plants. The fact that the public sector recruitment system gave priority to the lignite villages (the ones that were relocated/expropriated or were awaiting expropriation) fueled disputes in the courts, media and communities that tore the social fabric of the wider region. Most importantly, it brought to light deeper social conflicts, often played out in cultural/ ethnic terms. Indeed, Western Macedonia is a region with historically vast demographic and economic transformations, following the compulsory exchange of minority populations after the Greco–Turkish War (1919–22), recurrent waves of radical agrarian reform but also the emigration of many of those politically defeated after the civil war. Many of the villages around the mines and power plants had been settled by Greco–Turkish War refugees from Pontus (southern coast of the Black Sea), as many Turkish settlements were abandoned and as the Greek state wanted to boost the Greek ethnic identity in a border region with a significant Slavophone population. As elsewhere in Greece, the refugee arrival was met with hostility. Conflicts—often violent—erupted over the distribution of annexed land, entangled in identity politics over degrees of "Greekness" and translated into polarized political standings (ex. liberals vs. royalists) (Kontogiorgi 2006; Mavrogordatos 1983; Pelagidis 1994).

Discourses of inter-ethnic competition over state employment and resources were omnipresent among Kozanian interlocutors, as present tensions were expressed in terms of the past, revitalizing historical animosities (see Van Boeschoten 2000). From the 1970s onwards, as the energy sector expanded, villages were expropriated and relocated to serve the national interest. But as expropriated villagers received considerable compensation for their lost homes and land, workers in other zones did not understand their current priority in recruitment. The Pontioi were again stigmatized as outsiders who had come to take over everything, greedy people "milking the DEI cow" only for their own interests: "we [the state? Greeks?] accepted these people when they came [in 1920s]," said a Kozanian worker, echoing a widely shared view. "We gave them land. Then work. Now they want to keep these privileges for ever. No! The grandpa 'ate' well. His son too. Even his son-in-law! Now they want Mama-DEI to feed the grandkids too? There is no end to their greed."

Perceived undeservingness in accessing labor was exacerbated by the strong ties maintained by workers from these villages, cross-cutting the casual/permanent divide. For example, despite the animosity between permanent and precarious staff, the moment of recruitment for eight-month contracts signaled a race to mobilize ties of kinship and vicinity in order to access "good positions." Time and again, I witnessed permanent workers promising such an intervention, assuring their interlocutors "don't worry, you are not going to be among the stupid ones, working in the mud. I'll take you at the machine." Such favors were not simply providing better working conditions but often meant facilitating future advancement in the conveyor belt by offering skills that could not be obtained elsewhere. Taking somebody to the machine was in fact a huge privilege as, at the time, there was no official license for excavator conductors and the permit was acquired after a period of "craft" apprenticeship alongside a permanent worker. Such skills not only offered better working conditions and pay; knowing how to operate old, complex machinery strengthened these workers' positions against potential redundancy (Trevisani 2018).

Other workers had more nuanced reactions, seeing a degree of fairness in the residency requirement but demanding stricter criteria for defining residency (many beneficiaries were only officially registered in the villages but lived in the cities) and for applying the home-grown rule (only to currently affected populations and not to those relocated 30 years ago). They stressed that proximity should become part of the points system, as one criterion among many, so that transparency would not be realized by sacrificing meritocracy: "It is comico-tragic that people enter the company only because of where they were born, although they have no skills. How do you think this makes you feel, when for years you were getting license after license [to practice], educating yourself?" Although it is true that there were previously no educational requirements for eight-month contracts and many people were hired as non-qualified labor, DEI recently changed its policy to only accept candidates who have at minimum a technician's license from a technical high school. Whereas some men were no longer eligible, many women from the villages had enrolled in four-year technical night schools. At the time of my fieldwork, a few had already started working while many more were about to be employed.

This was the first time women were taking jobs at the front line of production in this setting of archetypal masculine work, not without triggering new kinds of conflicts. "And now we have all these women from these villages," complained Sotiris, Thomas' colleague:

They were smart, finished school with good grades and got the jobs. I'm fine with this. The problem is that once they enter, they look for their kin [among the regular workers] who transfer them to offices to make coffee and to do unrelated jobs. And who is gonna do their job? Me, I have to work for two, and I'm already doing the work of the permanent! Many say, come on it's women! The truth is, it is tough, imagine there are not even toilets in the mine, they don't even have a place to go pee. But, on the other hand, let's ask for toilets! I mean why should I feel sorry for them? If they don't want to do this job, they should stay at home.

Interestingly, Sotiris was a university graduate who would have been overqualified (and thus non-qualified) for his job had he declared his degree. This was a common pattern as there were few jobs for university graduates, while hired university graduates often merely wanted to establish contacts with regular workers before opening their own consulting/planning firms. However, I never heard anyone accusing these workers of stealing the jobs of others, as they all did about women, revealing deeper discriminatory perceptions and attitudes towards gender. Once again, it was the remnants of DEI's public character that was deemed responsible for tolerating such situations undermining productivity. Idle permanents, lazy unionists, undeserving villagers, unsuitable women—all were proof that DEI was not a serious business. "What kind of company," lamented many, "cannot choose its workers? DEI here is doing social policy." In many of our conversations, the conclusion was the same: "Let's completely privatize it then, to hell with it all!"

Conclusion: On Public/Private Frictions

In the early 2010s organized energy workers in Greece actively participated in the wave of anti-austerity rallies that shook the country. Despite violent repression, demonstrations in several cities were massive and recurrent; the demands far exceeding sectoral economic interests and extending to reclaiming democratic participation and dignity. But whereas the privatization of healthcare, water, public infrastructure and land fueled spontaneous responses as well as movements of solidarity, nothing similar took place to defend electricity as a public good, not even in Kozani where thousands of jobs were at stake. At the time of my fieldwork, responses to DEI's further privatization were limited to unions drafting letters to members of parliament and ministers, and organizing protests at the municipality which, in a town dependent on DEI employment, drew only 20 people. Unity against the company's privatization could not be taken for granted, even among DEI workers, as the casualization of labor had fueled divisions and disorganization.

Despite union efforts to deploy an inclusive "language of contention" (Roseberry 1994) that highlighted the more general interest in their particular struggles, DEI's public sector workers did not manage to bridge what Raymond Williams' (1989) called the scales of "particular militantism" and "abstract universalism" (cf. Narotzky 2014 and Collins 2012). Explaining political positions, I have argued in this chapter, requires digging into the contradictions and fuzziness of the public/private dichotomy. Methodologically, the categories of public and private cannot simply be accepted as sociological givens, but need to be deconstructed in a way that takes into account workers' entitlements as well as their differential expectations and moral significations. Although the inequalities between permanent and precarious staff in the production line were obvious and harsh, they did not automatically translate into antagonistic political views. Rather, their contradictory engagements with public/private signifiers made them feel that they were in a lose-lose limbo. If DEI was still a semi-public company, why were their contracts regulated by private employment laws? If DEI was a semi-private company, why were they recruited through the public sector employment points system? If DEI was a public company, why did they not have the right to have their work regularized? If private, why were certain workers allowed to be underproductive? Why couldn't DEI freely choose its personnel as in any other company?

Casual work always also means casual unemployment. But for many of DEI's fixed-term workers, the quest for public sector transparency created a peculiar regime of bondage unemployment. In contrast to other cases of industrial restructuring, where strategies to accumulate capital led to geographically dispersed employment and unemployment (see Collins 2003), the restructuring of DEI in the wake of austerity simultaneously produced wage labor and wagelessness, the latter being the precondition of the former. The boundaries created by this employability system triggered intra-class conflict, wedded to wider inequalities and exclusions based on gender, generation and residence. The home-grown rule [εν-τοπιότητα] proved to be a particularly serious bone of contention. For some, it was reasonable compensation for their sacrifices, of becoming collateral damage for the country's energy production. For many more, its imposition through the public sector employment points system contradicted the latter's very raison d'être: transparency and meritocracy based on credentials and skills. Worse, the inclusions and exclusions created by the system did not end with labor issues but seemed to erode the very social fabric of the region, bringing up historical tensions between locals and past refugee newcomers. Outside of bureaucratic definitions, who should be seen as "native" was open to translation and moral judgment. The outspoken ethnic rivalries were intrinsically tied to the distribution of state-given entitlements to land and labor, and thus to the problematic relations between citizens and the state.

As discontent could not find expression through organized labor, insecurity, material and moral devaluation produced a race-to-the bottom attitude. The leading unions—ironically nicknamed *Kozan Nostra*—were bounded, exclusionary communities for the casual workforce and functioned more as mechanisms to distribute favors (faster access to company credit, better positions in the conveyor belt, days off, and so forth). Behind their aggressive masculine posturing, they posed no serious threat to ongoing privatization and disinvestment; they had, in fact, already contributed to it by agreeing to the initial privatization. Yet, increased vulnerability and precarity did not lead to isolation and social detachment; nor did they create dispersed identities or atomized subjectivities. My ethnographic research in fact revealed the opposite tendencies: labor fragmentation meant deeper social embeddedness as the support networks of kinship and common origins as well as unequal relations of obligation became more important than ever. Such ties of dependency in their turn called forth notions of meritocracy and enriched existing maps of (un)deserving others.

To return to issues of organization and contestation, because unity is a political challenge—a struggle around the very definition of struggle—labor disunity is not the automatic result of labor differentiation. DEI unions indeed framed their specific labor problems as an attack on public property and an erosion of rights stemming from economic citizenship (e.g. the right to cheap electricity). What they failed to address, however, were the very flaws of the public sector, its hierarchies and undemocratic features. For casual workers, regulars were treating their jobs as a private property right. Their complaints and fights seemed arrogant, oriented towards safeguarding their established working conditions rather than serving some common general interest. They were seen more as protective "protests of desperation" (Lee 2007) than as acts of transformative politics. For many—and not only for the most excluded—privatization thus meant a kind of catharsis, a "sanitizing" of endemic corruption and a possibility for employment based on merit. Unfortunately, the public character of such a crucial good as energy was experienced by many as a privilege of the few.

Notes

1. Lignite extraction reached 1.3 million tons in 1959, 11.7 million tons in 1975, 27.3 million tons in 1985 and its peak of 70.3 million tons in 2002. Since then, production has continuously fallen to, at the time of my fieldwork in 2016, 31.4 million tons. The remaining lignite reserves amount to 1.7 billion tons.
2. http://ec.europa.eu/competition/antitrust/cases/dec_docs/38700/38700_2053_3.pdf (last accessed March 2019).
3. Like other southern European countries, the large number of self-employed and SMEs manifest how accumulation works through peripheralization and subcontracting (Vaiou and Hadjimichalis 1997) and an ideological desire for autonomy.
4. https://www.dei.gr/el/i-dei/kentro-tupou/deltia-tupou/deltia-tupou-2015/martios-2015/dieukriniseis-gia-ti-sullogiki-sumvasi-ergasias-mi/param/t/ECPrint.aspx (last accessed March 2019).
5. The recruitment criteria and points system are explained in the document "Fixed-term Contract of Employment" [Σύμβαση εργασίας ορισμένου χρόνου (ΣΟΧ/ΔΕΗ)] https://www.e-dimosio.gr/entypa-asep/40740/entipo-asep-gia-prokirixis-tis-dei/ (last accessed April 2019).
6. DEI as a semi-public company used to offer "permanent" contracts, setting the age for establishing pension rights to 62 years for administrative staff, 65 years for managers and 60 years for technical staff in the mines and power plants. In 2012, following the austerity memorandum, the company transformed these permanent contracts into contracts of indefinite time, thus abolishing the pension threshold. Workers could choose to leave or stay until they were fired.

References

Athanasiou, A. 2012. *Crisis as "State of Emergency."* Athens: Savalas [in Greek].
Baca, G. 2004. "Legends Of Fordism: Between Myth, History, And Foregone Conclusions." *Social Analysis* 48(3): 169–78.
Beynon, H., R. Hudson and D. Sadler. 1994. *A Place Called Teesside: A Locality in a Global Economy.* Edinburgh: Edinburgh University Press.
Breman, J. 2013. "A Bogus Concept?" *New Left Review* 84: 130–38.
Carbonella, A. and S. Kasmir. 2014. "Introduction: Toward a Global Anthropology of Labor." In S. Kasmir and A. Carbonella, eds. *Blood and Fire: Toward a Global Anthropology of Labor.* New York: Berghahn.
Collins, J. 2003. *Threads: Gender Labor and Power in the Global Apparel Industry.* Chicago: University of Chicago Press.

Collins, J. 2012. "Theorizing Wisconsin's 2011 protests: Community-based Unionism Confronts Accumulation by Dispossession". *American Ethnologist* 39 (1): 6-20.
Dertilis, G. 2016 [2004]. *History of the Greek State 1830-1920*. Athens: Estia [in Greek].
European Commission. 2014. *European Energy Security Strategy*. https://eur-lex.europa.eu/legal-content/EN/TXT/PDF/?uri=CELEX:52014DC0330&from=EN (last accessed March 2019).
European Commission. 2015. *Energy Union Package*. https://eur-lex.europa.eu/resource.html?uri=cellar:a5bfdc21-bdd7-11e4-bbe1-01aa75ed71a1.0003.01/DOC_1&format=PDF (last accessed March 2019).
European Commission. 2016. *Clean Energy for All Europeans*. https://eur-lex.europa.eu/resource.html?uri=cellar:fa6ea15b-b7b0-11e6-9e3c-01aa75ed71a1.0001.02/DOC_1&format=PDF (last accessed March 2019).
Gill, L. 2016. *A Century of Violence in a Red City: Popular Struggles, Counterinsurgency, and Human Rights in Colombia*. Durham: Duke University Press.
Grigorakis, A. 2014 *Les stratégies familiales dans la reproduction et la transformation sociale dans la Grèce d'après-guerre*. PhD Thesis, University Paris 8.
Hadjimichalis, C. 2014a. "Crisis and Land Dispossession in Greece as Part of the Global 'Land Fever'." *City: Analysis of Urban Trends, Culture, Theory, Policy, Action* 18(4-5): 502–8.
Hadjimichalis, C. 2014b. *Debt Crisis and Land Dispossession*. Athens: KΨM Publications [in Greek].
Hadjimichalis, C. 2017. *Crisis Spaces: Structures, Struggles and Solidarity in Southern Europe*. London: Routledge.
Hann, C. and J. Parry. 2018. *Industrial Labor on the Margins of Capitalism: Precarity, Class, and the Neoliberal Subject*. New York: Berghahn.
Kavouridis, K. 2008. "Lignite Industry in Greece Within a World Context: Mining, Energy Supply and Environment.". *Energy Policy* 36(4): 1257–72.
Kofti, D. 2016. "Moral Economy of Flexible Production: Fabricating Precarity Between the Conveyor Belt and the Household." *Anthropological Theory* 16(4): 433–53.
Kofti, D. 2018. "Regular Work in Decline, Precarious Households, and Changing Solidarities in Bulgaria." In C. Hann and J. Parry, eds. *Industrial Labor on the Margins of Capitalism: Precarity, Class, and the Neoliberal Subject*. New York: Berghahn.
Kontogiorgi, E. 2006. *Population Exchange in Greek Macedonia: The Rural Settlement of Refugees 1922–1930*. New York: Oxford University Press.
Lapavitsas, C. 2012. *Crisis in the Eurozone*. London: Verso.
Lazar, S. 2017. *The Social Life of Politics. Ethics, Kinship, and Union Activism in Argentina*. Stanford: Stanford University Press.
Lee, C.K. 2007. *Against the Law: Labor Protests in China's Rustbelt and Sunbelt*. Berkeley: University California Press.
Lyrintzis, C. 1984. "Political Parties in Post-Junta Greece: A Case of Bureaucratic Clientelism." *West European Politics* 7(2): 99–118.

Maniatis, T. and C. Passas. 2013. "Profitability, Capital Accumulation and Crisis in the Greek Economy 1958–2009: A Marxist Analysis." *Review of Political Economy* 25(4): 624–49.

Mavridis, S. 2000. "The Union Movement of Public Utility Companies and the Crisis of Public Enterprises in Greece." In *Structures and Power Relations in Contemporary Greece*. Athens: Sakis Karagiorgas Foundation [in Greek].

Mavrogordatos, George Th. 1983. *Stillborn Republic: Social Coalitions and Party Strategies in Greece, 1922-1936*. Berkeley and Los Angeles: University of California Press.

Mavroudeas, S. 2014. *Greek Capitalism in Crisis: Marxist Analyses*. London: Routledge.

Mollona, M. 2009. *Made in Sheffield: An Ethnography of Industrial Work and Politics*. Oxford: Berghahn.

Mylonas, Y. 2014. "Crisis, Austerity and Opposition in Mainstream Media Discourses of Greece." *Critical Discourse Studies* 11(3): 305–21.

Mylonas, Y. 2017. "Social Media as Propaganda Tools: The Greek Conservative Party and National Elections." In M. Barisione and A. Michailidou, eds. *Social Media and European Politics: Rethinking Power and Legitimacy in the Digital Era*. London: Palgrave Macmillan.

Narotzky, S. 2014. "Structures Without Soul and Immediate Struggles: Rethinking Militant Particularism in Contemporary Spain." In S. Kasmir and A. Carbonella, eds. *Blood and Fire: Toward a New Anthropology of Labor*. New York: Berghahn.

Narotzky, S. 2016. "Between Inequality and Injustice: Dignity as a Motive for Mobilization During the Crisis." *History and Anthropology* 27(1): 74–92.

Narotzky, S. and V. Goddard. 2017. *Work and Livelihoods in Times of Crisis: History, Ethnography and Models in Times of Crisis*. New York: Routledge.

Papagaroufali, E. 2013. "The Industry of Cvs: The Construction of the Self as Active and Flexible Citizen." *Sygxrona Themata* 122–3: 112–18 [in Greek].

Parry, J.P. 2013. "Company and Contract Labour in a Central Indian Steel Town." *Economy and Society* 42(3): 348–74.

Pelagidis, E. 1994. *The Restitution of Refugees in Western Macedonia: 1923-1930*. Thessaloniki: Afoi Kiriakidi [in Greek].

Psimmenos, I. 1999. *Globalization and Workers' Participation: The Case of DEI*. Athens: Gutenberg [in Greek].

Roseberry, W. 1994. "Hegemony and the Language of Contention." In G. Joseph and D. Nugent, eds. *Everyday Forms of State Formation: Revolution and the Negotiation of Rule in Modern Mexico*. Durham: Duke University Press.

Samiou, D. 1998. *The Takeover of Electricity Companies by DEI*. Athens: Institute of Neohellenic Research [in Greek].

Sotiropoulos, D. 2004. "Two Faces of Politicization of the Civil Service: The Greek Case." In B.G. Peters and J. Pierre, eds. *The Politicization of the Civil Service in Comparative Perspective: The Quest for Control*. London: Routledge.

Tsakiris, A. 2004. "State-Party-Union 1980-2001: Between Incorporation and Contestation." In *Social Change in Modern Greece*. Athens: Sakis Karagiorgas Foundation [in Greek].

Tsoukalas, C. 1986. *State, Society, Labor in Postwar Greece*. Athens: Themelio [in Greek].

Trevisani, T. 2018. "Work, Precarity, and Resistance: Company and Contract Labor in Kazakhstan's Former Soviet Steel Town." In C. Hann and J. Parry, eds. *Industrial Labor on the Margins of Capitalism: Precarity, Class, and the Neoliberal Subject.* New York: Berghahn.

Vaiou, D. and C. Hadjimichalis. 1997. *With the Sewing Machine in the Kitchen and the Poles in the Fields: Cities, Regions and Informal Work.* Athens: Exandas [in Greek].

Van Boeschoten, Riki. 2000. "When Difference Matters: Sociopolitical Dimensions of Ethnicity in the District of Florina." In Cowan, Jane (ed) *Macedonia: The Politics of Identity and Difference.* London: Pluto. pp. 28–46.

Vetta, T. Forthcoming. "Households in Trial: Over-Indebtedness, State and Moral Struggles in Greece." In Streinzer, Andreas and Jelena Tošić (eds) *Ethnographies of Deservingness: Unpacking Ideologies of Distribution and Inequality.* EASA series. New York: Berghahn Books.

Vetta, T. and J. Palomera. 2020 forthcoming. "Concrete Stories: Financialization and Inequality in the Construction Chain." *Antipode* 52(3).

Williams, R. 1989. Resources of Hope: Culture, Democracy, Socialism. London: Verso.

Zamparloukou, S. 1997. *State and Labor Unionism in Greece.* Athens: Sakkoulas [in Greek].

3
Work, Wage and Subsidy: Making a Living Between Regulation and Informalization

Antonio Maria Pusceddu

Goodbye Welfare, the Future is Workfare

A 1997 article in *La Repubblica* hailed the post-welfare turn of Tony Blair and Bill Clinton with the headline "Goodbye Welfare the Future is Workfare."[1] In that same year, the Italian government was overhauling the country's labor legislation, which included the first organic systematization of active labor market policies[2] under the banner of "Socially Useful Jobs" (*Lavori Socialmente Utili*, hereafter LSU).[3] The new LSU policies endowed public administrations with special funds to subsidize redundant workers and the long-term unemployed to participate in programs that advanced the "collective utility." Initially welcomed as Italy's first experiment in workfare, LSU projects were later criticized for reinstating "assistentialist" policies in Italy's economically fragile southern regions—Campania, Apulia, Basilicata, Calabria, Sicily and Sardinia—where they were mostly concentrated.

In the mid-2010s, two decades after LSU projects were first implemented in Brindisi, a mid-sized industrial town in the region of Apulia, the uneven trajectories of the early beneficiaries—the "socially useful workers" (hereafter Lsu)—remained a source of contention, echoing broader unrest and collective mobilization in southern Italy. Lsu workers who had been assigned to the outsourced public-school cleaning service in the early 2000s were demanding stable public employment; those in the municipal administration were demanding formal contracts rather than reliance on continuously renewed subsidies. In the same years (2015 and 2016), regional institutions were experimenting with new workfare measures to tackle the long-term effects of the 2007 financial crisis and the austerity policies that followed in its wake. Unlike the LSU—a national scheme territorially managed by job centers—these short-lived regional experiments involved caseworkers determining the eligibility of participants. Developed by regional governments, they were an outcome of the devolution of welfare responsibilities that had begun in the mid-1990s. Whereas Lsu workers had their subsidies regularly renewed by the National Institute of Social Security until they found employment, participation in these regional schemes, which were limited in time and resources, offered no real prospects for future employment. One of these programs, *Cantieri di Cittadinanza* ("Citizenship in the Making", hereafter CDC), targeted the long-term unemployed in households suffering from material deprivation, disability or socio-psychological distress.[4] Through six-month apprenticeships, the CDC sought to foster the "employability" and "social inclusion" of its beneficiaries (see Salvati 2017).

This chapter examines how ambiguity, difference and worthiness are tied to "work" in the neoliberal "workfare state" and in its concrete regional rescaling in southern Italy (Peck 2001, 2002). Drawing on my ethnographic study of Lsu workers and CDC care assistant apprentices in Brindisi's Home Care Assistance Program, I examine how subsidized workers experienced the distinction between *working for a wage* and *working for a subsidy*.

The past decade has witnessed a growing anthropological interest in *time* (Bear 2014; Ringel and Moroşanu 2016), including the emergence of distinct temporal agencies and temporalities during the austerity crisis (Bear 2015; Knight and Stewart 2017; Muehlebach 2016). This chapter is driven by similar concerns about how people relate to the temporal frameworks that structure their livelihoods and how they live with the temporalities of crisis and austerity—the short-term extractive demands and constraints of public debt repayment and the temporal shrinking of their future-making projects (Stubb 2017). Focusing on two different workfare programs allows me to show the different temporalities entangled in the articulation of the Italian workfare state in the 1990s crisis and in the 2010s austerity crisis. Whereas the two phases of workfare maintain the centrality of the work/employment–citizenship nexus, their different temporalities—the duration of work and income as well as the temporal horizon of participants' expectations—reveal the changing constraints and prospects for local beneficiaries and the moral worth attached to "being a wageworker." By focusing on the distinct trajectories of male and female recipients, the chapter also highlights how the gender-based search for social worth is differently enacted by men and women.

I develop my argument by examining the interplay between *regulation* and *informalization* in the trajectories of subsidized workers—two critical aspects of the territorial articulations of state structures and powers in southern Italy (Mingione 1991). Regulation provides a general framework for thinking about both the internationalized tenets of work-for-benefit policies (Peck 2002) and the actual regulatory processes and practices through which they are implemented in specific contexts. As Peck (2001) observes, pure workfare has been more of an ideological program than a historically observable phenomenon. The trajectories of the "subsidized workers" I followed highlight the localization of workfare in contemporary Italy as an emerging regime of mandatory labor, while the regulations enforced by the state for coping with unemployment in Italy's southern regions relied on, and in turn enhanced, informalization in the bureaucratic and institutional sphere and in the broader life-sustaining practices of the unemployed.

The comparative analysis of workfare programs over two decades sheds light on ongoing strategies to regulate surplus labor. Here my argument revisits past debates on the "crisis of employment" and the role of the state in managing the contradictions inherent in the accumulation process— between the commodification of social reproduction and the formation of a surplus population of the unemployed and underemployed (Mingione 1985; Collins and Gimenez 1991). Within this framework, I examine workfare as a coping strategy for addressing the social implications of mass unemployment. The state is a central actor for two reasons. First, as both workfare programs studied in this chapter consist of subsidized jobs in the public services, the state has a dual position as subsidy provider and employer. Second, state regulations differentiate between "subsidy receivers" and "wage workers." Especially for the unemployed, being a *worker* means achieving the social worth attached to "work" (Narotzky 2018).[5] Whether one is a *wage-earner* or a *subsidy-receiver* also has important implications for entitlements and obligations and for how people's subjectivities are constructed and underpinned by moral frameworks of "autonomy" and "dependency" (Gibson-Graham 2006; Narotzky and Besnier 2014).

I suggest that *collective utility*—an elusive concept encompassing public services ranging from caregiving to administrative tasks—informs a framework of devaluation in which "subsidized work" is saddled with all the attributes that characterize reproductive housework, beginning with its gratuitousness. Despite its implicit utilitarianism, "collective utility" informs a non-economic valuation framework that deems the social worth of this work closer to "voluntary work" (without its unselfish and ethical connotations) than to "true" labor.[6] In sum, whereas subsidized work is part of normal labor processes, its economic value is denied—precisely in the sense captured by the "housewifisation" of labor (Mies 1986, 2014; cf. Vantaggiato 1996).

My understanding of "employment for collective utility" draws on Jane Collins' study of the battle over public sector downsizing in the US state of Wisconsin, where proponents of cuts to the public sector pointed to its allegedly "unproductive" role in the economy. In Wisconsin, the "revaluation struggles" of public sector workers invoked long-standing feminist arguments about unpaid reproductive housework, largely invisible to "all the official frameworks that assess economic transactions" (Collins 2017: 7). Building on this line of argument, I suggest that the "collective utility" framework that informs workfare programs institutionalizes uneven relationships between waged and unwaged labor in the broader public sphere of labor surplus regulation, where the moral frameworks of "autonomy" and "dependency" are recast through the difference between wage and subsidy.

Workfare Italian Style

The normative and historical evolution of "socially useful jobs" (Mingione et al. 1999; Saracini 2002) in some ways parallels the international introduction of work-for-benefit programs.[7] Although the use of unemployed workers in activities of "public utility" dates back to the post-World War Two period, it was only after the crises of the 1970s that policies to promote youth employment referred to socially useful jobs (Saracini 2003). Following the closure, privatization and restructuring of public firms, a proper LSU scheme was created in the 1980s for redundant workers receiving unemployment insurance benefits in the deindustrializing regions of southern Italy. In the face of industrial crisis, major jobs losses[8] and rising unemployment in the early 1990s, the scheme was extended to redundant workers nationwide and later to the long-term unemployed. "Socially useful jobs" were part of the broader reform of labor legislation known as *Pacchetto Treu* in 1997, where they were defined as "activities aiming at the realization of works and service provision of collective utility, through the employment of particular categories of subjects."[9] The *Pacchetto Treu* also clarifies that "the use" of workers in activities of public utility "does not establish an employment relationship" (art. 8, paragraph 1).

Between 1995 and 1999, the number of LSU beneficiaries grew from 55,413 to 169,307. Reflecting the regional pattern of structural unemployment in Italy (Pugliese and Rebeggiani 2005),[10] more than 80 percent of them were in southern Italy (cf. Mingione et al. 1999). To reverse this growth of Lsu workers, a process of "emptying the historic pool" of beneficiaries was instituted in the early 2000s. While fiscal incentives were offered to private firms to absorb workers, the job stabilization plans were usually implemented in the public sector.[11]

Although the workfare-oriented LSU scheme was lauded in the mid-1990s as a move to overcome passive "assistentialist" welfare, its expansion raised questions about its workfare-orientation and transformation into a mere "assistance scheme" (Fargion 2001: 53). Critics observed how institutional improvements were hampered by the de-centralized management of active labor policies in which "the implementing actors often work[ed] within traditional organisational settings" (Mingione et al. 1999: 17). The de-centralization of public employment services, within the broader devolution of powers to Italy's regions, marked an important shift in the transfer of responsibilities. The localization of welfare-to-work policies and the proliferation of "socially useful jobs" in areas of chronic mass unemployment were then controversially identified as "workfare Italian style" (*workfare all'italiana*) (Beretta 1999). Criticism of the LSU, which had failed to "activate" the unemployed and push them to re-enter the job market, fueled the stigmatization of LSU beneficiaries as "welfare dependent." In Brindisi, LSU projects came to be identified with access to public employment, thus orienting "activation" policies towards what they were supposed to overcome: the allegedly "assistentialist" nature of public intervention in southern Italy.

The recurrent renewal of LSU subsidies over the years, with the prospect of formal employment, changed the nature of the measure and expanded its temporal scale, turning short-term goals of labor market activation into long-term collective expectations of public jobs. Two decades after the massive growth of LSU workers, the workfare experiments undertaken during the austerity crisis, though underpinned by the same work-for-benefit principle, were shaped by a different relationship to time which left no room for feasible expectations of stable jobs and income, while fully individualizing labor market insertion strategies.

In the five years following the outbreak of the crisis in 2007, unemployment rates in Italy doubled from 6.1 percent to 12.1 percent. Although indicators of material deprivation were rising rapidly, very few national measures sought to address the rapid deterioration of social welfare (Saraceno 2015: 109–15). Regional differences further underscored the dire situation in southern Italy, where 19.9 percent of the population was suffering from severe material deprivation in 2015 (the corresponding numbers were 7.4 percent for central Italy and 7.1 percent for northern Italy) (ISTAT 2016: 2–3). In response, the Regional Government of Apulia agreed with trade union confederations to develop a "Work of Citizenship" framework to bolster social inclusion through active labor policies and workfare-oriented measures of income support.[12] Within this general framework, the CDC scheme was a conditional cash transfer measure, providing income support through specifically designed job training projects. Shortly after its implementation in 2015–16, it was replaced by a new regional scheme, *Reddito di Dignità* (Dignity Income). These same years also witnessed the launch of the national poverty relief scheme *Sostegno di Inclusione Attiva* (Active Inclusion Support), replaced in 2018 by a new conditional cash transfer scheme, *Reddito di Inclusione* (Inclusion Income). Finally, a new national scheme, *Reddito di Cittadinanza* (Citizenship Income) was passed in January 2019.[13] All of these measures have in common their short duration and a strong workfarist approach. Despite variations in rules of access and the resources earmarked for each scheme, they all converge in their emphasis on work that advances the "collective utility." Taken together, these "austerity schemes" differ from the earlier LSU on a significant point: whereas the LSU was conceived as a labor activation policy, the former conflate labor policies with anti-poverty measures, implying the double moralization of beneficiaries as "unemployed" and "poor"—a difference further conveyed through the symbolic packaging of policies with terms such as "dignity," "inclusion" and "citizenship."

All of these schemes can be read along a continuum defined by the different temporalities that construct beneficiaries as workers or non-workers. While the LSU set the stage for long-term collective mobilization and negotiations around "work" and "citizenship," short-term measures such as the CDC more clearly reveal that the tensions between needs and aspirations has become individualized and confined to the sphere of personal responsibility. In the following section, I describe how workfare was localized in Brindisi.

Locating Workfare in Brindisi

The two main groups of Lsu—redundant workers and the long-term unemployed—reflect the extended phase of industrial restructuring in the 1980s and chronically high rates of unemployment (see Table 3.1). The job center selected the beneficiaries employed by the municipal administration in specifically designed projects. Some 130 redundant workers—most of them male and drawn from the "mobility list"—were admitted in 1995–6. Another 120 long-term unemployed persons were admitted in 1998 and initially employed in a biennial waste recycling promotion project. Many in this group were women.

The first group of Lsu (the redundant workers) reflected the national restructuring and downsizing of the petrochemical sector in the 1980s,

Table 3.1

		1991	2001	2011		
		Brindisi	Brindisi	Brindisi	Apulia	Italy
Labor force participation	Total	47.5	42.7	45.7	45.4	50.8
	Male	67.5	57.6	58.4	58.3	60.7
	Female	29.3	29.3	34.4	33.5	41.8
Employed	Total	33	33.1	36.5	37.5	45
	Male	50.2	48.1	49.3	50.2	54.8
	Female	17.3	19.5	25	25.8	36.1
	Youth	20.9	24.3	28.1	29.9	36.3
	Agriculture	7.5	5.4	6.7	12.1	5.5
	Industry	29.6	28.6	23.2	22.4	27.1
	Service	63	66	70.1	65.6	67.4
Unemployed	Total	30.5	22.5	20.2	17.3	11.4
	Male	25.6	16.5	15.6	13.9	9.8
	Female	40.9	33.3	27.3	22.8	13.6
	Youth	73.4	56.1	52.1	43.1	34.7

Source: ISTAT – National Institute of Statistics, National Census
http://ottomilacensus.istat.it/comune/074/074001/ (last accessed April 2019).

which hit the large-scale state-sponsored project of heavy industrialization in Brindisi that had begun in the early 1960s (Ginsborg 1990: 229–31). In a period of four years between 1978 and 1982, 1,500 out of 7,500 workers were laid off while investments in labor saving technologies further reduced future employment opportunities (Greco 2002). To compensate for the loss of industrial employment, public authorities in the early 1980s agreed to locate a new ENEL (the public electricity company) power plant in Brindisi. Its construction was completed in the early 1990s; the Lsu redundant workers came from this laid-off construction workforce. Lsu from this group, both blue- and white-collar workers (e.g. accountants), were hired by the municipal administration in 2001. A larger group of about a hundred workers were attached to the outsourced public-school cleaning service, to be employed by the successful contractor in 2001.

The second group of Lsu beneficiaries (the long-term unemployed) reflected the prevailing situation in the south of Italy: high rates of female unemployment (see Table 3.1) including for women with secondary education,[14] historically precarious and discontinuous work in the construction sector, and the large informal sector in which many "unemployed" workers earned their livelihoods (Mingione 1991: 380–414).[15] Within this group, a large majority of the women had secondary education and came from single-income families where the husband was the sole wage-earner. Marta (54), married with two children, was typical; she had worked on and off with short-term contracts in the public administration. Most men, in contrast, lacked secondary education and combined informal employment, temporary jobs and other welfare provisions. Francesco (61) had held numerous jobs (gravedigger, butcher, caretaker, etc.) following a short period of work in Turin. Living with his wife in a council house, he eventually obtained a small disability pension due to an accident at work. Many male beneficiaries were also involved in cigarette smuggling, prominent in Brindisi in the 1980s and 1990s until its final dismantling with a massive police operation in 2000. Official reports estimated that more than 5,000 households in the province earned their livelihoods through cigarette smuggling.[16]

In this second group (the long-term unemployed), only a small number of beneficiaries were selected for training and assigned to the outsourced tax collection service in 2002. Following the end of the waste recycling project in 2001, the remaining Lsu were distributed in different branches of the municipal administration without changes to their status. Since then, they have been performing a variety of tasks—from administrative work to cleaning, gardening and maintenance, most of the time filling personnel gaps in the administration. They continued receiving the subsidy (580 euros per month for 80 hours of work) from Social Security, which was renewed on a six-month or yearly basis. They could earn more (up to 1,000 euros) only when funds from the municipal budget were earmarked for supplementary hours, which fluctuated with the demands of the administration (e.g. employees' vacation schedules or an increase in workload).

The *Cantieri di Cittadinanza* scheme targeted a specific segment of the unemployed already known to the municipal welfare services. Under the supervision of case managers, recipients were enrolled in a six-month apprenticeship (20 hours per week) for a monthly stipend of 500 euros, getting paid only for the actual hours spent in the apprenticeship. But according to the local coordinator, the lack of information provided to potential private partners and the poor coordination between institutions jeopardized the program's local implementation.[17] As a result, the only projects submitted were those by the municipal social services.[18]

The care assistant apprenticeship project in the municipal Home Care Assistance Program was also the only case of a public–private partnership, run by a cooperative contracted to deliver care to people with special needs. The apprentices (*tirocinanti*) were five women and a man who asked to join the project. The man, Mario (42), was single and lived in a council house with his aged mother, whose pension (380 euros) was their only regular income, supplemented by the little he earned as an occasional house painter. Out of the five women in the program, four had experience with informal paid care work.[19] The youngest woman in the group, a 26-year-old single mother, was disappointed by her assignment. She had grown up in Cremona in northern Italy, where her family moved in the early 2000s, and returned to Brindisi after quitting her job in a beauty salon. After splitting up with her partner, she could not afford to raise her children alone. She lived in a council house with her father, who received a disability pension.

Similar arrangements were common among the women. Manuela (40), married with a child, occasionally worked as a seamstress to supplement the meager household income. When her husband lost his job in a service company, they moved into her mother's house, unable to pay rent on their own. The household income was made up of different subsidies, casual jobs, charity assistance and her mother's pension. Giuliana (58) lived with two children and a disabled brother, whose pension was the only regular income in the household. She ran a small cleaning service firm, which she eventually closed due to distress caused by family events. While serving the apprenticeship, she received a three-year rent subsidy and daily meals from a soup kitchen. She earned some additional money by recycling clothing and children's toys that she sold to a second-hand shop.

The importance of participating in the CDC apprenticeship was twofold. First, it ensured a stable income, relieving chronic material insecurity for at least several months. Second, it gave grounds for hope that job training would eventually improve one's "employability," not least by providing visibility and recognition to one's care work. But as the program approached its end, its participants were left disappointed. In the following three sections, I illustrate how struggles for recognition, social worth and material security interact with the ambiguous boundaries between work, wage and subsidy.

A Wage, Not a Subsidy

In July 2015, the ex-Lsu-Ata—the ex-Lsu workers now formally employed by the firm cleaning the schools—were demonstrating throughout Apulia against the decision of the contracting company to temporarily lay them off until a new tranche of public funds was confirmed. In Brindisi, workers were clashing with their employer, a subcontracting cooperative, due to a reversal in the mechanism of "hours banking" (*banca ore*). Rather than accumulating extra work hours—to be used as time off rather than as paid overtime—workers were accumulating "non-worked hours" and becoming "indebted" to their employer. This happened when, for lack of proper planning, some workers were "left at home" (*lasciati a casa*) with their wages docked accordingly. But while some workers were losing hours, others were being pressured to increase their productivity, to clean more square meters per hour to the detriment of quality. The "time debt" (*debito orario*) was denounced by unions nationwide and was a recurrent source of friction between workers and employers—mainly subcontracting cooperatives (USB 2012). Workers and unions contended that the "hours banking" system transferred to workers the negative consequences of firms underbidding each other to win public contracts. In the face of continuous tensions, payment delays, the uncertainty of public fund transfers and exhausting negotiations, unions and workers asked for the cancellation of all accumulated negative hours. The fact that some workers were left at home while others were not was also having a divisive effect on the workers themselves. The same happened when a group of cleaners were selected to form a team of "decorators"—a differentiation that implied privileged treatment.

In the following months, I started following a small group of "decorators" in a local school. Although they were by contract "cleaners," they worked as decorators in an extraordinary building maintenance plan funded by the national government in 2014 to settle a conflict between workers and their contracting company over the reduction of working hours. They were among the selected group of specifically trained workers who hoped to become a permanent team of decorators for the local public-school network. Their actual situation, however, was not as positive as they had hoped since they still did not know whether new projects were scheduled or whether they were running the risk of being "left at home." Bitter and disappointed, they did not feel "encouraged to do good work." As ex-Lsu-Ata "cleaners," they worked either part-time or on 35-hour week contracts, earning a salary of 900 euros or less. Until the crisis reduced opportunities in the informal labor market, most of them had second jobs[20] which many enjoyed more than working as "cleaners." Cosimo's (48) story illustrates a common trajectory. In the mid-1980s, he started working in a mechanical workshop in the petrochemical sector. From 1987 to 1992, he was employed in the power station construction works. Laid off and registered in the mobility lists for two years, he was then admitted to the LSU scheme. In the meantime, married with two children, Cosimo managed to supplement the family income through informal jobs (e.g. paper collector) and even cigarette smuggling—"like everyone here in Brindisi."

A closer look at the terminology—*ex-Lsu-Ata*—can help us disentangle the ambiguities surrounding their condition as wageworkers and how their "temporal agency" is constrained by the moralization of their occupational trajectories. The social implications of this specific denomination suggest how the allusion to "subsidized jobs" continues to affect their categorization as "workers," even when they are regularly employed, and how regulation and informalization intersect to affect their incomes as well as how work identities are made socially meaningful. Whereas *ex-Lsu* tracks their previous status as subsidy receivers, the acronym *Ata* (Administrative, Technical and Auxiliary personnel employed in public schools) describes what they do (cleaning and maintenance work), but not what they are. Ata workers are in fact public employees, while the ex-Lsu-Ata are a "protected" category of workers employed through public tendering by private firms contracted for taking over the outsourced cleaning services previously done by Ata personnel. In their "liminal" denomination—"ex-Lsu" but "not-yet-Ata"—their connection to the LSU prevails even in the ways they are implicitly categorized in workplaces as "welfare dependent." For example, Cosimo and his colleagues complained that public school employees called them *cassintegrati* (workers on redundancy payment), which they considered disrespectful, a way of diminishing their dignity as workers (*la dignità di lavoratori*).

The "misrecognition" (Fraser 2000) implied in the tendency to bind workers to their former status as "subsidy receivers" also explains the social meaning of usually informal "second jobs." In addition to their economic value, second jobs can be a source of social legitimacy for male breadwinners, for unlike "socially useful jobs," they are not branded with negative connotations of welfare dependency. The friction between the ambiguity of institutional normative frameworks and the legitimacy of informal social norms suggests how meanings of work are produced as well as how "difference" (Carbonella and Kasmir 2014) weighs on workers' subjectivities and creates effective hierarchies among workers. The struggle for direct employment in the public sector shaped the collective agency of ex-Lsu-Ata workers. Internal conflicts and short-term livelihood arrangements had to be carefully—and often with difficulty—balanced with long-term collective expectations of stable work and income as well as social and moral recognition.

A Subsidy, Not a Wage

Lsu workers in the municipal administration faced a more institutionalized form of misrecognition (Fraser 2000). While they shared the precarious situation of the ex-Lsu-Ata—living through payment delays, last-minute renewals, etc.—unlike them, they technically remained "subsidy-receivers." This formal difference had substantial implications for labor relations, for their lack of bargaining power and thus subordination. They were not entitled to the benefits of the wage relationship, for example pension contributions, labor protection, productivity bonuses or performance-related pay, which could only be allocated after an informal agreement among employees to renounce their own shares. After 18 years of back-to-back subsidies, they were still hoping to achieve permanent positions. In 2015, new national legislation to reform public administration (L. 124/2015) set the framework for definitive Lsu "stabilization" in the administrations where they were employed.

In the early summer of 2016, a union assembly was summoned in the town hall to discuss the job stabilization plan elaborated by the human resources executive. The triennial plan outlined that workers could be hired as A (the lowest rank) or B, according to financial resources and organizational demands. The proposal was received with tepid enthusiasm by Lsu as previous expectations of job stabilization had been repeatedly frustrated.[21] Mistrust and disappointment had come to prevail over time, undermining solidarity. In 2014, Lsu workers had decided to undertake a 15-day work-to-rule action (*sciopero bianco*). As their tasks had never been specified, their plan was to do nothing. Anna (50), a committed union member, explained that "they say we abstained from work, but I have been working now for 14 years in the General Records Office, and I have never seen my tasks written down anywhere." The action demonstrated how important they had become for the regular functioning of the administrative machine. When Anna returned to work, she found piles of unregistered mail on her desk. But the action was ineffective; those who joined (90 percent) had their allowances cut in half. Despite being able to undertake collective action, Lsu realized the predicament of the unions in dealing with their case: "the Lsu situation," Anna explained, "is so 'messy' (*ingarbugliata*) that even for the unions it is a real pain to understand what it implies… it's a matter of legal frameworks… in terms of representativeness, it is not about 'workers' (*lavoratori*)."

At the union assembly, several women quarreled about who was going to get the A or B rank. Filomena, complaining that she had not even been "entitled to a writing desk," was suspicious that another woman was receiving special help thanks to her connections in the administrative hierarchy. Maria (52), a Lsu worker in the municipal housing service, told me that "those who didn't manage to get a desk" were the ones who "did not want to work." "I have never said no, bring the paper and I went, bring that… and I went, do that… and I have always done it… It is by doing so that I earned the desk because I have shown that I deserve it." During the assembly, male Lsu stayed silent. Maria stated that "since they have their [second] jobs, they are fine just getting the regular subsidy." Competitive concerns about "worthiness" and "deservingness" were more common among women who committed themselves to learning administrative jobs and who sought to be acknowledged for it.

Such was the case for Anna. She had married young to a man employed in the military arsenal, with whom she had two children. Theirs was a common single-income family—a breadwinning father and "a full-time mother," as she put it. Once the children had grown up, she applied to the LSU, which she saw as "an opportunity to start doing something." When her project (1998–2000) ended, Anna was sent to the mayor's office as an informal "administrative collaborator" and eventually to the General Records Office. Thanks to basic computing skills acquired by attending a regional training course for the unemployed, she supervised the transition to the digital records. In 2016 she was in charge of controlling and verifying the General Records Office, basically checking all the incoming and outgoing mail. Yet she remained "invisible." When she complained to the executive officer about the excessive workload for a Lsu, he responded in a patronizing way: "Shall I send you with the cleaners? You should be grateful for us letting you do a job that gives you dignity (*un lavoro che ti da dignità*)." Anna remained speechless. She told me: "you can't say anything, you can't do anything, you're nothing! Meanwhile, you sign resolutions; they bring you tender documentation, legal documents... though, who am I? Nothing!"

This episode and the quarrel during the union assembly reveal the gender dynamics among Lsu workers in the municipal administration. Like the ex-Lsu-Ata, male Lsu continued to have informal "second" jobs which brought them additional income and augmented their worth as breadwinners. Women often explained how their male co-workers showed little interest in claiming supplementary hours (funded by the municipal budget) since they "have a profession" (*hanno il mestiere*) and do not need more LSU work hours. While male workers associated the LSU subsidy with dependency and informal self-employment with autonomy, for women, their "informal activities" consisted of unpaid domestic housework, which implied financial dependency on their husbands. It was thus in the sphere of state regulation that their struggle for recognition and autonomy could be waged. At the same time, they experienced "working without a wage" as a double form of misrecognition and subordination, exemplified by the combination of unpaid domestic labor (reproductive work) and "working for a subsidy" (socially useful work). While the lens of gender throws into sharp relief how men and women must make a living between regulation and informalization—and how "worthiness" is differently pursued in their livelihood strategies—the burden of inequality weighs more heavily on some women (care assistant apprentices in the Home Care Assistance Program) than others (Lsu workers). In the following section, I illustrate how the interaction between informalization and regulation underlies the temporality of workfare in the era of austerity.

Working Citizenship

In March 2016, a union officer introduced me to Rosaria (52) who, at the time, had not yet been informed of her admission to the *Cantieri di Cittadinanza* program. Rosaria lived with her son (21) and daughter (18). While waiting for council housing, she was receiving a three-year rent subsidy. Although she had separated from her husband in the late 1990s, she only obtained child support many years afterwards. In the meantime, she struggled to make ends meet by taking on all possible jobs and receiving support from relatives, institutions and charities. She cared for a disabled woman for four hours per day, for which she received 10 euros. Several times per month, she cleaned offices and private homes. When called, she washed dishes in restaurants, usually on weekends or on special occasions. As she could only get jobs in the black labor market (*lavoro a nero*), Rosaria saw the CDC as a chance to come out of the shadow of informal labor and have a recognized position. As she explained: "I have worked a lot, everywhere, but it does not appear anywhere; this [CDC] would give me the chance of having my name written somewhere… finally I will have a job… I don't know, [a job which is] not illegal."

Thanks to an extended network of friends and acquaintances, Rosaria could rely on horizontal relationships of mutual aid as well as vertical relationships of the patron–client type. Through the former, she often received used clothes, food and help, including information about possible jobs. Through the patron–client relationship, she hoped to climb the social housing waiting list in exchange for actively supporting a council candidate during mayoral elections. Toiling day after day to make ends meet, Rosaria also had to cope with indebtedness as she had secured several small bank loans when she started receiving child support. Even after starting her CDC apprenticeship, she continued to clean offices and private houses. On her only free mornings, on Saturdays and Sundays, she began caring for an old lady. And despite being embittered by the treatment she received, she continued her four hours of care work each evening. Rosaria never complained: "I have to stay silent and do whatever they say because I need the money."

Rosaria's situation was common to all of the CDC recipients I met. They had applied to the program with high hopes. Participation in the CDC provided an important supplement to their meagre family incomes and held the promise of making their care work "visible." Most had worked, or continued to work, informally as caregivers; they saw the apprenticeship as a chance to become professionally recognized as such. Informal caregiving generally entails exploitative working conditions (e.g. low pay and lack of social protection) which weighed on the precarious livelihoods of the (mostly female) workers. Obtaining formal employment in the local service cooperatives was thus an important goal. But "citizenship" came in the shape of a low salary in the subcontracting chain of caregiving, while official recognition would entail fitting into one of the professional categories set by the regional planning of social services. Another option was to be included in the upcoming Income of Dignity scheme, which was planned to last for one year, though with a lower stipend and strict control over recipients' use of money.

Despite the intentions of the CDC scheme to provide the basis for "active inclusion," most of the subjects involved—from social workers to recipients, union officers to the cooperative's employees—were skeptical of the program's efficacy. While all were positive about the underlying idea and framework, many were disappointed by the manner of its implementation, especially the lack of coordination, limited funding and scarce publicity. In the end, all recognized that recipients earned some badly needed money. But when CDC participants realized that the apprenticeship was "real" work, some tried to blow the whistle on its exploitative practices. Before the end of the six-month apprenticeship, a "spontaneous committee of CDC unemployed," supported by the COBAS (Confederazione dei Comitati di Base) rank and file union, issued a statement in which no particular demands were made. It was a generic request for help against exploitation, with their experiences qualified as "modern slavery."[22]

In the end, participating in Citizenship in the Making underlined workfare recipients' own uncertain citizenship, as though citizenship was a process always in the making—and continuously postponed. Their experience was further shaped by the tension between two co-existing temporalities: the temporary relief of the monthly stipend and the long-term expectation of being able to pursue their life projects.

Conclusion

This chapter has presented a diachronic comparison of workfare schemes in southern Italy, with the aim of highlighting how ambiguity, personal worth and difference are variously entangled in the articulations of work, wage and subsidy. In this concluding section, I return to the main points raised at the chapter's outset: "collective utility" as the framework for rephrasing the unequal relationship between waged and unwaged work in the public sphere; the pursuit of livelihood and "worthiness" in the interaction of regulation and informalization; and the tension between shifting temporalities of crisis and the temporal horizon of workfare recipients' expectations.

I have addressed the local implications of categorizing workers as *wage-earning* or *subsidy-receiving*. Although the LSU framework sought to tackle unemployment by implementing "active" labor policies, in the long run it led to the growing precariousness and segmentation of the public sector labor force, along the cleavages of intra-national territorial inequality. The regional devolution of workfare policies and the process of differentiation this implied created spaces of conflict in which claims, obligations and entitlements were ambiguously produced in the interaction between regulation and informalization. The moral designation of "collective utility" underlying the categorization of "socially useful workers" rescaled the issue of care in the public sphere by exposing the ambiguous boundaries between "working for a wage" and "working for a subsidy." The experience of the CDC caregiver apprentices was even bitterer since participation in the program replicated the exploitative conditions of caregiving in informal settings. Inevitably, "public utility" was held responsible for the burden of inequality they had come to experience in their everyday pursuit of livelihood. "Public utility" jobs can therefore be seen as an experimental moment in reconfiguring the regulatory role of the state in scaling-up the uneven relationship of waged and unwaged labor in the macro-process of social reproduction.

My analysis has identified the twofold dynamic of regulation and informalization as fundamental to understanding the production of differences, ambiguities and worthiness. Regulation and informalization are inter-related dynamics that cannot be disentangled in the workfarist perspective of "getting people back to work." As the Lsu struggles for recognition showed, the informalization of labor is implied in the state's regulation of "socially useful jobs" as work-out-of-employment. At the same time, the regulatory framework that brought ex-Lsu-Ata under the controversial system of outsourcing and sub-contracting public services entailed a devaluation of labor, counterbalanced by the social worth of informal jobs. Finally, the dynamics operating in the CDC scheme expose labor devaluation as a necessary condition of "citizenship" while reinforcing labor informalization in its exploitative form. The "collective utility" framework here appears as a moralizing force operating through a set of oppositions (wage/subsidy, productive/unproductive, market/state, autonomy/dependency) which eventually erodes the employment–citizenship nexus. Only non-remunerated work of "collective utility" (e.g. voluntary work) with unselfish ethical content can serve as an alternative basis for citizenship (Muehlebach 2012).

The comparison of workfare schemes implemented in two distinct phases of crisis and mass unemployment—in the 1990s and in the post-2008 era—show how the temporalities of livelihood incorporate essential shifts in the temporalities of the state, which provided the grounds for different possibilities of conflict, struggle, (gendered) individual and collective expectations. While the early LSU could still be understood within a national Keynesian framework (Barbu 2013) with the long-term goal of "formal employment," the CDC more clearly exemplifies the shift towards a territorially fragmented and temporally limited workfare—a shift that reveals the state's attempts to shape socio-economic relations in order to manage a contradiction inherent in the accumulation process. On the one hand, the state enhances its extractive functions by cutting public services; on the other, the state finds it increasingly difficult to deal with a growing surplus population through the creation of jobs and minimum welfare provisions. The temporally limited workfarist mobilization of the surplus population is thus enabled by the interaction of regulation and informalization, where people's search for social worth—underpinned by socially defined and gender-based expectations of "work"—plays a central role. Paradoxically, this workfare state functions only because of the large-scale informalization of the livelihoods of the surplus population, which sets the ground for disciplining the boundaries of "citizenship" through "work" and "non-work."

Different temporalities and orientations towards the future are reflected in workers' capacity and possibilities to build horizontal and vertical alliances. The Lsu workers, and especially the ex-Lsu-Ata workers when talking about quitting their uncertain jobs as cleaners, emphasized two key points: collective strength—"together we are 20,000"—and temporal horizons, with real public employment as the goal. CDC recipients, in contrast, experienced the contradiction between piecemeal workfare and the rhetoric of individual activation which underpinned a more immediate, individualized temporality. Finally, whereas the two main phases of workfare in Italy reveal how the work/employment–citizenship nexus remains central, they also show essential differences of temporal scale, revealing fundamental shifts in the constraints and prospects of local beneficiaries and their capacity to imagine long-term collective engagements.

Notes

1. "Welfare addio il future è del workfare," *La Repubblica*, June 15, 1997. On the "geopolitical etymology" of workfare, see Peck (2001: 83–122).
2. See "European Semester: Thematic factsheet—Active labour market policies—2017," November 16, 2016: https://ec.europa.eu/info/sites/info/files/european-semester_thematic-factsheet_active-labour-market-policies_en.pdf (last accessed March 2019).
3. I use the acronym LSU, in capital letters, to refer to the scheme, and Lsu (*Lavoratori socialmente utili*) to refer to its beneficiaries, the "socially useful workers." LSU are sometimes called LPU (Lavori di Pubblica Utilità)—jobs of public utility. Lsu are divided into two general categories. The *transitoristi* depend on ministerial funds and are targeted by special measures for stable employment in the public or private sector. This category includes beneficiaries from the late 1990s who are conventionally referred to as the "historic pool" (*platea storica*). The *autofinanziati* (literally "self-funded") are directly subsidized by local administrations and are excluded from special measures for stable employment. See: https://www.inps.it/nuovoportaleinps/default.aspx?itemdir=46860 (last accessed February 2019). This chapter refers only to the first category of Lsu workers.
4. See http://www.sistema.puglia.it/SistemaPuglia/cantieridicittadinanza (last accessed March 2019). A parallel program, *Lavoro Minimo di Cittadinanza* (Minimum Work of Citizenship), targeted redundant workers receiving unemployment benefits; it received far fewer applications than the CDC.
5. In the Italian language there is a single word for work, labor or jobs, *lavoro*, which generally conveys the meaning of "paid employment" or "salaried work." In Brindisi, the word used in the local dialect is *fatìa*, the meaning of which is closer to "toil."
6. In the 1990s a group of Italian economists debated "socially useful jobs" (not the workfare program) as a possible solution to mass unemployment, aiming to satisfy "unmet social needs" such as underdeveloped or neglected public services (Lunghini et al. 1995). The tricky question was how such jobs were to be understood in relation to the market and the wage relationship.
7. For a chronological reconstruction of the introduction of compulsory work-for-benefit programs, see Lødemel and Trickey (2001). In France, the Travaux d'Utilité Collective was a short-lived work-based insertion program targeting young people in the mid-1980s.
8. The scheme exclusively targeted redundant workers registered on "mobility lists"—workers dismissed from industrial firms or recipients of extraordinary unemployment insurance benefits.
9. Legislative Decree December 1, 1997, n. 468. The financed projects covered a wide range of activities in the public services from gardening, waste recycling, activities in museums and home care assistance to tasks in

public administration, ranging from administrative support to cleaning and maintenance.
10. Unemployment rates in the south of Italy more than doubled from 8 percent in 1977 to 17.2 percent in 2012. The center and north of the country recorded more modest increases (from 5.5 percent to 9.5 percent and from 5.8 percent to 7.4 percent). For an overview of employment and unemployment trends from 1977 to 2012 see: https://www.istat.it/it/files//2013/04/Report-serie-storiche_Occupati-e-disoccupati2.pdf (last accessed February 2019). For a broader temporal perspective on unemployment in Italy and its statistical treatment, see Alberti (2016).
11. Following the approval of the special measures (Legislative Decree 81/2000 and art. 50 of Finance Bill, 2003), their numbers dropped to 69,268 in 2003 and to 19,984 in 2010. According to the National Institute of Social Security, there were around 15,000 beneficiaries in 2015. See: https://www.inps.it/nuovoportaleinps/default.aspx?itemdir=46860 (last accessed February 2019).
12. "Il Piano straordinario per il lavoro—Per un lavoro di cittadinanza" http://cgilpuglia.it/archive/news/documenti/1146_PQ62D.pdf (last accessed February 2019).
13. The decree was passed in January 2019. See: https://www.repubblica.it/economia/2019/01/17/news/reddito_di_cittadinanza-216790041/ (last accessed April 2019). For a critical appraisal, see Saraceno (2018).
14. This can be explained by the prominence of women with secondary education on the public job center's unemployment lists. Women with only compulsory education are less present, meaning they are not even registered among the "active population" in the unemployment lists (see Mingione et al. 1999: 15). This aspect of inequality and misrecognition within the female population is not addressed in this chapter.
15. In the early 1990s, unemployment increased to 30.5 percent of the labor force, with even higher rates for women (40.9 percent) and youth (73.4 percent)—corresponding to employment rates of 17.3 percent and 20.9 percent respectively (see Table 3.1). Between 2015 and 2016, the job centers recorded that 30 percent of the active population was in search of employment.
16. Commissione Parlamentare Antimafia, *Relazione sul fenomeno criminale del contrabbando di tabacchi lavorati esteri in Italia e in Europa*, March 6, 2001, p. 58. See also "La seconda vita dei contrabbandieri," *La Repubblica*, April 4, 2005.
17. Brindisian residents could only apply to the projects submitted to their sub-provincial unit (called *ambito*), which included the urban area plus a nearby town, with a total population of almost 110,000.
18. The projects were: public administration (archive digitalization); urban green maintenance; network for social inclusion (Home Care Assistance Program); preservation and fruition of environmental heritage.
19. According to ISTAT (2018), service jobs (including caregiving, mostly done by immigrant female workers) accounted for the largest share of estimated irregular employment (47.2 percent) in 2016. CENSIS/Confcooperative (2018) estimates an 8.3 percent increase in irregular employment during the crisis years (2012–15), with higher incidence in southern Italy. In 2015,

paid domestic labor and caregiving accounted for 58.3 percent of estimated irregular employment.
20. Households would save money by doing house repairs on their own or by postponing regular maintenance work. One interlocutor also stressed that the availability of cheap materials and online do-it-yourself tutorials had further reduced the informal market for house repairs and maintenance.
21. The job stabilization plan was eventually approved and implemented in two phases in 2018, leading to the formal hiring of all workers on part-time contracts. The situation of the Lsu workers described in this chapter, based on research carried out in 2015 and 2016, is common to all subsidized workers who remain employed in public administrations. In 2017 the national public broadcasting company RAI addressed the issue with a dedicated reportage with the telling title "Socially humiliated" https://www.youtube.com/watch?v=U3q7MjniZrs (last accessed March 2019).
22. http://www.brindisitime.it/nasce-con-i-cobas-un-comitato-spontaneo-dei-disoccupati-del-cantieri-di-cittadinanza/ (last accessed February 2019).

References

Alberti, M. 2016. *Senza lavoro. La disoccupazione in Italia dall'Unità a oggi*. Rome: Laterza.
Barbu, M. 2013. *Socially Useful Jobs: The Last Keynesian Labour Market Policy in Italy. Policy Process Evaluation*. Unpublished PhD thesis, University of Sussex.
Bear, L., ed. 2014. "Doubt, Conflict, Mediation: The Anthropology of Modern Time." *Journal of the Royal Anthropological Institute*, special issue, 20(S1): vii–ix, 3–186.
Bear, L. 2015. *Navigating Austerity: Currents of Debt along a South Asian River*. Stanford: Stanford University Press.
Beretta, G. 1999. "L'arcipelago dei lavori socialmente utili." *Il Diritto del Mercato del Lavoro* 2.
Carbonella, A. and S. Kasmir. 2014. "Introduction: Toward A Global Anthropology of Labor." In S. Kasmir and A. Carbonella, eds. *Blood and Fire: Toward a Global Anthropology of Labor*. New York: Berghahn.
CENSIS/Confcooperative. 2018. *Negato, irregolare, sommerso: il lato oscuro del lavoro*. http://www.regione.puglia.it/documents/3652161/6413143/Focus-Censis-Confcooperative-gen18-1.pdf/c910e84c-07e8-4ec0-ba65-8dec9b9bb374 (last accessed March 2019).
Collins, J. and M. Gimenez, eds. 1990. *Work without Wages: Domestic Labor and Self-Employment within Capitalism*. New York: SUNY Press.
Collins, J.L. 2017. *The Politics of Value: Three Movements to Change How We Think about the Economy*. Chicago: University of Chicago Press.
Fargion, V. 2001. "Creeping Workfare Policies: The Case of Italy." In N. Gilbert, ed. *Activating the Unemployed: A Comparative Appraisal of Work-Oriented Policies*. Rutgers: Transaction.
Gibson-Graham, J.K. 2006. *A Postcapitalist Politics*. Minneapolis: Minnesota University Press.

Ginsborg, P. 1990. *A History of Contemporary Italy: 1943-1980*. London: Penguin.
Fraser, N. 2000. "Rethinking Recognition." *New Left Review* 3: 107–20.
Greco, L. 2002. *Industrial Redundancies: A Comparative Analysis of the Chemical and Clothing Industries in the UK and Italy*. Aldershot: Ashgate.
ISTAT. 2016. *Condizioni di vita e reddito. Anno 2015.* https://www.istat.it/it/files//2016/12/Reddito-e-Condizioni-di-vita-Anno-2015.pdf (last accessed April 2019).
ISTAT. 2018. *L'economia non osservata nei conti nazionali. Anni 2013-16.* https://www.istat.it/it/files//2018/10/Economia-non-osservata_2013-2016_rev.pdf (last accessed March 2019).
Knight, D.M. and C. Stewart, eds. 2017. *Ethnographies of Austerity: Temporality, Crisis and Affect in Southern Europe*. London: Routledge.
Lødemel, I. and H. Trickey, eds. 2001. *An Offer You Can't Refuse: Workfare in International Perspective*. Bristol: Policy Press.
Lunghini, G. et al. 1995. *Disoccupazione e lavori socialmente utili*. Rome: Il Manifesto.
Mies, M. 1986. *Patriarchy and Accumulation on a World Scale*. London: Zed Books.
Mies, M. 2014. "Housewifisation–Globalisation–Subsistence-Perspective." In M. van der Linden and K.H. Roth, eds. *Beyond Marx: Theorising the Global Labour Relations of the Twenty-First Century*. Brill: Leiden.
Mingione, E. 1985. "Social Reproduction of the Surplus Labour Force: The Case of Southern Italy." In N. Redclift and E. Mingione, eds. *Beyond Employment: Household, Gender, and Subsistence*. Oxford: Blackwell.
Mingione, E. 1991. *Fragmented Societies: A Sociology of Economic Life beyond the Market Paradigm*. Oxford: Basil Blackwell.
Mingione, E., Y. Kazepov, A. Andreotti and M. Ruttico. 1999. "The Italian Case: The Socially Useful Jobs." *Comparative Social Inclusion Policies and Citizenship in Europe: Towards a New European Social Model (CSIP)*. http://fondazionebignaschi.it/CSIP-Wp3-it.pdf (last accessed April 2019).
Muehlebach, A. 2012. *The Moral Neoliberal: Welfare and Citizenship in Italy*. Chicago: University of Chicago Press.
Muehlebach, A. 2016. "Anthropologies of Austerity." *History and Anthropology* 27(3): 359–72.
Narotzky, S. 2018. "Rethinking the Concept of Labour." *Journal of the Royal Anthropological Institute* 24(S1): 29–43.
Narotzky, S. and N. Besnier. 2014. "Crisis, Value, and Hope: Rethinking Economy." *Current Anthropology* 55(S9): S4–S16.
Peck, J. 2001. *Workfare States*. New York: Guildford Press.
Peck, J. 2002. "Political Economies of Scale: Fast Policy, Interscalar Relations, and Neoliberal Workfare." *Economic Geography* 78(3): 331–60.
Pugliese, E. and E. Rebeggiani. 2005. *Occupazione e disoccupazione in Italia dal dopoguerra ai giorni nostril*. Rome: Edizioni Lavoro.
Ringel, F. and R. Moroşanu, eds. 2016. "Time-Tricking: Reconsidering Temporal Agency in Troubled Times." *The Cambridge Journal of Anthropology*, special issue, 34(1): 1–133.
Salvati, A. 2017. "Dai Cantieri di Cittadinanza al Reddito di dignità. Prove di contrasto alla povertà in Puglia." *Politiche Sociali* 2: 245–58.

Saracini, P. 2003. "Lavori socialmente utili e cittadinanza sociale. Spunti per una prima riflessione." In G. Ferraro, ed. *Sviluppo e occupazione nell'Europa federale: Itinerari giuridici e socioeconomici su regioni e autonomie locali*. Milan: Giuffrè.

Saraceno, C. 2015. *Il lavoro non basta. La povertà in Europa negli anni della crisi*. Milan: Feltrinelli.

Saraceno, C. 2018. "Metamorfosi del reddito di cittadinanza." *Menabò di Etica ed Economia* 91.https://www.eticaeconomia.it/metamorfosi-del-reddito-di-cittadinanza/ (last accessed February 2019).

Stubbs, P. 2017. "Slow, Slow, Quick, Quick, Slow: Power, Expertise and the Hegemonic Temporalities of Austerity." *Innovation: The European Journal of Social Science Research* 31(1): 25–39.

USB (Unione Sindacale di Base). 2012. *Libro bianco. Appalti di pulizia nelle scuole. Ex-LSU – una storia infinita*. http://agenziastampaitalia.it/immagini/LIBRO_BIANCO_-_USB.pdf (last accessed February 2019).

Vantaggiato, I. 1996. "La 'femminilizzazione' del lavoro." In M. Bascetta et al., eds. *Stato e diritti nel postfordismo*. Rome: Il Manifesto.

4

Criminalizing Livelihoods: "Illegal Vegetables" and the Return to the Home

Carmen Leidereiter

It is the first days of March 2016 and the municipal market hall in the northern Portuguese city of Guimarães is seeing its usual steady morning traffic. Shoppers move between the stalls while the predominantly female vendors attempt to chat them up, sometimes gently tugging at their sleeves, quoting the prices and quality of the produce they have on offer. Maria is tending to a client interested in the honey while her sister is downstairs, unloading the van. But before Maria's sister can return, the two main entrances at the ends of the market hall are suddenly filled with men wearing blue windbreaker jackets emblazoned with yellow logos. Most mill around the entrances while three teams slowly begin to make their way from stall to stall, checking permits and questioning vendors. Looking around the hall, I see backs bending to hide produce under the tables and to retrieve cloths to cover up the "illegal vegetables." Previously occupied stalls are suddenly left unattended as vendors slip away through the backdoors; where there were several salespeople, only one remains. In all cases, the remaining vendor is either the renter of the stall or can produce proof of employment by the trader.

When the men in blue reach Maria's stall, they are already carrying several boxes piled high with confiscated goods. Upon their request, Maria produces a permit which the head officer proceeds to meticulously check against a list of his own. He calls out the number and weight of associated vegetables, which one of his underlings holds up, counts or weighs before reporting back. In the end, Maria receives a fine of 500 euros and a warning notice (*carta da advertencia*). The notice threatens prosecution and the suspension of her license should she be caught again, in the next 12 months, with undeclared produce or—and I quote the notice—"illegal vegetables." Maria refuses to accept the letter; crying, she pleads with the men, citing her sick husband and unemployed grandchildren as reasons for her transgressions. Later, I learn that it was not only her produce that was checked. The men in blue also checked her tax-reported sales against the produce she had available, her bookkeeping and the contents of her till.

About an hour into the inspection, a small crowd had gathered in the corridors, following the inspectors. As the head inspector demanded to see another vendor's permit and accounting, which he could not produce, a chorus of voices grew louder. Complaints, pleas and threats echoed around the room as more and more boxes of produce accompanied the tax authority officials. Whether in response to the raised voices or because it had been planned this way, an extra unit of uniformed men flooded the hall, soon outnumbering the female vendors. When they finally left, they took with them three vans loaded with impounded produce.

In an unusual show of conversation between competitors, the vendors and spectators gathered around. By this time, many others besides Maria were crying. The news had traveled fast and as more people arrived, a discussion quickly ensued: many of the vendors, lamenting the injustice they had just suffered, were left wondering how they would earn cash in the weeks to come. Never before had the tax authority visited the market; people described it as a "raid" rather than as an "inspection." Several of the older vendors, Maria among them, compared what just happened to the impounding of produce in their home farms which they remembered from the era of food rationing during the fascist dictatorship in the 1940s and 50s. Back then, inspectors, usually aided by the National Guard and sometimes even the secret police, would inspect the production of family farms and, following a grid not unlike the one used by the chief inspector today, ascertain how much produce to impound and to redistribute as food rations to the urban population. "Are they going to *redistribute* this food, too?" Maria asked, her fingers sketching quotation marks around the word "redistribute." "Back then, at least they pretended it was for the common good, stealing from the '*gente à baixo*'[1]... Now they just make our life impossible, without bothering to even lie."

I begin with this ethnographic moment because it—and the many discussions that followed—is emblematic of the time I spent in Guimarães between 2015 and 2017. As I show in this chapter, the articulation between formal and informal ways of making a living changes in contexts of austerity, as do the conditions of possibility for pursuing a livelihood. Drawing on this ethnographic moment and on the wider process of social control and sanctioning that it represents, I suggest that state interventions under the austerity regime have rendered benign, everyday practices of livelihood-making in Guimarães impossible. Under the pretext that practices are "informal" and need to be regulated, both age-old and novel means of livelihood have been criminalized although no alternative formal or legal means of making a living are available. I term this predicament a *livelihood dilemma* and ethnographically explore how the families and households I worked with cope with its material and social effects. In what follows, I first place austerity in a broader genealogy of governance and state control and highlight how it is experienced by my interlocutors as a continuation of state repression and abandonment. I then focus on the current moment to highlight how far austerity—and its criminalizing of livelihood—marks a radical break from previous forms of state intervention. Finally, I trace what avenues of livelihood are available to households. Scaling up from these observations then introduces questions about the conditions of possibility for livelihood-making under austerity, as well as the statist orthodoxies that govern how populations are managed in times of "exception" and "crisis."

Livelihood Under "Draconian Regulation"

Guimarães, capital of the Vale do Ave sub-region, used to be the center of Portuguese textile production. Industrialized during the capitalist expansion of industry towards Porto's hinterlands in the mid-1800s, it was, until recently, the site of many Italian and Spanish fashion brands' factories and subcontractors. But with the opening of EU markets to international competition in 2001 and the expiration of the multi fiber agreement in 2005, around 40 percent of the factories downscaled or closed altogether. Five years later, the subprime mortgage crisis hit Portugal, swelling unemployment in the region from 4.5 percent (below the national average) in 2000 to 20.1 percent in 2014 (INE 2014).

Although the textile manufacturing sector generally experiences cycles of boom and bust, the latest crisis differs from those of the past in that the surplus labor made redundant through the closure of large production sites could no longer be absorbed by a mushrooming undercurrent of SMEs, self-employment opportunities and other smaller manufacturing units. In the persistent crisis and decline of the past decade, livelihoods derived solely from full employment in what we may call the "formal" sector have become unattainable. People are therefore resorting to informal practices as avenues to organize for survival—practices that many believed they had left behind them in the past.

Whatever reasons I offered for my extended stay in the peripheral areas of Guimarães, people continuously searched for their own explanations as to why I had moved there. Fernando, one of Maria's sons, told me shortly after the market inspection: "You are here because we once again live like people in the past! You want to see how we get by without jobs, or help… or respect." While true in essence, Fernando's assertion also alluded to the often-repeated claim that the achievements in living standards gained since the Carnation Revolution—the 1974 coup that overthrew the authoritarian Estado Novo regime—were slowly being undone by persistent economic decline and abandonment by the state. The "past" in Fernando's rendering was a time when the textile industry existed but employment in it was so unpredictable that people relied on a variety of non-wage, often informal activities to supplement their meager wages: petty, home-based outworking arrangements, subsistence agriculture, day-laboring, small commodity production, petty rent and others. That they could rely on this particular combination of formal and informal livelihood strategies was due to a particular absence of state regulation. Although it is not my aim to theorize the peculiarities of state intervention in the north of Portugal, regulation and intervention bear directly on this story because, as Fernando reminds us, the past conditions people's current expectations of the state's role in their everyday lives.

Since its beginnings in the nineteenth century, the development of industry in northern Portugal depended on the peculiar absence and simultaneous presence of the regulatory powers of the state (Cabral 1981). During the time of capitalist expansion, state regulation only sought to secure the conditions of possibility for the emergence of an industrial working class,[2] while its withdrawal from modes of everyday livelihood allowed people to organize for survival in whatever manner they saw fit. During the Estado Novo, this present absence (Santos 1991) expanded into a model of industrial paternalism that involved the state only when it came to ensuring social peace. While frequently lamented, my interlocutors seemed to take the absence and neglect of the state for granted, as a basic fact of life. In the face of the state's most recent interventions, they frequently even recast this abandonment as an entitlement, insofar as it permitted the co-existence of formal and informal livelihood strategies and, more generally, the possibility to organize for survival in whatever manner they saw fit.

When the current return to informal livelihoods is equated with "going back" to the past, this rendering of the past refers to a time when—in the absence of waged labor with stable, predictable returns—informality was the "only chance we had to get by" (Fernando). What is different now is that the state no longer facilitates this informality by looking the other way. Instead, events like the market inspection, Fernando told me, are

> a way to illegalize making a livelihood. Especially in terms of pushing into illegality the benign things we have always done to survive... It's like they pretend we love to do this, but it's from need, you understand. We could not pay for electricity, or gas, or petrol if it wasn't for the market income.

Not only are their ways of getting by rendered illegal; people feel that their livelihoods are increasingly at the center of a statist gaze that seeks to sanction them as "tax avoidance." Maria asserted:

> The big producers, you know, just like the big supermarkets... they break all the laws. And when they get caught, they pay the fine and continue on just like that. But us... a little fruit vendor like myself, I get fined once at the market, I go bankrupt trying to pay the fine... and if I don't pay, they take my license. Anyway, we're out of business! How can we live with these draconian regulations?

Maria's is a common lament—one that points to what is perceived as deeply entrenched inequality in how different societal groups are treated by the state and its selective and arbitrary interventions. There is a deeply political dimension to this lament as well, one that becomes apparent when people are asked when this "change" in the enforcing of regulations began. Maria's views on this are clear:

> It's a thing that comes from the EU. It was in the 1990s that this standardization of everything happened.... Probably the big businesses always got away with breaking the laws... But back then, so did we! Us, up here in the north... They left us alone for a long time, to take care of ourselves even with the EU. Some things we weren't allowed to do... But well, until recently, very recently, this year, until this raid at the market, they left us... It is only now, with this crisis that they make us into an example... that what they do is as violent as back in the old days.

Two points emerge from these quotes. First, Maria's claim that she lacks options other than to produce, trade and sell informally implies that the basis upon which the state regulates her market trading have little or nothing to do with the real reasons behind her actions. The policy not only misunderstands her motivations, but mounts this misinterpretation on a disciplinary strategy that ends up treating her like an ignorant child—a child who, out of greed and selfishness, does not want to pay her taxes. As Maria sees it, informal trading is rather her only chance to supplement her meager pension and declining household income. If we take her assertion at face value, what Maria is alleging is a massive disarticulation between the orthodoxies that govern how populations are administered (and their underlying premises) vis-a-vis the livelihood practices and motivations that drive people in their everyday lives. The very premises that underpin the raid on the Guimarães municipal market, however, can be disproven by looking at the social and material relationships and conditions Maria is engaged in on a daily basis, which I detail in the third section.

Second, and in light of the historically conditioned expectations of the state's role in people's lives, Maria and her son identify a fundamental change in how they are treated by the state. What distinguishes the present are not only the more repressive laws but the intensity with which both old and new laws are enforced. It is in this way that Maria and Fernando view the inspection at the municipal market as an unprecedented event, albeit one that epitomizes their livelihood dilemma in the absence of formal ways of getting by. On the one hand, they remember what it was like to get by without the security of a stable job, a living wage and social protections; this was their lived reality except for a short period between 1974 and 2000. In fact, they are only continuing with some informal strategies, and re-initiating others, out of sheer necessity. On the other hand, all the avenues for making a livelihood available today are not only considered to belong to the past but are persecuted as criminal or as tax evasion under austerity. Their dilemma, in short, is that whichever avenue for making a livelihood they choose, impossibility, illegalization and criminalization await at every turn.

By situating the inspection at the municipal market in the longue durée, Maria and Fernando posit it as the culmination of a historical process, one that has been underway from well before the most recent financial crisis, indeed since the beginning of the European Union. The language of habitual crisis that so many of the region's most disenfranchised use to speak about their daily struggles stands in sharp contrast to the novelty and exceptionality narrative employed by policymakers and politicians. For the disenfranchised, abandonment by the state under the austerity regime is not experienced as a radical break from previous modes of governance. Rather, what is experienced as novel and radical is the intensity and intentionality of current regulatory enforcement. To my interlocutors, the austerity memorandum the Portuguese government signed in 2011 alongside the legal and bureaucratic changes it heralded was merely the most recent in a long line of comparable state interventions. While past interventions sought to make people available for waged labor but left them alone to organize survival outside of it, today's interventions treat informal practices as criminal tax evasion and persecute their practitioners accordingly. The radical break is not austerity itself, but the forms of control that have become legitimate in its wake, alongside their pauperizing impact on the daily realms of social reproduction. To understand how this is possible, I detail how the governing of the municipal market has changed in recent years, followed by an examination of the activities that enable the livelihood of Maria's household.

Governing Illegal Vegetables

There are numerous regulations contained in the municipal ordinances governing market use and vending, most of which have been in effect since 1999 (amended in 2002). First, all vendors must be licensed; the main requirement for obtaining a license is the holding of a commercial license prior to applying. A commercial license, which authorizes the production and distribution of goods, obliges its holder to report sales and income to the tax office as well as to pay the corresponding contributions. The municipality only issues vending licenses for the market hall after traders have completed this process. Vending licenses stipulate not only the title holder, their tax ID and employees, but also the stalls or shops they occupy in the market, the allowable activities and the products which are authorized for sale (Articles 2, 3 and 20).

Second, all licensed vendors must abide by the municipal ordinances that govern market trading. One crucial stipulation is the vendor's cooperation with the municipal services, the police and other public functionaries in carrying out their duties of control (Art 35 para 1&2; Art 42). This includes presenting unobscured all information requested by officials such as the book-keeping, names, license numbers and tax IDs of trading partners and employees, the origin and production processes of goods

(Art 36); aiding in the carrying out of the duties (Art 35) of law enforcement; and reporting all infractions, misdemeanors and other irregular occurrences at the market that they have knowledge of (Art 42). Failure to comply with any of these stipulations is punishable by fines ranging from 50 to 2,500 euros, depending on the gravity of the infringement (Art 44). The first offence will lead to a fine and a warning notice. Repeat offenses will lead to the suspension and eventually withdrawal of a vending license (Art 44 footnote).

During the market inspection, vendors were found to be in violation of both the municipal ordinances and the tax authority's regulations that govern holders of commercial licenses. Most notably, they had failed to report irregularities amongst themselves and tried to obscure their involvement in unregistered trading. For tax purposes, however, the most important violations were both selling unauthorized produce and at quantities higher than they had declared. There is, then, a host of regulations governing market vending. Although virtually all have been in effect since the late 1990s, no efforts to enforce them have been made until very recently, as we can glean from the vendors' shock at the inspection. So, when my informants say that something has changed in the way that market trading is policed in particular, and in the way local populations are treated in general, they seem quite correct. But the question remains: what it is that has changed?

I want to suggest that the timing of the raid on the market was no coincidence. Laws that had been in existence for decades were suddenly used to discipline alleged "tax informality" at the very moment that Portugal was being pushed by its European creditors to adopt austerity measures and to maintain international creditworthiness by securing further loans, repaying its debt and controlling its internal deficit through cuts to national spending, tax hikes and the privatization of national industries and services. It then appears logical that the only violation that was penalized during the inspection was traders' petty tax avoidance, found in their failure to declare the correct produce, sales and income to the authorities. The tax authorities levied fines on Maria and others, alleging that the failure to report all produce and sales constituted an effort to evade paying taxes, thereby withholding potential revenue from the state. Implicitly, the argument might be extended to say that this tax revenue could contribute to the country's ability to balance its internal deficit, thereby reducing its debt and retaining international creditworthiness.

A further moral dimension is also at work. The argument often begins with the allegation that people have spent the last few decades consuming on borrowed money, enabled by the extension of popular credit which has led people to live beyond their means in a luxury often referred to in the media and elsewhere as a sickness. The era of lavishness, people are reminded, is now over; it is time to come together as a country, forget individual desires and greed and collectively pay the price for having wanted too much. The country and its people must be "cured" of the "sickness" of individual greed, overconsumption and the overestimation of one's own means, and the medicine for tightening one's belt is austerity.[3]

This framing of petty tax evasion as the culprit behind austerity—and the registers of blame and shame that come with it—distinguish present interventions from those of the past. The almost violent intervention in the municipal market could only be legitimized by recasting and re-signifying it as an attempt to curb the "evil" of tax evasion, an expression of the selfish greed and lavishness behind "overconsumption." Maria and Fernando's claim that their treatment by the state has changed is thus correct. The Portuguese state has shifted from being a welfare provider to becoming the agency responsible for collecting and containing national debt. What has changed is the intentionality and positionality of the state: it must now execute the saving and deficit-curbing activities mandated from above, while also legitimizing policies of repression, illegalization and the sanctioning of its population. This is why it is only in the present moment that the conjuncture of formal and informal activities that made livelihood possible is genuinely under threat, as Maria correctly observed.

Curbing illegal activities with inspections and fines becomes the logical medicine for ignorant, selfish or simply greedy people who work informally in order to avoid paying taxes. The revenue generated may be negligible compared to what the national tax evasion statistics allege is missed, but the moral lessons of such a performance for the people it targets are likely to be long-lasting and will likely discipline them into obedient officialism. Media-disseminated raids of this kind also have the added benefit of broadcasting good will to the country's creditors and European auditors. This shift towards international exercises of control may well constitute an alteration of governmental morality (Rose and Miller 1992) in which the state is pushed to find new frameworks to legitimize what is effectively an exclusively repressive function.

Examining the orthodoxies of population management (Brown 1992; Abrams 1989) and the discrepancies between their foundational premises and people's livelihood-making suggests that the stress environment of austerity has only strengthened these governmental orthodoxies, with laws and regulations that have been on the books for decades suddenly informing new kinds of intervention. From the perspective of population management, discipline and governance, the municipal market raid can be seen as performative: a performance designed to instill in a reluctant, deviant local population the fear and awe of state power (Taussig 1992), where the blame and shame for austerity can be placed on individuals rather than on national and international banks and governments.

Whether performative or not, the point remains that these novel types of intervention have very real consequences for the people they target. How did the people of Guimarães deal with this contradictory and seemingly arbitrarily applied field of rules and regulations, apparently enforced to discipline and instill fear? I first introduce the moral frameworks that currently inform unofficial livelihood-making before returning to the example of Maria's household and the avenues that remain available to its members.

Negotiating the Livelihood Dilemma: Retreat to the Home

Conscious of living in changing, depressing times, the inhabitants of Guimarães I came to know were acutely aware of both the malfunctions of the (local) state and the structural problems of economic "crisis" and wider society that had come to impact their lives. They continuously weighed their available assets and opportunities, accounting for and managing what little lay in their power. They did so in the midst of an unpredictable environment filled with apparently arbitrary, constantly changing regulations—an environment that seemed to offer little but deprivation, with which they have no choice but to contend. In doing so, they strove to define a moral framework that distinguishes between activities that are not strictly legal but nonetheless acceptable/legitimate and those that are obviously criminal or illicit. Their definitions of illegal but acceptable, and criminal and unacceptable, were complex and almost never corresponded to the legislative provisions of the Portuguese state; nor could they be mounted onto the formal/informal distinction that has informed criminal justice definitions of formality (Portes and Sassen-Koob 1987; Portes, Castells and Benton 1989). As I hope to have shown through Maria's dilemma, a growing number of the livelihood strategies that my interlocutors consider legitimate are currently rendered illegal or impossible by state control. In light of these seeming impossibilities, we need to understand how people can organize for their livelihood on a daily basis.

More often than not, the families and households I lived with tried to conceal their avenues of livelihood-making in order to avoid surveillance, taxation, or sanctioning. The most common strategy lay in capitalizing on what was often the only asset left to families: their home and the security and control it offered. Taking inspiration from the "retreat to the household" that Frances Pine (2002) famously described for post-socialist Poland, I term this move a "retreat to the home," by which I mean quite literally a spatial move of the means of livelihood from public and often formal to private and mostly informal spaces. I trace how this happens through the example of Maria's household, as it is emblematic of the multi-generational, downwardly mobile households in Guimarães.

The members of Maria's household, the protagonists of this account, were all formally unemployed. Nevertheless, they were involved in a complex and seemingly ever-changing array of activities that I can provide only a snapshot of. Maria's household is comprised of an extended family inhabiting two adjacent multi-generational houses in the north of Guimarães city center. The family owns two modest plots of land which they farm; the two older-generation women, Maria (born 1949) and her sister (1947), sell the produce they do not consume themselves at the municipal market. This business has formed the backbone of their household income for the last 60 years, with their dependence on its returns varying considerably over time. Maria's husband passed away over a decade ago and her sister never married. Maria's youngest son emigrated to France where he operates an unregistered import-export business with cars, and in 2015 two of the grandsons went to join him in Lyon. From the mid-1960s until the early 2000s, Maria's two other sons, along with the oldest grandsons, were employed as operators in several medium-sized textile factories, which in the past yielded sufficient income for the sons to build a second, modern house adjacent to Maria's, in which they raised their two families. Today, the fathers and sons are unemployed and try to get by on small jobs, usually day-laboring in agriculture and construction. They also do virtually all the farming.

The son's wives run an out-working, subcontracted sewing and embroidery workshop in their garage. The enterprise used to be an official business located in a nearby industrial park but was moved to the house two years ago in an effort to ensure continued profits, which had begun to dwindle between the very low piecemeal prices and rising production costs, mainly taxes and social security expenses. Although the business had never been run completely formally—they relied on unregistered piecemeal workers to complete their orders, never declared all their revenue and often struck under-the-table deals in cash—the relocation to the home still constituted a major shift in their operations. It meant letting go of some informal employees to better hide their practice and to instead rely on free family labor to operate the machines when orders would come in.

Alongside the increased reliance on family help and obligation, relocating the workshop to the home constituted a major shift in the temporality of future planning. Running the workshop even semi-formally in the industrial park meant the sisters paid taxes and social security contributions, even if only on the tax-declared part of their income. This was likely to yield income and security in the distant future, following retirement or a workplace accident. Relocating the business meant that they now only gained its short-term profits as direct income. While this allowed them to pay the gas and electricity bills at the end of the month, it offered neither security in case of an accident nor a pension. Relocating the formerly externalized business to the home shrunk the household's temporal horizon for planning, from more long-term to immediate.

Alongside the relocation of already existing businesses to the private home, new activities were added to the livelihood strategy, the most notable being petty rent derived from AirBnB. In trying to make the most of their assets, households across Guimarães began to rent their spare spaces out to anyone willing to pay. In Maria's household, rooms and attics in both homes were hastily refurbished, furnished and posted on online platforms to attract paying tenants. As petty rent proved successful where many other strategies had not, further attempts were made to capitalize on rent extraction. The two granddaughters were asked to share a room in their grandparents' house, while the still-resident grandsons had to abandon their rooms and move into the moldy cellar. In the older house, the sons fixed up the garage to rent to friends for storage, while Maria's daughter and her husband moved to the second floor so that their former bedroom, with a private entrance from the garden, could be freed up for tenants. In the new house, the couch in the living room was replaced with a sleeping sofa, on which the other married couple now slept, while their bedroom became a boarding room. Over the course of ten months, five rooms were made available to rent while the number of household residents almost doubled, from ten to nineteen.

While successful in providing cash income, the shifting articulation of formal and informal livelihood strategies not only had material consequences but directly impacted on relations between family members, with far-reaching consequences for their well-being. Most immediately, relations between family members suffered due to shrinking personal space, as the removal of the public/private distinction brought both businesses and paying tenants into one's home, leading to an increase in stress and conflict. In the longer run, the lack of privacy and the sheer noise and discomfort of the place affected their physical and psychological well-being. The strain was often heightened by attempts to keep paying tenants happy as their needs and wants were routinely privileged over those of family members.

Although filled with conflict between its members and their divergent interests and activities, the household nevertheless, somewhat inevitably, became the place to negotiate the dilemmas of livelihood. Given unemployment, the cut-backs to social provisions, the illegalization of informal livelihoods and state surveillance, private property—and more specifically, the private home—became the only means for households to continue organizing for survival, as a liminal space between formality and informality in which livelihood activities that would otherwise be persecuted in public space could continue. In addition, the house provided opportunities for generating income through rent. The house thus emerged as central to household strategies to avoid state surveillance and repression and to continue informal practices of livelihood-making.

Despite its performative violence, the criminalization of pursuing informal livelihood in public spaces did not lead to the formalization of all economic activities, as was arguably the state's intention. Among the people with whom I worked, state intervention encouraged the shift of informal activities to the home alongside the expansion of other, possibly traditional forms of household production that still took place beneath the radar of the state. To what extent, however, were state interventions met with the docility and obedient officiality that such disciplinary strategies ostensibly demand?

Resistance to Regulation as a Livelihood Strategy

Let us leave aside for a moment the anthropological given that informality always exists (Portes and Sassen-Koob 1987) and ask instead what the criminalization of informality is likely to mean for its practitioners. If the objective is to foreclose informality as a means of livelihood-making, people who previously relied on it must then find other sources of income. Let us assume, as the state apparatus presumably does, that they will seek this income in the formal realm, for example by looking for a job. As I have shown above, in the current context of Guimarães, finding stable, long-term employment in a specialized or professional setting is, if anything, a dream of the past, one of the 1980s and 90s when the textile and service industries were booming, and upward social mobility appeared possible. Today, however, what job could, say, a former market vendor pushed out of her livelihood expect to find?

A telling case is that of Joana, Maria's youngest granddaughter. Joana runs a hair parlor in the bedroom she shares with her sister. Her sister, who has a degree in computer engineering, repairs private PCs at home and is also responsible for posting the rooms they rent on online platforms. For both of them, what they now do for a living is what they feel will likely be their future. Although they have career aspirations, they feel that stable, long-term employment in a professional setting is simply unattainable. Their only opportunities for formal employment are low-wage, low-skill, dead-end jobs in the service sector.

During my stay in Maria's household, Joana applied to and received an offer for a service sector job in a fashion outlet in the nearby city of Porto. Joana ran the numbers with her mother and grandmother: the offer was for minimum wage, which in 2015 was 494 euros per month for a 39-hour week. She would have to work five or six days a week, four days full-time and two days half-time in alternating shifts. The cheapest return train ticket to Porto was 6.20 euros; 25 days per month would amount to 150 euros in transportation costs. Including commuting time, Joana would be out of the house for at least 12 hours a day, and her lunches and dinners would be another expense. Even though what would remain after transportation and food was a little more than her revenue from her hair parlor, with the commute, she would have very little time to help in her mother's workshop, or on the land. After a few days of discussion, Joana decided not to take the job, although she would "feel better for not taking all the risks, like with my business now."

In Joana's choice not to pursue formal minimum-wage employment, we find a clear calculation of both the subjective and objective factors in which the merits of subsistence, petty production and home-based services are weighed against the opportunity of a wage foregone. Joana's case reveals the manifold considerations informing people's behaviors and decisions, which the state's bureaucratic gaze can neither grasp nor apprehend. Like Joana and her elders, all the members of the families I worked with continuously weighed strategies and sources of income against each other, with the most important consideration being how much each would contribute to survival and family income. Personal preferences and concerns about the risks of being caught and fined were decidedly secondary. Despite the dangers and inconveniences of working informally at home, Joana, like her grandmother, insisted on continuing these activities. However, she did not turn her back on a low-wage job because she was greedy, selfish, uneducated or lazy. She turned her back because of her felt obligation to support the group she is part of, and calculated that she could better contribute at home than being out all day for scant pay.

Joana's case can be seen as an example of people not accepting the kind of disciplining that the state assumes will push them into accepting low-wage, dead-end jobs. Instead of the passive acceptance that the state's disciplinary strategy arguably calls for, Joana's example extrapolates the care, responsibility and mutual obligation that underlie the rationale for continuing to practice informally. In choosing against that which the criminalization of informal livelihood ostensibly demands—i.e. the acceptance of low-wage labor—Joana's case highlights how personal preference and familial obligation can supersede the governing efforts of state control and sanction. In every measure of complexity, Joana's beliefs and choices differ so starkly from what the state seems to assume motivates people that the logics and orthodoxies devised to control and sanction people such as her hardly apply.

In conclusion, I hope to have shown that the interests and needs of household members could hardly be further from the assumptions of the state apparatus regarding what drives people towards informality. Most family livelihood activities did not feature at all in the state's regulatory framework; when they did, they were of a completely different nature and scale than those assumed by the bureaucratic gaze. The members of Maria's household did not opt for informality because they were greedy, selfish or too uneducated to realize the dangers and pitfalls of so doing. The continuation of informal activities by relocating them to the private home was not, as much of the literature on the urban poor and international "precariat" would have us believe, the only option left to a marginalized group. Nor was it the choice of selfish individuals seeking to further their own gains. Instead, the return to the home was a desirable response to the crisis for this household, precisely because it allowed them to negotiate livelihood dilemmas against the backdrop of increased taxation, surveillance and sanctioning.

The combining of informal and formal livelihood strategies within a single multi-generational household is eminently logical, the result of a thoughtful calculation of risks, benefits and family needs. Engagement in all manner of economic activity was thus determined by family and personal needs, which were negotiated in the complex interplay of self-interests and self-worth, mutual obligation and care, family solidarity, the livelihood dilemma and strained financial capacities. They are, in short, highly tactical yet uncertain choices aimed more tacitly at ensuring the continuation of livelihood in spite of falling piecemeal production rates and the absence of socially secure, long-term employment options. Maria's household and the many others like hers are thus grappling with the possibilities for making a living, based not only on what is possible and permissible, but also on what is desirable in reciprocal, social and caring terms.

Rather than simply reverting to old forms of household production, households responding to the austerity-compounded livelihood dilemma have simultaneously retreated into subsistence and home-based outwork accompanied by new forms of income generation such as petty rent. In this retreat to the home, private property was the crucial asset, albeit as an ambivalent space ridden with tensions and conflict. Pine (2002) has shown how in post-socialist Poland, entering a chaotic, fragmented post-Fordist globalism and returning to the livelihood practices of the past were compatible experiences, reflecting the contradictory realities of living through socio-economic crisis and political upheaval. I observed a similar dual temporality in Guimarães: while people resented being pushed back into the hardships of farming and informality, which they believed they had left behind them, memories of the not-too-distant past also allowed them to resurrect its livelihood practices, informing their determination to continue informality today as they had back then. At the same time, the novel forms of social control and governance that accompanied austerity have instituted policies that not only curtail possibilities for upward mobility but also criminalize and scapegoat informal livelihood-making. While not radically new, austerity and the interventions it legitimized have remade the conditions of possibility for livelihood.

My ethnography of state-citizen relations during austerity furthermore questions the narratives of novelty and exceptionalism that have become common tropes in discussions of austerity and crisis. Officially introduced with the 2011 memorandum, austerity as intervention did not feel particularly exceptional or new to Guimaraes citizens. For people like Maria, her family members and many others, it merely cemented and intensified existing arbitrary rules and regulations with which they had no choice but to contend, while magnifying a history of state abandonment. What was radically new were the blaming and moralizing registers that accompanied austerity—handmaidens to governmental orthodoxies that sought to limit the informal economy in order to secure and retain national creditworthiness. But what was intended as a public performance to appease international creditors and discipline an unruly public worked—if at all—only achieved to publicly expose and shame informal traders, the chosen scapegoats of austerity. If the intended objective of violent interventions such as the market raid was truly the abolition of informality, this objective remains unfulfilled.

With this ethnography, I hope to have provided at least one example of how people accustomed to repressive modes of governance and institutional neglect refuse to silently accept the blame for austerity, to be pushed into low-wage labor or to buy into the narrative of austerity as exception. Instead, they insist on making their living regardless, negotiating whatever formal and informal avenues are within their reach while juggling familial, personal and caring responsibilities. But it is important to remember that despite all of their, at-times ingenious, strategies, the financial situation of Maria's household continued to decline. To pay the fine incurred at the municipal market, Maria had to sacrifice over a month's worth of income from pensions and petty rent; and the income left from agriculture, services and petty production barely sufficed to pay the monthly bills. At the same time, her grandsons are thinking of joining their brothers in France in search of livelihood opportunities, relieving Maria of some responsibilities while depriving her of emotional support. These material conditions remind us that it is deprivation and unpredictability—the struggle to pay the bills or manage an unexpected expense, alongside fear for the future—that remain the structuring narratives of livelihood during austerity. Informality neither helped overcome this pattern, nor did it abate the dilemma of livelihood: whichever avenue for making a living people turn to, impossibility, illegality and criminalization await at every turn.

Notes

1. Literally: people at/from the bottom.
2. For a detailed historical account of industrial expansion and the emergence of a waged-labour system in the Vale do Ave, see Marques (1988), Fereira (2014) and Cortesao et al. (2012).
3. For an example of the medicalized jargon used by newspapers across the EU to discuss austerity, see: http://www.ft.com/intl/cms/s/0/2009bb08-d3a5-11e3-b0be-00144feabdc0.html# axzz31h4JOKqr (last accessed June 2019).

References

Abrams, P. 1988. "Notes on the Difficulty of Studying the State." *Journal of Historical Sociology* 1(1): 58–89.

Alves, J.F. 1999. *Fiar e tecer: uma perspectiva histórica da indústria têxtil a partir do vale do Ave*. Vila Nova de Famalicao: Camara Municipal.

Brown, W. 1992. "Finding the Man in the State." *Feminist Studies* 18(1): 7–34.

Cabral, M.V. 1981. *O desenvolvimento do capitalismo em Portugal no século XIX*. Lisbon: A Regra do Jogo.

Camara Municipal de Guimarães. 2002[1999]. *Regulamento de Organizacao e Funcionamento do Mercado Municipal de Guimaraes*. CMdG.

Cortesao, L., A. Cavalho, R. Silva, et al. 2012. *"Oh Mae, Deia-Nos Pao!": Escutando Quotidianos de Pobreza*. Guimaraes Capital Europeia da Cultura, Publicacoes. Porto: Projecto Raizes.

Cortesao, L., C. Viera and M. da Luz Sampaio. 2012. *"Quando Eu Nasci, Aquela fabrica já Alí Estava": Mémorias, Vivencias e Opinoes Sobre o Trabalho na Indústria em Guimaraes*. Guimaraes Capital Europeia da Cultura, Publicacoes. Porto: Projecto Raizes.

Fereira, D. 2014. *Paisagem Industrial Do Vale do Ave*. Thesis presented at FCTUC, Universidade do Porto.

Hart, K. 1973. "Informal Income Opportunities and Urban Employment in Ghana." *Journal of Modern African Studies* 11(1): 61–89.

Instituto Nacional da Estatistica. 2015. *Inquérito às Condições de Vida e Rendimentos* (ICOR/EU-SILC). Lisbon: INE.

Marques, T.S. 1988. "Sistema produtivo industria e territorio. Um estudo do textile em Guimaraes." *Revista da Faculadade das Letras* 1(4): 55–103.

Pine, F. 2002. "Retreat to the Household: Gendered Domains in Postsocialist Poland." In C. Hann, ed. *Postsocialism: Ideals, Ideologies and Practices in Eurasia*. London: Routledge.

Portes, A., M. Castells and L. Benton, eds. 1989. *The Informal Economy: Studies in Advanced and Less Developed Countries*. Baltimore: Johns Hopkins University Press.

Portes, A. and S. Sassen-Koob. 1987. "Making it Underground: Comparative Material on The Informal Sector in Western Economies." *American Journal of Sociology* 93(1): 30–61.

Rodrigues, C.F., R. Figueiras and V. Junqueira. 2016. *Desigualidade do Rendimento e Probreza em Portugal: As Consequencias Sociais do Programma do Adjustamento*. Fundacao Fransisco Manuel dos Santos.

Rose, N. and P. Miller. 1992. "Political Power Beyond the State: Problematics of Government." *British Journal of Sociology* 43(2): 173–205.

Santos, B.S. 1991. *State, Wage Relations and Social Welfare in the Semiperiphery: The Case of Portugal*. Centro de Estudos Sociais. https://estudogeral.sib.uc.pt/handle/10316/10931 (last accessed October 2015).

Taussig, M. 1992. *The Nervous System*. London: Routledge.

5
Austerity, Social Values and Value: The Social Economy and Entrepreneurship in Catalonia

Patricia Homs

From Unemployment to Entrepreneurship

The destruction of thousands of jobs since 2008 and the resulting vast increase in unemployment and precariousness across Europe has led local, regional, national and European authorities to embrace entrepreneurship as a strategy to boost self-employment. The social and solidarity economy—and in particular work cooperatives—have been lauded as collective projects of social entrepreneurship embodying values such as environmental sustainability, cooperation and social justice, resilient to the crisis due to their flexibility and capacity to adapt to different economic contexts.

Cooperative, social economy and entrepreneurship discourses and practices have been articulated at different scales. This chapter examines the tensions between the ideologies and practices of entrepreneurship and those of the social and solidarity economy in the region of Catalonia in northeast Spain. By focusing on how people active in cooperatives, the social economy and entrepreneurship programs understand "social entrepreneurship," I examine the diverse meanings conferred on activation policies and self-employment as well as how government institutions use these discourses to promote self-employment in a devastated labor landscape. Although the values of solidarity and cooperation add a consciously moral dimension to the social economy and social entrepreneurship, the domain of exchange in which cooperatives must participate continues to be structured by competition. Despite their stated aims of transforming society, I argue that social economy and social entrepreneurship in their current forms do not challenge the hegemony of the capitalist economy.

Structural unemployment tends to legitimize public policies that transfer responsibilities of livelihood and employability to individual citizens. It is thus hardly surprising that since the 1990s, and especially since the latest financial and socio-economic crisis, policymakers at various scales have embraced the ideology of entrepreneurship as a means to promote employment. With unemployment in the European Union reaching alarming levels in the late 1990s, the 1997 *European Employment Strategy* sought to establish common policy objectives and targets for EU member states.[1] The strategy consisted of four pillars: fostering employability, an entrepreneurial attitude, adaptability and equality of opportunities. Employability meant that citizens had to be sufficiently trained to improve their prospects; the "entrepreneurial attitude" posited that workers, driven by self-motivation, should be "able to create their own jobs." Workers had to be willing to adapt to the positions offered them concerning schedules, locations and working conditions, while measures favoring the employment of women were encouraged. These guidelines (amended repeatedly) expressed the priorities and targets proposed by the European Commission, agreed by national governments, and adopted by the European Council (European Council 2018). In 2000, the *Lisbon Strategy* proposed another broad set of measures to promote employment along economic, social and environmental lines (European Council 2000). The *Europe 2020 Strategy* followed in 2010, billed as "a strategy for smart, sustainable and inclusive growth" to "overcome the structural weaknesses in Europe's economy, improve its competitiveness and productivity and underpin a sustainable social market economy" (European Commission 2010).

These strategies were all accompanied by programs to encourage entrepreneurship: *Promoting Entrepreneurship in Europe: Priorities for the Future* (European Commission 1998), *The European Program for Entrepreneurship* (European Commission 2004) and the *2020 Entrepreneurship Action Plan* (European Commission 2013). The latter gathered recommendations to foster the entrepreneurial spirit in three areas: education and training in entrepreneurial skills to promote new businesses; creation of a favorable environment for entrepreneurial development and growth; and the establishment of entrepreneurial models to reach specific groups. Reaching women, the unemployed, youth, seniors and immigrants was a key objective, as can be gleaned from the report *The Missing Entrepreneurs: Policies for Inclusive Entrepreneurship* (OECD/European Union 2017).

In many official documents, "entrepreneurship" appears as a synonym or euphemism for self-employment (Valenzuela et al. 2015; Lobato and

Valenzuela 2014). In Spain, to be a self-employed worker means being registered under the special tax regime for "autonomous work" (Régimen Especial de Trabajadores Autónomos, RETA).[2] Nevertheless, local development agencies routinely associate entrepreneurship with positive qualities such as motivation, freedom, opportunity, creativity, dynamism and self-satisfaction rather than simply self-employment, while unemployment and insertion into the labor market are terms reserved for occupational training. Numerous official reports also frame peoples' preferences and expectations for salaried positions—rather than creating their own opportunities as entrepreneurs—as problematic. Martínez and Bogino (2015) point to the "high degree of correspondence between the form and content of the European recommendations and the measures adopted by the Spanish government." Indeed, the 2013 Spanish law on entrepreneurship (BOE 28/9/2013) offers fiscal benefits, training and facilities to finance entrepreneurship.

The lauding of the entrepreneurial spirit extends to changing people's beliefs about employment and entrepreneurship by making them school subjects from an early age. The Spanish Education Law (enacted in 2006 and modified in 2013) stipulates the need to strengthen ties between the educational system and the labor market and to develop the entrepreneurial spirit among children.[3] Developing entrepreneurial skills has become a key part of labor market integration and employability schemes as well as in courses offered by local development agencies. Universities and private firms, including banks, promote the entrepreneurial ideology through public prizes and programs designed for potential entrepreneurs.

In this context, self-employment initiatives such as cooperatives and other social economy projects have been revalued and praised for fostering entrepreneurship as well as adding to individual self-employment values such as cooperation, solidarity, resilience, community and social justice. In the words of a member of the Regional Ministry of Labor, "cooperatives and the social economy turn social entrepreneurship into a safe bet" (Field notes 2017). But although the values underpinning the social and solidarity economy reinforce the moral discourse and community involvement—even evoking empowerment and social transformation—the ideology and practice of "social entrepreneurship" is flourishing in a context where neoliberal policies are privatizing what were once public safety nets (Molina et al. 2014). The articulation and endorsement of the social economy and entrepreneurship is thus underpinned by the neoliberal state's disengagement from its responsibilities for public welfare (Moulaert and Ailenei 2005).

Social and Solidarity Economy in Catalonia

Over the past decade, the social and solidarity economy has spread throughout the Catalan region. Through the activities of over 4,600 initiatives, it accounts for 7 percent of Barcelona City's gross domestic product (Fernández and Miró 2016). The social and solidarity economy has been variously defined as "an alternative to the market economy" (Intercontinental Network for the Promotion of Social Solidarity Economy, RIPESS), as the economic domain of cooperatives, mutual entities, foundations, associations and other legal formulas (Spanish Law on Social Economy, Ley 5/2011), and as a set of socio-economic initiatives that seek to meet the needs of people through solidarity, cooperation, donation and reciprocity (Solidarity Economy Network, XES). It has received increasing institutional support since 2015 partially because its projects, with their capacity for adaptability and flexibility, are deemed more resilient to the consequences of crisis. By embodying values such as environmental sustainability, cooperation and social justice, social and solidarity economy projects are said to offer benefits to society as a whole.

The research underpinning this chapter had two main goals. First, I sought to better understand the multiple meanings and practices of entrepreneurship and their articulation within the social and solidarity economy. What are the tensions between their ideologies and practices? Have social economy practices become more widespread in society? Have they been domesticated and emptied of critical political perspective? Second, I sought to understand whether and to what extent initiatives from the social and solidarity economy introduce values that may configure a different or even an alternative economic logic. What is the role of intercooperation and competition in the so-called social market?

My research in Catalonia included 19 semi-structured interviews, informal conversations and participant observation over a period of ten months in 2017 and 2018. To provide context, I carried out a statistical analysis of the labor market; reviewed European, national, regional and local documents and public policies; and analyzed the findings of ten surveys focusing on two specific issues: entrepreneurship and health. My fieldwork focused on four case studies: two *Ateneus Cooperatius* (Cooperative Athenaeums), each a network of diverse entities from the social and solidarity economy led by small cooperatives dedicated to social transformation; the collective entrepreneurship training program *Estarter* organized by the Institut de Govern i Polítiques Públiques (Public Policy and Government Institute) at the Autonomous University of Barcelona; and the *Xarxa d'Economia Solidària de Catalunya* (Solidarity Economy Network of Catalonia, commonly known as XES), one of the leading actors in the regional social and solidarity economy.

In one of the Cooperative Athenaeums, public administration intervenes through town councils, regional councils, local development agencies and so on. Since October 2016, these networks, which seek to encourage the creation of new cooperative enterprises and to improve labor market conditions, have been fully subsidized by the Government of Catalonia. In 2018, they were discussing the continuation of these networks as a public-community-cooperative service. The collective entrepreneurship training program Estarter[4] ran between 2013 and 2016 and offered practical tools, knowledge and resources to projects in the city of Barcelona with a "social transforming vocation." Unlike the conventional entrepreneur ideology that lauds individual initiative and obscures socio-economic inequalities, Estarter deliberately considered the inequality of opportunities and did not hold individuals responsible for the project's failure. The Solidarity Economy Network, officially founded in 2003, has since then experienced exponential growth. At present, it consists of over 100 members, 15 support entities and 190 entities pursuing economic activity.

I also carried out fieldwork in institutions linked to the four case studies (Barcelona City Council, especially the new department dedicated to the development of the social and solidarity economy in the city; Barcelona Activa, the major local development agency; and the Catalan Government, specifically the social economy department) as well as in other cooperatives, associations and institutions in Catalonia. All of the cooperatives I studied were quite small (between three and eight partners), linked to social movements and committed to social transformation. Some authors have classified these cooperatives as belonging to the *cooperative solidarity model*, which allegedly differs from the *commodified cooperative* by not being organized around competitiveness and economic benefits (Mansilla et al. 2014). But as we will see below, most *solidarity cooperatives* still need to be part of the market economy and, consequently, to compete.

Social Entrepreneurship Meets the Social Economy

Although entrepreneurship has grown during the crisis—and has penetrated the unemployed sector through incentives such as the possibility of capitalizing unemployment benefits and discounts on fees during the first 18 months of self-employment—critics argue that this discourse obscures the necessity of designing efficient public policies for employment (Pfeilstetter et al. 2014). Indeed, all of my interlocutors believed the ideology of entrepreneurship to be a strategy to hide the structural problems of unemployment. Nevertheless, many of them had incorporated entrepreneurship ideology in their discourses and practices, most often as "social entrepreneurship." Social entrepreneurship combines the passion for a social mission with an image of business-like discipline, innovation, creativity and change-oriented action (Dees 2001). Accordingly, the newly legitimized space of social entrepreneurship embraces three specific kinds of social agents: professionals displaced by cuts to social spending, members of cooperatives and associations who resignify themselves within this *fancier* category, and people *elected* by institutions to develop socio-economic initiatives (Molina et al. 2014).

In my fieldwork, I came across four main elaborations of entrepreneurship in the social and solidarity economy. *Social entrepreneurship* means that projects aim to satisfy social needs not met by the state or market.[5] *Collective entrepreneurship* (in contrast to individual entrepreneurship) considers inequalities among people from the outset; the basic idea is that "if we are more, it will be easier to make the project possible" (field notes 2017) as each person can contribute complementary knowledge and resources. *Cooperative entrepreneurship* means that the project has the legal status of a cooperative, while *collaborative entrepreneurship* signals that the project is part of the collaborative economy where producers and consumers "collaborate" through a digital platform in order to exchange goods and services.

Critics have charged that such typologies obscure the differences and tensions among heterogeneous groups of entrepreneurs (Pfeilstetter 2011); others have suggested using the term "socially oriented economy" to highlight the diversity of projects and meanings of entrepreneurship (Martinez et al. 2015). The "socially oriented economy" includes the solidarity economy, the traditional cooperative movement, the social economy, social entrepreneurship, social enterprises and even corporate social responsibility. Thus, most of these bottom-up initiatives (Rakopoulos 2014) are articulated with top-down processes and vice-versa. Other authors argue that entrepreneurial dynamics were introduced into the very heart of the third sector in the 1980s and 1990s due to changes in its public funding (Defourny and Nyssens 2010). Structural unemployment in many European countries, the reduction of state funding for social action, and the need for more active integration policies raised the question of how the third sector could adapt to this new context (Moulaert and Alenei 2005). The answer was clear: the third sector should reorganize itself in order to appear as a provider of welfare services and start working with the market (Lipietz 1996). Most present entities belonging to the third sector as well as to the social economy thus rely on income raised from the market, state redistribution and reciprocity (volunteers and donations), and tend to hybridize these different economic exchanges in their activities.

During my fieldwork, I encountered cooperative members expressing very different views about making use of the entrepreneurship discourse. Some flatly refused to link their social and solidarity projects to entrepreneurship because:

> It is a theoretical tradition that comes from Schumpeter, from creative destruction, from the entrepreneur, from the model of capitalism of creative destruction and of the competitive advantages of the entrepreneur and the innovator... Each conceptual tradition has burdens and we have chosen others. Furthermore, it's linked to European public policies of taking advantage of this social energy and commodifying it. (Member of a worker cooperative and a Cooperative Athenaeum)

Cooperative members who rejected the entrepreneurship discourse pointed to its role in legitimizing institutional demands to deregulate and individualize the labor market, tracing the emergence of the social entrepreneur to the inability of the state and the market to satisfy social needs. The entrepreneur as a white man whose mission is to look for innovative solutions to social problems is the most suitable agent that fits into the market economy, assuming in his discourses and practices the theoretical postulates of neoliberalism: personal effort, individual freedom and the so-called equality of opportunities (Pfeilstetter 2011). Embodying a subjectivist and economistic approach to entrepreneurship, the figure of the entrepreneur obscures the social and historical conditions that facilitate the emergence of entrepreneurship. My interlocutors who refused to articulate the social and solidarity economy in a language of social entrepreneurship further emphasized that the former not only addresses questions of labor but other areas such as consumption and reproduction.

Other cooperative members used the discourse strategically for the purposes of outreach:

> Why have we made such an approach? I think that we have been utilitarian, that is to say, "we will use the entrepreneurship services to reach our own goals." We have told them [conventional public entrepreneurship services]: "send us people." Of course, it depends with whom you make alliances, you will then get different kinds of people. Then, we use "entrepreneurship" to attract audiences... We have used it to reach more people without giving much thought to the concept. (Member of a worker cooperative and a Cooperative Athenaeum)

Other cooperative members told me that it's a battle of meanings and that it's necessary to translate the ideology of entrepreneurship into the terms of the social and solidarity economy, for instance by adding social values to the ideology of entrepreneurship. Many projects also used mainstream concepts to access resources that would otherwise have remained elusive:

> You can understand it from a purely capitalist mercantile logic or you can understand it from a logic of social and solidarity economy... In the end, the economy, the circular economy, entrepreneurship, social innovation... are things that come from above, that determine the allocation of public resources and then, for that reason, I say that there is a struggle for meanings. You fit here and try to make this happen in your political color.

Members of Estarter explained that they understood the idea of collective entrepreneurship as an opportunity to make the social economy more sustainable and to pool knowledge from domains that have usually been opposed: social movements' experience with collective management and the business world's experience in running economically sustainable projects. Some criticized the tendency of social movements to remain isolated in order to avoid losing their political edge and being redefined and domesticated. The activist and ex-member of Estarter, who nowadays has a post in the Barcelona City Council, declared that entrepreneurship:

is a discourse that can politically be a trap or can depoliticize and so on, but I have always claimed that for most transformation positions, we have to come out of our comfort zones and we have to fight. Some spaces will surely be co-opted or things will be used in such a way... and it is true. But we must have a discourse of entrepreneurship from the left, from the social transformation movements.

Although many of the projects that participated in this research had elaborated a discourse on entrepreneurship, my interlocutors, when asked, often proposed alternative concepts in order to avoid using a term that they perceived as tainted. Some referred to "economic democracy" or "economic self-organization" to clarify that it's not only about adding social values to the economy but about "radical change," a "different way of doing economics." Their perspectives on entrepreneurship thus encompassed both economic-material and socio-cultural dimensions, implying an awareness of an economy embedded in culture, history and social relations. For activists explicitly following Polanyi (1989[1944]) and Laville (2004), the social economy model indeed held the promise of overcoming the separation between market and society, of combining "the state and the market," "people and things," "economics and politics." That said, all economic models are embedded in social relations; it is capitalist ideology that hides people's relations within exchanges and, in general, in the economy (Marx 1999 [1867]: 36–47; Hart 1986; Booth 1994; Granovetter 1985; Zelizer 1994).

While some of my interlocutors preferred the terminology of "transformative entrepreneurship" to highlight that the goal is social transformation, others preferred to talk about "collective entrepreneurship" to underline the importance of the collective dimension (as opposed to the individual entrepreneur). Projects that sought to avoid the term *entrepreneur* used words such as "people," "future cooperativists," "people motivated to start a project," "people wanting to start a self-employment project," etc. All of these terms reveal the difficulties of finding an effective, inclusive synonym for "entrepreneur." Despite the growing importance of the phenomenon, there is a stark lack of agreement on the conceptual framework, definitions, motivations and purposes of entrepreneurship (Parente et al. 2012; Shane and Venkataraman 2000; Alonso and Galve 2008).

This theoretical and conceptual murkiness extends to the arena of social entrepreneurship, with each actor adapting the term to fit her own needs and priorities. The discourses and practices of the social and solidarity economy and entrepreneurship allow for multiple articulations. But even as entrepreneurship remains an ambiguous term capable of subsuming different content and political positions, at its core it is part of a neoliberal ideology that resignifies employment through specific capacities and attitudes.

Values in the Social Economy and Entrepreneurship

While entrepreneurship is often presented as an opportunity for the social economy, many small cooperatives rooted in social movements argue that the resources delivered to social entrepreneurship are meagre, that salaries and workloads leave much to be desired, that a lack of demand hinders the economic viability of some projects, and that institutional support is forcing the agenda, which often clashes with self-management and political criteria. As I have described elsewhere (Homs 2019), the often-repeated claim that cooperatives are *resilient* is better understood as *resistance* by people—or more precisely, by their bodies—living in precarious situations rather than as an effective business formula to overcome economic difficulties. Cooperative members face precarity collectively, or as many interlocutors put it, as "collective self-exploitation." Resilience is in fact an embodiment of the consequences of socioeconomic crisis and resistance to a capitalist economy that tries to subjugate and commodify every human sphere (Narotzky 2004; Homs et al. 2019).

All of my interlocutors stated that the social and solidarity economy is embedded in political, social and moral values. According to a member of the Cooperative and Social Economy Department of the Catalan Government:

> The capitalist market only takes into account the supply and the demand and the price, generally. And the social market takes into account an ethical dimension. Is it an anti-capitalist or non-monetary market? No, we're not talking about that. This is another area… it is a market, a social market.

This "new" socioeconomic model is guided by values such as cooperation, quality of life, sustainability and equity. Others underline values such as commitment, solidarity, justice and democracy, while more critical voices espouse direct democracy, social justice, quality stable employment, collective property, limited profit and the redistribution of surplus. They thus range from explicitly political values that seek to configure collective internal praxis (Alquézar 2016) to moral values that "remoralize" the economy (Narotzky 2010).

In any case, the capitalist economy also invokes social values when referring to products deemed to benefit people or the environment, reconfiguring social values as market values and giving capitalism its socially responsible face. Numerous social economy actors also recognize that social values award market position. A report by the Catalan Federation of Workers Cooperatives—citing Porter and Kramer's (2011) theory of "shared value creation" which posits that "values can be a solvency factor and a competitive advantage even in a capitalist framework"—explains that "nowadays we have to change the neoclassic perspective of value creation that only considers the short-term interests of shareholders" (Alternativas Económicas 2018).

Such points of view are common among larger social enterprises such as Mondragon and social economy business groups such as Clade which declare that cooperation is an added value that facilitates the development of the social economy and improves its market competitiveness. Txomin Garcia, president of Laboral Kutxa, expressed the same idea at the 2018 Global Social Economy Forum in Bilbao: "Cooperation is essential, but it has to go together with competitiveness." Indeed, the forum had as its title *Values and Competitiveness for Local, Inclusive and Sustainable Development*. In a similar vein, a member of the Cooperative and Social Economy Department of the Catalan Government explains that the social economy consists of enterprises guided by social and cooperative values, but which still need the market—where exchanges are guided by competitiveness—to sell their goods and services. Nevertheless, members of the small cooperatives and networks that participated in this research emphasized that social values are the seeds of social transformation as they imply internal practices such as recognizing collective property, redistributing surplus and democratic decision-making within horizontal assemblies—the main goal of which is not the reproduction of capital but the reproduction of life (Coraggio 2004; Federici 2013; Pérez-Orozco 2014). In other words, these practices privilege the social value of work (Marx 1999 [1867]) and life, with social values extending beyond the "social" and "environmental" features of products and beyond market logic.

The promotion of *intercooperation* between entities in the social and solidarity economy stands out among the strategies to expand this sector. It works through three mechanisms. First, the purchase of goods and services from social economy entities facilitates growth of the so-called social market. Second, it allows for the articulation of networks that contribute to greater social visibility and the possibility of exerting greater pressure on public policymaking. Third, intercooperation is seen as a pooling of resources among entities that favors both growth and the consolidation of the social economy: "the axis that must allow forging a model for a more just and respectful society, based on community values such as solidarity, equality and respect, differentiated from individualism and competitiveness" (member of a worker cooperative and a Cooperative Athenaeum). In this last case, intercooperation is presented as an alternative to competitiveness and as a tool for social transformation, in contrast to large-scale social economy actors such as Mondragon and Clade which have also framed cooperation as a tool that enables positioning in the capitalist market.

Different economic logics are thus in tension and conflict. On the one hand, the hegemonic market is guided by market value; its ultimate goal is the expanded reproduction of capital. On the other hand, the logic of social reproduction seeks to extend the reproduction of life. Many social and solidarity economy activists end up proposing a *harmonious* coexistence between these two economic logics, thereby downplaying the many existing tensions and conflicts and the power of the market to co-opt social economy projects. According to them, the social economy can operate in a parallel social market guided by social values; some explicitly argue that it is impossible to get rid of competition. This is why the "new model" should consider the possibility of cohabitation of different economic logics, with cooperation guiding the social market and competition guiding the capitalist market. As a member of the Solidarity Economy Network stated:

> If you try to cancel the private market economy, surely you are annulling a part of human nature. In fact, the individualistic selfish impulse coexists with our cooperative, altruistic impulse. Trying to override the private market economy is, I think, a bad idea, because it's not possible. We then have this framework of coexistence of the market, the public and the cooperative [economy]. The idea is that the public and cooperative economy removes the hegemony of the market economy.

This recalls the multi-centric economy that Bohannan (1965) found among the Tiv in Nigeria, where several spheres of exchange, each following their own logic, co-existed and interacted with each other. Recent studies of social currencies also highlight parallels with Bohannan's idea of spheres of exchange. In some cases, there is a clear delimitation of the interactions between the hegemonic economy and the exchange networks based on social currency; in other cases, interactions are not prevented, precisely to ensure the sustainability of the projects (Alcañiz, Sanz and Estevez 2014). All in all, my ethnographic fieldwork revealed that cooperative members interpret interactions between the social economy and the market economy as opportunities to socialize, expand, and to "remove the hegemony" of the market economy.

Structural Opportunities

The strategic development of social entrepreneurship and its identification as an opportunity by social and solidarity economy activists reveal both bottom-up and top-down dynamics. As a member of the Cooperative and Social Economy Department of the Catalan Government argues, the "social economy is part of the trend towards social entrepreneurship" but differs from it because it is a collective endeavor: "It doesn't assume risks individually which dramatically reduces the risks. One is not alone. Each person is capable of assuming a specific role in entrepreneurship. Maybe not everyone can be a leader, but they can do other things." More optimistically, a member of the Social Economy Department of the Barcelona City Council, in a debate about the role of the social economy in local economies, argued that the social economy may even change the business economy and conventional entrepreneurship.

Although most of my interlocutors (except those who saw it as a capitalist perversion) saw the entrepreneurial discourse as an opportunity for the social economy to attract greater resources, for activists to reach positions of power and for introducing social values into the conventional economy, the discourse of entrepreneurship, I argue, legitimizes the transfer of responsibilities from the state and the market to individuals. It is only by obscuring structural factors such as the destruction of thousands of jobs and the massive social cuts brought by austerity that people's *needs* can be performed as *opportunities*. The discourse of entrepreneurship thus reformulates the need for work and welfare in the context of crisis as an opportunity to create one's own job, one that will offer benefits to society. It also provides opportunities to channel political militancy and activism into economic initiatives such as cooperatives.

Indeed, the crisis itself is seen as an opportunity as it has brought the social economy, through the discourse of social entrepreneurship, onto the agendas of regional and local institutions. Some social movements have lost sight of the structural causes of the crisis and the social and historical conditions that have enabled the development of the social economy and social entrepreneurship. My analysis here parallels that of critical scholars who have concluded that student struggles in the 1980s which sought to make minorities more visible without addressing the socio-economic inequalities between groups were eventually co-opted and depoliticized by the marketing departments of multinational corporations (Klein 1999).

The growth of the social and solidarity economy thus contains the risks of appropriation and political domestication: "We cannot always be the same people; we need to involve more people in this process of expansion and growth. And with more people, who also have the right to their opinions… the social economy sector will have to change" (member of the Cooperative and Social Economy Department, field notes 2018). While this may dilute the transformative dimension that many micro and small cooperatives want to achieve, it is still interpreted as an opportunity: "it may be a watered-down social economy. This is a danger, but it can also be an opportunity. It's a risk because there will certainly be lobbies but… let's profit from it!"

When asked about the accomplishments of these social entrepreneurship programs, members of several cooperatives answered that more people have been exposed to the cooperative formula but there remains a need for in-depth analysis. Some activists wondered who really ends up starting a social entrepreneurship project and, in any case, how long their projects survive: "In the end, people who take advantage of these programs are people that knew you before, who already had some affinity with the social economy. People coming from conventional entrepreneurship take the information and never come back again." These initiatives to develop the social economy thus often seem to preach to the converted, while the allocation of institutional resources creates dependencies on institutions as well.

In the end, the crisis, the social economy and entrepreneurship are presented as opportunities, as part of a discourse that dovetails with the ideology dominant during the last financial and socioeconomic crisis—one that absolves the state of responsibility, as well as the market and financial institutions, while holding individuals responsible for not having work, for not creating their own opportunities, for not saving enough money, for overspending in the past, for being indebted, for not having enough training, for not being innovative enough and so on (Fine et al. 2016; Guérin 2012).

Small cooperatives rooted in social movements claim that their aim is to not only add social values but transform the wider capitalist economy through their praxis: "we do not understand the social economy as a third sector dedicated to what the market or the state does not want; we want to transform the whole economy" (member of a worker cooperative and a Cooperative Athenaeum). Nevertheless, these cooperatives continue to sell their goods and services within a capitalist framework where exchange is guided by market value. In the final analysis, social values are measured in terms of market value and are added to the final price of goods and services (Homs and Narotzky 2019).

Although many of my interlocutors referred to two economic models with different goals and values coexisting under the paradigm of the plural economy (Laville 2013; Gibson-Graham 2008; Surinach 2017), we can find the same concepts, and even praxis, in both models. Capitalism presents a kinder, gentler face by giving lip service to social values, while some cooperatives mobilize social values to improve their positioning on the market. As a member of the Cooperative and Social Economy Department of the Catalan Government stated:

> A cooperative of workers is a company. So, whether you like it or not, it will be a part… it will compete and be part of a post-capitalist economy if you want to say it like this, it will be a cooperative economy. But it will not stop competing, it will not stop selling the product, using money… because it is a company… It wants to change the market but it does not want to stop existing in the current economic market because in the end, it is a company that competes, it uses money, it is different, it is ethical, but in the end… it is "I sell the product and they give me some money; I live thanks to this."

In conclusion, capital and the state are externalizing the costs of the politics of austerity as governments transfer their responsibilities for safeguarding welfare onto individuals, communities and specific sectors of labor (MacKinnon and Driscoll 2012)—including through the practices of the social economy and social entrepreneurship. While the development of the social economy is presented as a process of "contamination," "hybridization", "pollination" or "coexistence"—as adding social values to the conventional economy—this does not make explicit the social struggle and resistance to dispossession and exploitation in a capitalocentric world. Some of these projects are not only *different* but opposed in their purposes to capitalist accumulation. Nevertheless, they must operate in the market, are subject to capitalist economic logics and resist/exist through precariousness, competitiveness and self-exploitation. Although social values add a consciously moral dimension to the social economy and social entrepreneurship, the domain of exchange continues to be structured by competition and the logics of capitalism. Although some cooperatives espouse social transformation, the social economy and social entrepreneurship in their current forms do not challenge the hegemony of the capitalist economy.

Notes

1. See https://ec.europa.eu/social/
2. In general, workers registered in RETA have lower contributions than workers registered in the general regime. Lower contributions generally mean fewer benefits, and self-employed people must meet stricter requirements to access them. Workers registered in the general regime have an employment contract with the company and receive a salary; their employment relationship is framed by labor laws and collective agreements. In contrast, self-employed workers gain their income through contracts regulated by mercantile and civil laws.
3. The reform introduced the entrepreneurial spirit as one of the key competences to be achieved at each educational level for students from 6 to 18 years old. A new subject—"Initiation to Entrepreneurialism and Entrepreneurial Activity"—was proposed for Spain's different regions. In Catalonia, "Entrepreneurship" is currently an elective subject for students aged between 12 and 16, and is compulsory in vocational training.
4. Estarter is a training program sponsored by the Barcelona City Council and Barcelona Activa. Besides the Institut de Govern i Polítiques Públiques, nine other bodies from the social and solidarity economy collaborate in its organization.
5. Academics and activists have distinguished between four kinds of social entrepreneurship (Parente et al. 2012; Surinach 2017; Labcoop 2018). Social entrepreneurship *as social innovation* does not seek profit but reinvests it to maximize benefits for society. Social entrepreneurship *as a social business* can address social problems without involving the state as a stakeholder. Social entrepreneurship dependent on the welfare state, that is, on redistribution through subsidies. Finally, social entrepreneurship linked to *collective action* aims to transform society; examples in this chapter include XES and Estarter.

References

Alcañiz, G., J. Sanz and J.J. Estevez. 2014. "Monedas sociales, iniciativas socio-económicas emergentes y economía moral: notas a partir del estudio de la moneda complementaria 'La Bellota.'" *Actas Periferias, fronteras y diálogos XIII Congreso de Antropología de la FAAEE*, Tarragona.

Alonso, M.J. and C. Galve. 2008. "El emprendedor y la empresa: una revisión teórica de los determinantes a su constitución." *Acciones e Investigaciones Sociales* 26: 5–44.

Alquézar, R. 2016. "El problema del valor social añadido desde la perspectiva de la economía social y solidaria." *Jornada de Economía crítica: El análisis económico ante los límites del capitalism*: 818–28.

Alternativas Económicas. 2018. *Economies transformadores i cooperativisme. Oportunitats i riscos per al cooperativisme de treball*. Barcelona: Federació de Cooperatives de Treball de Catalunya.

Bohannan, P.Y. and G. Dalton. 1965. *Markets in Africa: Eight Subsistence Economies in Transition*. New York: Doubleday Anchor.

Boletín Oficial del Estado. 2013. "Ley 14/2013, de 27 de septiembre, de apoyo a los emprendedores y su internacionalización." No. 233: 78787-78882.

Booth, J.W. 1994. "On the Idea of the Moral Economy." *American Political Science Review* 88(3): 653–67.

Coraggio, J.L. 2004. "Economía del trabajo." In A.D. Cattani, ed. *La Otra Economia*. Buenos Aires: Editorial Altamira.

Dees, G. 2001. *The Meaning of Social Entrepreneurship*. https://entrepreneurship.duke.edu/news-item/the-meaning-of-social-entrepreneurship/ (last accessed May 2018).

Defourny, J. and M. Nyssens. 2010. "Social Enterprise in Europe: At the Crossroads of Market, Public Policies and Third Sector." *Policy and Society* 29: 231–42.

European Commission. 2010. *Europe 2020: A Strategy for Smart, Sustainable and Inclusive Growth*.

European Commission. 2011. *Iniciativa en favor del emprendimiento social. Construir un ecosistema para promover las empresas sociales en el centro de la economía y la innovación sociales*. 682 final.

European Council. 2000. *Conclusiones de la presidencia. Consejo Europeo de Lisboa. 23 y 24de marzo de 2000*.

European Council. 2018. *Council Decision (EU) 2018/1215 of 16 July 2018 on Guidelines for the Employment Policies of the Member States*. 224/9 final.

Federici, S. 2013. *Revolución en punto cero: trabajo doméstico, reproducción y luchas feministas*. Madrid: Traficantes de Sueños.

Fernández, A. and I. Miró. 2016. *L'economia social i solidària a Barcelona*. Barcelona: La Ciutat Invisible, SCCL and Barcelona City Council.

Fine, B., D. Johnston, A.C. Santos and E. Van Waeyenberge. 2016. "Nudging or Fudging: The World Development Report 2015." *Development and Change* 47(4): 640–63.

Gibson-Graham, J.K. 2008. "Diverse Economies: Performative Practices for 'Other Worlds'." *Progress in Human Geography* 32(5): 613–32.

Granovetter, M. 1985. "Economic Action and Social Structure: The Problem of Embeddedness." *American Journal of Sociology* 91(3): 481–510.

Guérin, I. 2012. "Households' Over-Indebtedness and the Fallacy of Financial Education: Insights from Economic Anthropology." *Microfinance in Crisis Working Papers Series 1*, Paris I Sorbonne University/IRD.

Hart, K. 1986. "Heads or Tails? Two Sides of the Coin." *Man* 21(4): 637–56.

Homs, P. 2019. "(Des)encuentros entre las instituciones y la economía social y solidaria en Cataluña." *Revista de Antropología Social* 28(2): 227–46.

Homs, P. and S. Narotzky. 2019. "Within and Beyond Market Allocation Systems: The Case of Organic Food Cooperatives in Catalonia." In: *Food Values in Europe: Economies, Ideologies, and Power in Practice*. London: Bloomsbury.

Homs, P., D. Sarkis, R. Alquézar and N. Morelló. 2019. "Cooperative Practices: Survival Strategies, "Alternative" Movements or Capitalism Re-Embedding?" In P. Simonic, ed. *Anthropological Perspectives on Solidarity and Reciprocity*. Ljubljana: Ljubljana University Press.

Klein, N. 1999. *No logo. Taking Aim at the Brand Bullies*. New York: Picador.

Labcoop. 2018. Escoles de Pensament en emprenedoria social. http://labcoop.coop/wp-content/uploads/2018/04/LabCoop_Escoles-de-pensament_CAT.pdf (last accessed May 2018).

Laville, J.L. 2004. "El marco conceptual de la economía solidaria." In J-L. Laville, ed. *Economía social y solidaria. Una visión europea*. Buenos Aires: Altamira.

Laville, J.L. 2013. "The Social and Solidarity Economy: A Theoretical and Plural Framework." Draft paper prepared for UNRISD conference *Potential and Limits of Social and Solidarity Economy*, 6–8 May 2013, Geneva.

Lipietz, A. 1996. "The Third Sector: Resolving the Crisis of the Welfare State." *City* 1(1–2): 141–4.

Lobato, M. and H. Valenzuela. 2014. Mercado de valores. Estrategias económicas emergentes en tiempos de crisis. *Actas Periferias, fronteras y diálogos XIII Congreso de Antropología de la FAAEE*, Tarragona.

MacKinnon, D. and K. Driscoll. 2012. "From Resilience to Resourcefulness: A Critique of Resilience Policy and Activism." *Progress in Human Geography* 37(2): 253–70.

Mansilla, E., J. Grenzner and S. Alberich. 2014. *Femení plural Les dones a l'economia cooperativa*. Barcelona: Diputació de Barcelona.

Martínez, L. and V. Bogino. 2015. "La instrumentación en España de las políticas europeas de emprendimiento ¿creación de empleo o profundización de la crisis del empleo asalariado?" *Revista Eletrônica de Ciência Política* 6(1).

Martínez, J, M.L. Molina and H. Valenzuela. 2015. "Del cooperativismo a la economía socialmente orientada." *GRAFO Working Papers 4*.

Marx, K. 1999 [1867]. *El Capital. Crítica de la economía política*. México City: Fondo de Cultura Económica.

Molina, J.L., S. Revilla and J. Pampalona. 2014. "Las redes sociales de la economía social." *Actas Periferias, fronteras y diálogos XIII Congreso de Antropología de la FAAEE*, Tarragona.

Moulaert, F. and O. Ailenei. 2005. "Social Economy, Third Sector and Solidarity Relations: A Conceptual Synthesis from History to Present." *Urban Studies* 42(11): 2037–53.

Narotzky, S. 2004. *Antropología económica. Nuevas tendencias.* Barcelona: Melusina.
Narotzky, S. 2010. Reciprocidad y capital social: modelos teóricos, políticas de desarrollo, economías alternativas. Una perspectiva antropológica. In V. Bretón, ed. *Saturno devora a sus hijos. Miradas críticas sobre el desarrollo y sus promesas.* Barcelona: Icária.
OECD/European Union. 2017. *The Missing Entrepreneurs. Policies for Inclusive Entrepreneurship.* Paris: OECD.
Parente, C., M. Santos, V. Marcos, D. Costa and L. Veloso. 2012. "Perspectives of Social Entrepreneurship in Portugal: Comparison and Contrast with International Theoretical Approaches." *International Review of Social Research* 2(2): 103–24.
Pérez-Orozco, A. 2014. *Subversión feminista de la economía.* Madrid: Traficantes de sueños.
Pfeilstetter, R. 2011. "El emprendedor. Una reflexión crítica sobre usos y significados actuales de un concepto." *Gazeta de Antropología* 27(1).
Pfeilstetter, R., H. Valenzuela and J.L. Molina. 2014. "Emprendimiento social e iniciativas socioeconómicas emergentes: fronteras y diálogos entre economía, cultura y sociedad." *Actas Periferias, fronteras y diálogos XIII Congreso de Antropología de la FAAEE,* Tarragona.
Polanyi, K. 1989 [1944]. *La gran trasformación: crítica al liberalismo económico.* Madrid: La Piqueta.
Porter, M. and M. Kramer. 2011. "Creating Shared Value. How to Reinvent Capitalism—And Unleash a Wave of Innovation and Growth." *Harvard Business Review* 89(January/February): 62–77.
Rakopoulos, T. 2014. "The Crisis Seen from Below, Within, and Against: From Solidarity Economy to Food Distribution Cooperatives in Greece." *Dialectical Anthropology* 38(2): 189–207.
Shane, S. and S. Venkataraman. 2000. "The Promise of Entrepreneurship as a Field of Research." *Academy of Management Review* 25(1): 217–26.
Surinach, R. 2017. *Economías Transformadoras de Barcelona.* Barcelona: Ajuntament de Barcelona.
Valenzuela, H., J.L. Molina, M. Lobato and M.J. Lubbers M.J. 2015. "Empresas sociales en Cataluña. Cambio de paradigma o estrategia de clase media?" *Otra Economía* 9(17): 177–86.
Zelizer, V. 1994. *The Social Meaning of Money.* New York: Basic Books.

PART II

SOCIAL REPRODUCTION

6

Austerity Welfare and the Moral Significance of Needs in Portugal

Patrícia Matos

Introduction

Portugal signed a four-year structural adjustment program with the "Troika" (the European Commission, European Central Bank and International Monetary Fund) in May 2011. The 78-billion-euro bailout was conditional upon severe cuts to state spending which, implemented under a right-wing coalition government, entailed harsh tax increases and the reduction of welfare benefits. Like other countries on the indebted periphery of the Eurozone, Portuguese policies of austerity entailed measures of "internal devaluation" (Blyth 2013)—wage repression, precarious employment and mass unemployment—contributing to the most violent and rapid transfer of income from labor to capital in democratic Portugal (Reis et al. 2013).

This conjuncture of austerity was shaped by the simultaneous *devaluation of human needs*[1] and political rhetoric that downplayed the language of rights and privileged the language of *national needs*, which became instrumental to legitimizing the coherence and validity of austerity measures. The government mobilized the *needs of the country/nation*—defined as financial sustainability—as a rhetorical device to legitimize austerity in light of the national condition of "emergency" and "exception." "Reforming the state and its welfare functions" was presented as essential in light of the *need* to avoid state bankruptcy, the *need* to make better use of available resources, to "make the social security system sustainable" (a phrase often used by politicians) and to be able to attend to *those in greater need*.

Talk of needs—in both political discourse and public policy—played a key role in legitimizing the new "architecture of need" (Haney 2003), justifying granting or depriving some persons of access to certain resources, rights to certain goods and claims to particular entitlements.² "Needs-talk" thus emerged as a site of struggle "where groups with unequal discursive (and extra-discursive) resources compete to establish as hegemonic their respective interpretations of legitimate social needs" (Fraser 2013: 59). Responding to *those in greater need* was part of the Program of Social Emergency implemented between 2011 and 2014, launched by the Ministry of Solidarity and Social Security to "fight the lack of efficiency" in state redistributive practices and to "change the paradigm of social response to severe material deprivation." The program, which targeted specific segments of the population including impoverished households, the long-term unemployed, the elderly and disabled persons with a budget of 630 million euros for 2012, instituted projects to be carried out in partnership with third-sector institutions and relevant interlocutors. As Joaquim (2015) notes, the Program of Social Emergency entailed decreased social spending and increased state funding to the third sector. It also implied a shift in the model and logic of welfare redistribution with the state delegating its responsibilities to the third sector while reinforcing the broader logic of charity and poor relief in welfare provisioning. One consequence was the number of soup kitchens in Portugal skyrocketing from 62 in 2011 to 843 in 2015.³

This chapter examines how individuals and households have struggled to fulfill and define their needs, wants and desires within the conjuncture of austerity welfare in post-crisis Portugal.⁴ I focus on the articulation of various forms of care work⁵—predominantly undertaken by women—that define and fulfill the material (food, shelter, wages) and immaterial (worth, entitlements, rights, recognition) needs of impoverished working-class households amidst unemployment, the lack of steady sources of monetary income, welfare retrenchment and the degradation of the entitlements of citizenship. In exploring the moral grounds and relational structure of the needs-claims that mediate the practices, motivations and dilemmas entailed in different kinds of care work—paid and unpaid, across public and private divides, within and between households—I suggest that welfare dispossession and the erosion of social rights have intensified the use of *needs* as a vernacular morality through which ordinary people seek to assert the legitimacy of their rights, claims and entitlements. At the same time, the government's political mobilization of "needs" to differentiate access to resources and entitlements ("real needs" as opposed to "subsidized livelihoods") renders the language of needs a *language of contention* (Roseberry 1994) that informs people's struggles to act upon broader processes of dispossession and disenfranchisement.

The chapter begins by examining how working-class women in Setúbal identified and justified their individual and household needs according to different *livelihood spheres of concern*.[6] This notion draws on Sayer's (2011) work on the relevance of attending to people's relations with the world as one of *concern*, which cannot be reduced to conventional, emotional or subjective attachments. In the context of women's articulations of different forms of care work to fulfill individual and household needs, livelihood spheres of concern define conceptions of vulnerability and well-being grounded in moral values and relations of interdependency, obligation and responsibility. The chapter then turns to how women's caring labors and efforts to fulfill their material and immaterial needs involved a valuation of livelihood conditions *and* an evaluation of the possibilities for preventing or promoting change. In doing so, they re-appropriated and re-signified the austerity language of national needs (focused on the sustainability of public debt) as a *language of contention* to underpin their pursuit of material resources and struggles for human worth. In particular, I examine how women's moral evaluation of human needs—in contrast to their framing as lack, deficiency or passivity by politicians, bureaucrats, charities and banks—was deployed to demand particular claims, entitlements and rights. In the conclusion, I discuss the political possibilities and limitations of an emergent needs-grounded morality of distribution and recognition for people's ability to dispute the unequal logics of welfare redistribution informed by hegemonic idioms of deservingness.

Identifying and Justifying Needs: Livelihood Spheres of Concern and Caring Dilemmas

While the austerity welfare regime in Portugal severely devalued human needs, the driving forces behind the destruction of jobs, wage cuts, welfare conditionality, diminished expectations and livelihood impoverishment were not specific to the country. In Europe and beyond, austerity policies reiterated the neoliberal mantra that "human well-being can best be advanced by liberating individual entrepreneurial freedoms and skills within an institutional framework characterized by strong private property rights, free markets, and free trade" (Harvey 2007). In Portugal and elsewhere, the policies of austerity entailed three major discontinuities: in the role and functions of the welfare state, in the financialization of capital extraction and in the breakdown of the models and expectations of social reproduction.

The austerity policies of spending cuts, privatizing healthcare and welfare reform—accompanied by the moral censure of those "who had been living beyond their means"—contributed to redefining moral obligations between citizens and the state, entailing a retrenchment of people's sense of citizenship entitlements and expectations of livelihoods improving over generations. This was facilitated by the fetishization of sovereign debt as *the* determining national collective obligation—a process through which financial capital has historically captured the national state's fiscal policies. Bear (2015: 178) argues that this capture led to the submission of people's needs, moralities and socialities to a "universe of calculi" pervaded by violence, destitution and abstraction. Indeed, in Portugal as well as in the other so-called PIGS countries in the years immediately following the sovereign debt crisis, politicians' embrace of technical terms such as "public debt," "deficit," the "spread of public bonds" and "fiscal adjustment" served to depoliticize and naturalize the growing social inequality and class polarization directly linked to the fiscal policies of austerity. It is by now well-documented that the fiscal policies of austerity have fueled a crisis of social reproduction, affecting people's ability to ensure even their physical reproduction, illustrated in the pronounced rise of food banks, the growing number of homeless people and widespread indebtedness. The policies of austerity have ushered in a "dynamics of reversal" (Knight and Stewart 2016: 2; cf. Knight 2015), undermining people's hopes and expectations of a *life worth living* for themselves and the next generation (Narotzky and Besnier 2014). What I designate by the phrase "austerity welfare" throughout this chapter is thus a conjuncture in which different livelihood spheres and scales have contributed to a reconfiguration of the articulation of the needs of states, capital and people, with the devaluation and subordination of the latter to the former.

The human and social costs of austerity in Portugal have been devastating. According to the Instituto Nacional de Estatística (National Institute of Statistics), in the second quarter of 2012, within a total active population of five million, 826,900 persons were unemployed (corresponding to an official unemployment rate of 15 percent); 217,400 persons were "inactive available to work" (i.e. "discouraged" from looking for work); and 261,000 persons were "underemployed" (i.e. working involuntarily in low-paid part-time positions) (Rosa 2012). More than one million people were either unemployed or living in conditions of heightened labor precarity. Moreover, 18.7 percent of the adult working population—that is, two million people—had to survive on an average monthly wage of 409 euros, which according to official data meant they were living below the poverty line. Levels of emigration rose to parallel those of the 1960s during the dictatorship.[7] In 2013 alone, 110,000 people left the country.[8] The policies of austerity reinforced a harsh economic recession with decidedly uneven effects upon the population; even before their implementation, Portugal was already one of the more unequal countries in Europe in terms of income distribution. Austerity reinforced this pattern, affecting, in particular, the disposable income of the poorest 10 percent of households (Carmo, Cantante and Carvalho 2012). One-fifth of households were affected by the consequences of unemployment, expressed in individuals' inability to ensure their organic survival and pay for housing, utilities, healthcare and education (Cunha 2012). The material and economic strain experienced by households and individuals had consequences for psychological and mental well-being, with the suicide rate climbing from 8.6 (in every 100,000 inhabitants) in 2006 to 10.1 in 2013 (Ribeiro et al. 2015).

How did ordinary people in Portugal identify and justify their needs under the conditions of austerity welfare? Struggling to fulfill their own material and immaterial needs as well as those of their impoverished households, the caring labor and relationships of working-class women in Setúbal reveal how the identification and justification of needs are mediated by morally bounded livelihood spheres of concern pertaining to kinship obligations and relations of interdependency and mutual help. The women had to make trade-offs in the process of taking care and pursuing livelihood, favoring some relations over others—all of which resulted in highly stressful situations.

I once asked Ana (46), living in a household with her husband (48) and son (27), how she organized her weekly preparation of meals. She explained to me the importance of hunting for local supermarket discounts, particularly for more expensive items such as meat and fish. Stocking up in advance was not an option as money was in short supply. She took advantage of the discounts and planned what to cook, trying to accommodate her husband and son's tastes. This was not the first time that Ana and her husband had experienced difficulties in sustaining the household. In 1999, they acquired a joint bank loan so she could open a small sewing business, which they had to close following the 2008 financial crisis. In 2010, due to the lack of other possibilities, Ana started working as a private cleaner; her husband migrated to Scotland to work in a frozen fish factory. In 2016 he returned to Portugal to become an unskilled worker in a local sugar factory.

When I met them in 2015, their livelihood was particularly precarious, having to repay debts while also having scant access to cash. Amid difficulties, Ana often framed her caring efforts, practices and investments—which she considered fundamental to the household's livelihood and dignity—as a constant struggle (*uma luta constante*). "We never went hungry. If we cannot eat steaks every day, we always have soup and the main dish," she once told me. During the years of austerity, patterns of food insecurity among the population reached alarming levels. In 2010 the Portuguese Catholic University initiated a survey on the well-being and livelihood conditions of welfare charity recipients in partnership with the national network of food banks (*Banco Alimentar Contra a Fome*). In 2014, 52 percent of surveyed households reported a monthly income of or below 400 euros; 53 percent declared that the family income was *never* enough to live on; 33 percent considered it was *sometimes* not enough. One in five respondents stated that they lacked food or felt hunger on *some* days of the week; 28 percent stated that they did not have enough money to buy food until the *end of the month*; and 43 percent replied that this happens *sometimes* (Correia, Costa and Policarpo 2015). Between 2014 and 2016, those who declared that they had gone without eating for the whole day *sometimes during the month* increased from 18 percent to 26 percent (Correia and Costa 2017).

The care work involved in household budgeting, shopping, planning meals, cooking and cleaning was for Ana—as for too many other women—motivated by instrumental, affective and moral reasons tied to livelihood spheres of concern, cross-cutting present and future temporalities. Ana did not disguise the physical and emotional exhaustion of having to manage the daily threats to her livelihood while struggling to ensure that her son would in the future become a "subject of value" (Skeggs and Loveday 2012). Ana was proud that her son was completing a master's program at the university, and neither she nor her husband expected him to work for wages while studying. It was important for them that their son would pursue a "better livelihood" (*uma vida melhor*) through studying, an opportunity they had never had. Although she knew that a university degree was no guarantee of stable employment, her son obtaining a degree and the need to ensure a sense of future was something Ana acted upon through care, with and against the precarious present.

My visits to Ana's household often took place after work during weekdays or on the weekends. I would arrive early in the evening and Ana would be starting to prepare dinner. Neighbors or friends would often pass by to leave fresh vegetables or fish that had not been sold that day at the market. Investing in relations of trust and reciprocity with friends, neighbors and acquaintances served to uphold "informal distributive networks" shaped by the constant flow of resources similar to the domestic networks studied by Carol Stack (1974). Once, Ana was preparing a fresh lettuce for dinner "brought to me by a colleague who also works in cleaning in a house nearby." On another occasion, "a friend I met on the bus brought me strawberries." Ana recounted how she made friends on the bus on her way to work by listening to them talk about their hardships. "Then people feel that they have to thank me. Sometimes I don't know how to thank them in return, but I try to do it in the way I can. The other day I gave one an apron, and she was thrilled." On another occasion, a neighbor asked Ana to prepare four dozen salty pastries made of cod and shrimp. In Ana's words:

> I decided to spend the last ten euros I had in my wallet because I knew she was going to pay for the pastries. I spent all the money because I don't use cheap ingredients. I only use good ingredients. I was in the kitchen all morning preparing the pastries. When I called her to come and pick up the pastries, she told me that she will be unable to keep them because she has to go to the hairdresser! She told me to try to sell them to another person, that she would pass by when she left the hairdresser in case she still had money, adding that "because I know that maybe you need the money."

Ana resented her neighbor's attitude. "I was furious because in her house 1,000 euros come in and in this one only 400, which is my wage, and she knows it." Informal distributive networks were shaped by conflict as much as by mutual aid and cooperation, while further investments of care were demanded to negotiate conflicts arising from the lack of reciprocity as part of an ethic of exchange among participants with unequal needs. Ana's husband suggested that she tell the neighbor she would never make pastries for her again. Ana explained to me that although she felt hurt, she decided to tell her neighbor that the pastries had already been sold to someone else: "in the end, we ended up eating the pastries during the week with salad."

Most of the working-class women I met in Setúbal identified and justified the fulfillment of their own and their household members' needs by referring to livelihood spheres of concern and lines of kin, generation, and networks of friends and acquaintances. These guided how women mobilized care work as a basis for action (Tronto 1993) to access and redistribute material and immaterial resources considered essential for survival and self-worth, to minimize material vulnerability and to enhance interdependent modalities of well-being.

The caring dilemmas women had to confront—for example, taking on further waged or non-waged work so that younger household members would not have to work for wages; managing tensions and conflicts with neighbors to maintain access to informal distributive networks—constituted livelihood trade-offs. I emphasize livelihood trade-offs rather than choice to stress that individual preferences and self-interest did not determine negotiations of tension and conflict. Instead, caring dilemmas entailed livelihood trade-offs underpinned by a normative ethics of livelihood reproduction shaped by interdependency, obligation and responsibility towards the vulnerability and well-being of oneself and others.[9]

Valuing and Evaluating Needs: Claims, Aspirations and Hopes

The devaluation of human needs—which lies at the core of austerity welfare regimes in southern Europe—has framed human needs as a form of deficiency conducive to dependency and passivity. This has been evident in policies of growing welfare residualization and conditionality,[10] in parallel with greater emphasis on the merits of having an entrepreneurial attitude towards work and life.[11] In Portugal, the prime minister implementing the austerity adjustment program went as far as to controversially suggest that people "should stop feeling sorry for themselves"[12] and perceive unemployment as "an opportunity to change lifestyles" rather than avoiding "risk" and "entrepreneurship."[13] Banking and economic elites stressed that ordinary people would need to adjust their behaviors to the new livelihood conditions, including being inventive and pro-active rather than passively expecting the paternalist support of the state. A noted representative of a national food bank charity commented in a television debate that people should "re-learn how to live with less" as a way of acting upon and satisfying their tangible and intangible needs. Underlying such comments was a tacit understanding that human needs should not inform social policy;

that—whilst the term is used for minimal charity-based policies of poor relief for the poorest of the poor, for *those in greater need*—human needs are an obstacle to the development of people's capabilities for independence, adaptation and self-sufficiency, thereby leading to Keynesian and paternalistic forms of welfare provision.

In stark counterpoint to the austerity-led definition of human needs as lack, passivity and deficiency, the caring efforts and labors of my female interlocutors reveal how human needs "do not merely passively register a difference between two states, one that is given and one that does not exist, but involve an impulse, drive or pressure to move towards the latter. They are thus world-guided in responding to the difference and action-guided in seeking to resolve it" (Sayer 2011: 54). For the working-class women I followed, the existence of needs implied a valuation of livelihood conditions and an evaluation of the possibilities for pursuing or preventing change. Needs triggered a morally grounded valuation of how to minimize the material vulnerability of those in need and an evaluation of how best to promote and sustain their claims, aspirations and hopes.

Caring for the needs of others and using these needs as a vernacular morality of claims to resources and entitlements was particularly prominent in the caring labors undertaken between women of different generations, within and between households, crossing public and private divides. Although their practices signal a trend towards the "re-familiarization" of care and welfare in the era of austerity, they can also challenge (or subvert) local administrative modes of satisfying needs as well as arbitrary typologies of moral deservingness. Let me provide an example. Sara (51), a part-time cleaner in a private medical office, lived with her second partner (62), two daughters (21 and 27) and one son (31) from a previous marriage. In the same neighborhood, in another house, lived her sister (42) and her mother (85), and in another her eldest daughter (35). The house where Sara lived was part of a social housing project run through a partnership between the municipality and a private company. The tenancy contract was in the name of Sara's mother. Sara explained that moving the tenancy contract to her name would mean losing the possibility of maintaining a low and "socially conditioned" rent. Sara's mother moved to her sister's house when Sara's first partner, the father of her children, died. This was a difficult moment as Sara found herself with few resources to sustain herself and her children. Over time, ensuring that the municipal authorities remained unaware of the arrangement enabled the fulfillment of various needs, as I explain below.

I followed Sara's daily care tasks between households and throughout the city. In the mornings, she would do the housework for her household (preparing meals for everyone, washing and ironing clothes, cleaning the house). Sometimes she would go shopping and deliver her mother's groceries to her house. In the afternoons she would go to work, except when she took her mother to the medical center or to the social security bureau. Sara felt obliged to follow her mother to the social security bureau because "they tend to think that just because we live in social housing, we are less worthy, and if you can't read or write [which was her mother's case] you can't defend yourself." Towards the end of my fieldwork, her eldest daughter gave birth. Sara began taking care of her eldest daughter's baby in the mornings and her two other daughters began helping with housework. Taking the baby to a nursery was not an option; there was no public nursery network and the private ones were too expensive. Sara once recounted how her son had returned home after pawning his wages to cover an unpaid debt to a private credit agency. "My daughters and my son are everything to me," she said. Sara's caring labors thus sustained the emotional, relational and affective capacities that enabled others to exercise agency beyond the sphere of the household: in her encounters with the state services (her mother), in overcoming dependency on a credit institution (her son) and in being both a worker and mother (her eldest daughter).

I conclude this section with two vignettes that represent a broader pattern I found among my older female interlocutors, pertaining to the inter-generational transfer of money from old age pensions, goods and care work. Most of my interlocutors framed these inter-related forms of care as a means to compensate for the breakdown of the social contract between citizens and the state, a social contract that once held the promise of supporting inter-generational projects of livelihood improvement. Vitória (69), retired for three years, lives alone in a small terraced house she owns in a fishing neighborhood. Before the arrival of heavy industry in the 1960s, Setúbal's formal and informal economy relied on the sea. Vitória had worked in canning factories since the age of 13, as a domestic laborer in private homes and commercial offices, and been a cleaner, later promoted to team-leader, in a reputable hotel in downtown Setúbal. She now earns a pension of around 500 euros per month. Her only son (40) had emigrated to Brazil with his partner and daughter some years ago after losing his job as a mechanic in a local aircraft company that relocated to another country. In our encounters, Vitória always linked her current economic difficulties to the fact that she had to help her son repay a bank loan he acquired to buy a flat, before he lost his job. Vitória regularly transfers money to her son's Portuguese bank account to meet the mortgage payments: "you want to see, I'm not lying, I have all the receipts here [showing me the bank receipts], sometimes I transfer 150 or 200, never more than 300 euros." More than half of Vitória's pension thus goes to her son. She earns some informal income by helping out a disabled senior woman in the neighborhood, shopping, cleaning her house, going to the pharmacy when needed and keeping her company during the afternoons.

Vitória understood her continuing care for her son as part of an inter-generational project of caregiving and life improvement. She also blamed the state for her son's unemployment, for not protecting the welfare and investments of working citizens through, for instance, legislating on regulations to prevent companies from leaving the country. Her perceptions of state negligence were only heightened by her experience of having her pension captured, a pension which she had trusted the state to protect. She told me about the many times she encountered in the local supermarket "people from the charity associations asking us to help with food goods," adding that "the state should help these people, and they ask us to help." She would compare her livelihood with that of her parents, saying that "my parents went through hunger, but they worked, they made their life (*fizeram a sua vida*), they raised me and went ahead. But now it is different, now the parents have to help the sons."

Teresa (63) lives with her husband in a house which belonged to her mother. She was married around age 20, first living at her mother-in-law's before moving to her own house, which was paid for in full after 30 years. When her mother suffered a stroke that left her unable to live alone or take care of herself, Teresa looked after her for 14 years. "I was the one who took care of her, which is why I inherited her house." Following her mother's death in 2000, Teresa worked seasonally as a domestic cleaner. She has two sons (42 and 32), both of whom are unemployed. Her eldest has two sons of his own (3 and 9) while her daughter-in-law works the evening shift (from 3 to 11 pm) cleaning at a local hospital, earning the minimum wage. During our conversations, Teresa often expressed concern for her two sons. As for her grandsons, she insisted that "if it weren't for us [the grandparents] they would have starved." Teresa's husband, Paulo (61), began his working life as a baker before working in the fisheries "almost all his life. He has been working for the same boss for the last 19 years. My eldest has now started going [informally] with his father to the sea...." On several occasions, Teresa emphasized the harshness of "making a living from the sea": "today he went to the sea, and he may return tomorrow, or in one week, it depends on what they can find." During our long talks, Teresa was invariably taking care of her two grandsons, which she has been doing since her eldest son became unemployed (before that, her daughter-in-law was not working at the hospital and took care of the children at home). In the summer, the boys spent all day with their grandmother, who provides all the daily meals; a pile of second-hand children's clothing was on her table, donated by a neighbor who had migrated to Switzerland. Teresa's trajectory illustrates the structured, feminized network of material and immaterial caregiving that sustains livelihood and worth-making pursuits across generations which was common among my older female interlocutors. Teresa moved to her mother's house to take care of her when she was ill, enabling her to inherit the house. At a later point in her life, her mother's house enabled Teresa to lend her own house to her son so that "he doesn't have to pay the rent" while also caring for, feeding and nurturing her eldest son's children.

Diane Elson (1992) notes that under conditions of economic crisis and structural adjustment, household strategies to confront the reallocation of resources at larger scales are not only symptoms of survival but may become engines of transformation. Struggle is what bridges the gap between survival and transformation, including struggles to maintain, promote, change or sustain the moral value of needs. The efforts of working-class women in Setúbal to respond to the needs of household members, extended family and loved ones were grounded in a morally oriented valuation and evaluation of needs. Caring with concern and acting upon the needs of others was not driven by arbitrary definitions of deservingness, but centered on fulfillling claims and expectations of human worth and changing entitlements to resources. Women's care work reinstated an embedded definition of need, acting upon the "ongoing contested and negotiated interpretative dimensions of needs" (Fraser 2013). In doing so, they re-affirmed that "inside every 'need' there is an affect, or 'want,' on its way to becoming an 'ought' (and vice-versa)" (Thompson 1978: 36, quoted by Sayer 2011: 42).

Conclusion

This chapter has approached the centrality of women's care work to ensuring household members' survival and ability to struggle as an expression of a *needs-grounded morality of distribution and recognition*. This notion is meant to capture how austerity, welfare dispossession and eroding social rights have intensified struggles around the concept of "need" and its use as a vernacular morality through which ordinary people seek to access material resources and to assert the legitimacy of their claims and entitlements. Drawing on James Ferguson (2015),[14] I suggest that austerity measures in Portugal have intensified the "feminization of distributive livelihoods." The latter is largely based on mobilizing women's distributive labor—various forms of care work to pool, allocate, hoard, transfer and access resources deemed necessary to fulfill material and recognition needs, both within and beyond the market, and which potentially penalize women's capabilities to challenge gendered idioms of deservingness and social value.

I conclude by addressing the political possibilities, value and limits of the needs-grounded morality of distribution and recognition underpinning women's care work and caring relationships. When I asked my female interlocutors what motivates them to pursue multiple and demanding efforts, what "despite everything, kept them going," they answered: "because I want my son to have a better life, to go to university," "because I have to help my daughter to maintain her work," "because I want to ensure my grandsons don't feel hunger," "because I want my mother to be treated with dignity at this stage of her life," "because my son is unemployed," "because they deserve better." These were not the only explanations, but they were the most recurrent ones. I am not suggesting that women accepted without complaints the sacrificial vocation of fulfillling the needs of others. What I wish to highlight instead are the moral and ethical premises underpinning what they care for, what they value and evaluate as worth struggling for (Sayer 2005; Narotzky and Besnier 2014).

What mattered most to the women I came to know was *minimizing the risk that the agency of those they cared for would be compromised in the present and in the future*. Their care work thus sought to fulfill needs required to exercise agency, not in spite of but because their actions were grounded in the ethical premises of vulnerability, interdependence, relationality, obligation and affect among kin, family, friends and neighbors. Their care work thus went well beyond conceptions of human agency based on the tenets of rationality, autonomy and independence espoused by orthodox economics and liberal philosophy (Miller 2012), underscoring the importance of attending to immediate material needs that increase the autonomous capacities of individuals (through the provision of food, shelter, clothing and money) as well as their interdependent and relational abilities (through affect, support and encouragement) to claim worth, value and recognition—in the present and in the future, and in private, public and institutional settings.

For Amartya Sen (1999), the fulfillment of needs is ultimately tied to the ability of political and institutional frameworks to increase people's capabilities for freedom and autonomy (Ferguson 2015: 143). Similarly, for Doyal and Gough (1991), health and autonomy are the preconditions for all human action and interaction. Martha Nussbaum's (2003) critical appraisal of Sen's capabilities approach, however, stresses the limits of freedom and autonomy as enablers of capability. Following Nussbaum (2003), I suggest that the needs-grounded morality of distribution and recognition underpinning women's caring practices shows that nurturing the abilities of interdependence, relationality, obligation and affect are as important as safeguarding the needs of rational autonomy and freedom. The needs required to exercise agency highlight the importance of attending to livelihood conditions of being and possibilities of becoming.

The needs-grounded morality of distribution and recognition addressed in this chapter raises questions about needs, care and welfare policy, within and beyond the current conjuncture of austerity. What sort of welfare policy could address both the human material needs of autonomy and those of moral interdependence? How can we give value to the caring values traditionally associated with women, as proposed by Tronto (1993), without legitimizing inequality? While these questions will remain unanswered here, women's caring labors to promote, nurture and maintain agency (including their own) through interdependence, relationality, obligation and affect show that the logic, orientations and abstractions of austerity are not a mechanically internalized, totalizing framework of action, thought and perception. Rather, women's caring labors and practices suggest that the moral significance of needs lies precisely in the struggle to counter the devaluing of human needs at the core of austerity welfare, while asserting the irreducibility of people's inherent vulnerability and the relational quality of their longings, expectations and hopes.

Notes

1. By "devaluation of human needs," I am referring in particular to labor, tax and welfare policies that subordinate people's needs of material well-being to the needs of national fiscal health as well as the moral censure of those "who have been living beyond their means," which implicitly evaluates citizens' consumption patterns as exceeding their "real needs" and entitlements.

2. Haney's (2003: 7) study of changing Hungarian welfare regimes in the latter part of the twentieth century highlights how "states not only create provisions to redistribute benefits but also articulate historically specific conceptions of need. By constructing 'architectures of need,' states define who is in need and how to satisfy those needs."
3. https://www.dn.pt/portugal/interior/cantinas-sociais-serviram-quase-48-mil-refeicoes-por-dia-no-primeiro-semestre-4723210.html (last accessed April 2019).
4. My empirical analysis draws on ethnographic research undertaken in 2015 and 2016 in Setúbal, a city of 117,000 residents located 50 km south of Portugal's capital city. Setúbal is a particularly well-suited site for ethnographic research on people's everyday responses to economic transition and crisis. Once a prosperous industrial city, it suffered decline—de-industrialization and high unemployment—through much of the twentieth century as well as ineffective top-down regional development plans backed by European funds following Portugal's accession to the EU in 1986. It has also been one of the areas of the country most affected by the 2008 financial crisis and ensuing austerity measures.
5. I follow the definition of care work proposed by Nancy Folbre (1995) as work that provides services based on sustained personal (usually face-to-face) interaction, motivated (at least in part) by concern about the recipient's welfare.
6. The women with whom I had contact spoke regularly about their needs, those of their kin, their household, neighbors and friends. Often, speaking of needs was a way of explaining the material impoverishment produced by austerity policies. On other occasions, the language of needs was mobilized as a form of moral critique of the dismantling of rights, claims and expectations.
7. An estimated two million Portuguese left the country between the 1950s and 1974.
8. https://expresso.pt/sociedade/2015-06-05-Emigracao-sobe-a-niveis-historicos-imigracao-desce.-E-agora-#gs.1r852u (last accessed April 2019).
9. With feminist theory, I emphasize the role of the household as the first sphere of provision (ensuring food, housing, care for children and elderly) and how social provisioning rather than choice (Ferber and Nelson 1993; Benería 2003) frames people's welfare projects.
10. Austerity policies furthered neoliberal reforms by targeting Keynesian "welfare dependency" (Fraser and Gordon 1994) by embracing the paradigm of the self-enterprising and flexible subject, the transfer of government-controlled welfare provision to the markets and civil society, and the spread of workfare programs grounded on the tenets of conditionality and personal responsibility (Peck 2001; Collins and Mayer 2010; Morgen, Acker and Weight 2010).
11. It may seem paradoxical that people are asked to be entrepreneurial in conditions of growing unemployment, welfare retrenchment and the dispossession of citizenship. In southern Europe, this paradox was given the fig leaf of coherence by morally condemning people's previously profligate behavior, unreasonable spending and an excessive sense of entitlement (Muehlebach 2016).

12. https://expresso.pt/actualidade/passos-pede-aos-portugueses-para-serem-menos-piegas=f703170 (last accessed April 2019).
13. https://www.publico.pt/2012/05/11/politica/noticia/passos-coelho-apela-a-cultura-de-risco-e-diz-que-desemprego-pode-ser-uma-oportunidade---1545696#gs.pkgRCCZ6 (last accessed April 2019).
14. Ferguson (2015) examines the simultaneous retreat of welfare state provisioning in the global north and the rise of social protection schemes based on conditional cash transfers in Latin America and Africa, the interactions between new state programs of distribution and long-established vernacular practices of distribution.

References

Bear, L. 2015. *Navigating Austerity: Currents of Debt along a South Asian River*. Stanford: Stanford University Press.

Benería, L. 2003. *Gender, Development and Globalization. Economics as if All People Mattered*. London: Routledge.

Blyth, M. 2013. *Austerity: The History of a Dangerous Idea*. New York: Oxford University Press.

Carmo, R.M., E. Cantante and M. Carvalho. 2012. *Inequalities in Portugal: Recent and Structural Trends*. http://observatorio-das-desigualdades.cies.iscte.pt/index.jsp?page=projects&lang=en&id=126 (last accessed April 2019).

Collins, J. and V. Mayer. 2010. *Both Hands Tied: Welfare Reform and the Race to the Bottom in the Low-Wage Labor Market*. Chicago: University of Chicago Press.

Correia, T. and L. Costa. 2017. *Utentes de Instituições de Solidariedade Social – Uma Abordagem à Pobreza nesta população*. http://www.entrajuda.pt/media/5644/estudo-2017-utentes-de-instituic%CC %A7o %CC %83es-de-solidariedade-uma-abordagem-a %CC %80-pobreza-nesta-populac %CC %A7a %CC %83o.pdf (last accessed April 2019).

Correia, T., L. Costa and V. Policarpo. 2015. *Utentes de Instituições de Solidariedade Social – Uma Abordagem à Pobreza nesta população*. http://www.entrajuda.pt/media/5489/estudo-aos-utentes-das-ipss-2015_relat%C3%B3rio-final.pdf (last accessed April 2019).

Cunha, L. 2012. *O Impacto da Crise no Bem-Estar dos Portugueses*. http://sedes.pt/multimedia/File/SEDES-lcc-Estudo.pdf (last accessed June 2019).

Doyal, L. and I. Gough. 1991. *A Theory of Human Need*. London: Palgrave Macmillan.

Elson, D. 1992. "From Survival Strategies To Transformation Strategies: Women's Needs And Structural Adjustment." In L. Beneria and S. Feldman, eds. *Unequal Burden: Economic Crises, Persistent Poverty, and Women's Work*. Boulder: Westview Press.

Ferber, M. and J. Nelson. 1993. *Beyond Economic Man*. Chicago: Chicago University Press.

Ferguson, J. 2015. *Give a Man a Fish: Reflections on the New Politics of Distribution*. Durham: Duke University Press.

Folbre N. 1995. "Holding Hands At Midnight: The Paradox of Caring Labor." *Feminist Economics* 1: 73–92.

Fraser, N. 2013. "Struggle Over Needs: Outline of a Socialist-Feminist Critical Theory of Late-Capitalist Political Culture." In *Fortunes of Feminism: From State-Managed Capitalism to Neoliberal Crisis*. London: Verso.
Fraser, N. and L. Gordon. 1994. "A Genealogy of Dependency: Tracing a Keyword of the U.S. Welfare State." *Signs* 19(2): 309–36.
Haney, L. 2003. *Inventing the Needy: Gender and the Politics of Welfare in Hungary*. Berkeley: University of California Press.
Harvey, D. 2007. *A Brief History of Neoliberalism*. Oxford: Oxford University Press.
Joaquim, C. 2015. *Proteção social, terceiro setor e equipamentos sociais: que modelos para Portugal*. https://www.ces.uc.pt/observatorios/crisalt/documentos/cadernos/CadernoObserv_III_fevereiro2015.pdf (last accessed April 2019).
Knight, D. and C. Stewart. 2016. "Ethnographies of Austerity: Temporality, Crisis, and Affect in Southern Europe." *History and Anthropology* 27(1): 1–18.
Knight, D. 2015. *History, Time, and Economic Crisis in Central Greece*. London: Palgrave Macmillan.
Miller, S. 2012. *The Ethics of Need: Agency, Dignity and Obligation*. London: Routledge.
Morgen, S., J. Acker and J. Weight. 2010. *Stretched Thin: Poor Families, Welfare Work and Welfare Reform*. Ithaca: Cornell University Press.
Muehlebach, A. 2016. "Anthropologies of Austerity." *History and Anthropology* 27(3): 359–72.
Narotzky, S. and N. Besnier. 2014. "Crisis, Value, and Hope: Rethinking the Economy." *Current Anthropology* 55(S9): S4–S16.
Nussbaum, M. 2003. "Capabilities as Fundamental Entitlements: Sen and Social Justice." *Feminist Economics* 9(2-3): 33–59.
Peck, J. 2001. *Workfare States*. New York: Guildford Press.
Reis, J. et al. 2013. *A Anatomia da Crise: identificar os problemas para construir alternativas*. Observatório da Crise e Alternativas. Coimbra: CES. https://www.ces.uc.pt/ficheiros2/files/Relatorio_Anatomia_Crise_final__.pdf (last accessed April 2019).
Ribeiro, R., Frade, C., Coelho, L., Valente, A. F. 2015. "Crise Economica em Portugal: Alteracoes nas Praticas Quotidianas e nas Relacoes Familiares." *Livro de Atas do 1.o Congresso da Associacao Internacional das Ciencias Sociais e Humanas em Lingua Portuguesa*. Lisbon: Universidade Nova de Lisboa.
Rosa, E. 2012. "O desemprego atinge já 1.3 milhões de Portugueses, mas não é um problema importante para o 1°ministro, pois no 'que é importante o governo nãofalhou'." https://www.eugeniorosa.com/Sites/eugeniorosa.com/Documentos/2012/33-2012-Desemprego-nao-e-problema-importante.pdf (last accessed April 2019).
Roseberry, W. 1994. "Hegemony and the Language of Contention." In Joseph, G.M. and Nugent, D., eds. *Everyday Forms of State Formation*. Durham: Duke University Press.
Sayer, A. 2005. *The Moral Significance of Class*. Cambridge: Cambridge University Press.
Sayer, A. 2011. *Why Things Matter to People: Social Sciences, Values and Ethical Life*. Cambridge: Cambridge University Press.
Sen, A. 1999. *Development as Freedom*. London: Anchor Books.

Skeggs, B. and V. Loveday. 2012. "Struggles for Value: Value Practices, Injustice, Judgment, Affect and the Idea of Class." *British Journal of Sociology* 63(3): 472–90.

Stack, C. 1974. *All Our Kin: Strategies for Survival in a Black Community.* New York: Harper & Row.

Thompson, E.P. 1978. *The Poverty of Theory, and Other Essays.* London: Merlin.

Tronto, J. 1993. *Moral Boundaries: A Political Argument for an Ethic of Care.* London: Routledge.

7
Family, Housing as an Asset, and the Production of Welfare

Jaime Palomera

Introduction

Southern European welfare systems have been characterized as following a conservative or corporative model whereby the family supplements or even replaces the state (Esping-Andersen 1990, 1999; Andreotti et al. 2001) and where kinship arrangements are more important than institutions. This arrangement—in which the state transfers its responsibilities for childcare, elderly care and other forms of support to families, voluntary associations and third-sector actors without providing and redistributing resources—has been termed "passive subsidiarity" (Kazepov 2010). As a result, the pressure on kinship networks and especially women, who are overburdened with caring responsibilities, is intense.

These analyses, I argue, have ignored the extent to which social reproduction in the past decades has become entangled with the role of credit and real estate, of how mortgages and housing properties owned by domestic economies inform arrangements of reciprocity between kin. While the articulation of family, the amassing of assets and rentier capitalism can be observed in many different locations around the world, it is particularly salient in the Mediterranean countries studied in the Grassroots Economics project. Contrary to what may be intuitively assumed, this article shows that the expansion of the credit market—a cornerstone of neoliberal, financialized capitalism—need not destroy kinship networks. Elsewhere, I have examined the corrosive impact of financialization on impoverished communities on the urban margins, showing that people tend to shelter from the abstract logics of capital accumulation that underpin their domination through interpersonal relations framed by moral values and mutual obligations (Palomera 2014a, 2014b). In this chapter, I argue that the penetration of financial credit can also lead to the expansion of social ties in a context of crisis and become entangled with kinship networks. Although neoliberalism and financial capitalism are commonly understood as political projects that privilege individualism, my ethnography reveals that it partly rests on the articulation of the entrepreneurial accumulation of assets (in the form of housing) with kinship networks.

This chapter draws on empirical research in a suburban neighborhood of Tarragona in Catalonia, Spain, among white working-class families that have experienced downward mobility or are losing ground. Although my informants, many of whom moved to Tarragona from different parts of Spain in the 1960s and 1970s, are not wealthy, they are better off than the migrant groups of foreign origin who arrived in the 1990s and especially in the 2000s. Tarragona is a mid-sized city with a sizable working class population that by and large enjoyed upward mobility from the 1970s up until 2008. Since the advent of the crisis, many have been experiencing growing precariousness.

The chapter begins by outlining the role of family reciprocity in coping with the crisis, especially the support provided by the baby-boomer generation in the face of dwindling incomes. I locate the roots of family support in historical experience, chiefly that of the post-war years. In the second part of the chapter, I argue that investment in housing as a form of wealth, asset and transferrable inheritance (via credit) plays a key role in kinship networks, a clear departure from previous historical periods. Families borrow heavily to invest in real estate as it has become the essential means for families trying to produce their own welfare, particularly in a context where real wages are constantly declining. In the chapter's final section, I argue that neoliberalism remains a project with political purchase precisely because its material elements (credit, debt, asset and rent making) are still articulated with a broad part of the social body.

Family Support and its Roots in History

While much of the recent work on responses to the great recession has focused on solidarity and alternative economies (Laville 2010; Rakopoulos 2014; Orlando 2017), the main response to the crisis has arguably taken the shape of kinship reciprocity, along the lines outlined by Narotzky (2002) and others. This was one of my most salient findings from fieldwork in Tarragona's working-class neighborhoods in 2015 and 2016. Indeed, the family solidarity I observed in the context of the great recession was nothing new: it is rooted in history and intergenerational experience.

Tarragona's urban peripheries and working-class neighborhoods have been molded by the experiences of the baby-boomer generation, whose members were born and raised during the years of rural–urban migration between the 1940s and 1960s. This is the generation that fled hunger and poverty in the deprived rural regions of Andalucía and other parts of Spain. Despite the stigmatizing discourse against working-class neighborhoods in popular culture (with the derogatory "*chonis*," "*quinquis*" and the like), the trajectories of these families are marked by stories of overcoming and by the aspirations that grandparents and ancestors were unable to fulfill: work and savings, purchase of a home (possibly including a second house) and access to education.

The amount of work that parents dedicate to supporting their children— motivated by a desire to spare the latter the kind of hardships that they themselves had to endure—is remarkable. As Paco Trago,[1] a retired man in Tarragona, told me: "We want to prevent our children from having to work for four cents [*cuatro duros*] like we did. So that there is no boss [*un patron*] that takes advantage of them." Although there is a clear wish that children will not have to start working at an early age, that they can study, go to university and emancipate themselves, many households are unable to fulfill these expectations, particularly due to obstacles in pursuing education and waged work.

The Limits of Formal Education

While education and meritocracy (and equal opportunity) are touted as the main paths to personal improvement and welfare, only a small minority of working-class youth currently enter the university system. Far from generating a system of equal chances in order to diminish inequality, the educational system in fact reproduces it (as was already noted by Bourdieu and Passeron in 1964). There are many reasons for this. On the one hand, working-class youths face numerous economic and cultural hurdles as they need to study *and* work at the same time to support their families, must depend on bursaries, and often encounter obstacles at school and a lack of support or faith from teachers, a situation that has worsened with rising tuition fees and austerity funding cuts to education. On the other hand, theirs is a context wherein stories of educational success are few and far between, while it remains unclear whether university is truly a means for promotion unless one has a network of personal contacts. The neighborhoods of Tarragona today contain a good number of young people with university degrees working typically working-class jobs: psychology graduates working as fast-food waiters, engineers working as street cleaners and so forth.

In this working-class world, self-esteem and respect are built by proving that one can work hard and make a living—a pattern also observed in the Grassroot Economics project's other field sites in Greece, Italy, Spain and Portugal. But although the ability to work hard is seen as a measure of personal worth, it remains difficult for the young—almost invariably—men to complete their studies and obtain their degrees given the absence of previous experiences of academic success or role models (i.e. social networks linking them to the academic world).

The Limits of Waged Work

The emphasis on work is particularly salient. Being employed (or not) is often used to justify people's wellbeing or poverty, to draw the line between the deserving and the undeserving, the hard working and the lazy. While notions of (un)deservingness have traditionally been imposed on the poor by external agents such as the state (Katz 1989; Wacquant 2009), here we see that the dominant neoliberal ideology is enmeshed in complex ways with grassroots forms of working-class pride. Mariela, a 60-year-old widow who had led a small construction firm with her husband, clearly expressed this view:

> We've always worked, we've carried on, we've taken different jobs… We've committed ourselves to working and living better… Others have not, and they've stayed the same: poor. Some people tell you: let's work, be formal, not be partying. You work and maybe in July you can go on holidays.

The paradox is that people's ability to live on their incomes (when there is one) has been undermined in recent years by the prolonged economic crisis. Wage stagnation and repression, coupled with the reduction of job opportunities and the rise in unemployment, have taken their toll on the social and economic landscape of working-class neighborhoods. The majority of households interviewed during fieldwork in the urban periphery of Tarragona had at least one-third of their adult members unemployed, while those who were employed often had low-paid jobs.

The Role of Kinship Reciprocity

That so many people can get by with so much less—and with negligible state support—has a lot to do with the role of kinship reciprocity. My fieldwork in Tarragona revealed that access to goods is not primarily an individual matter; first and foremost, goods are accessed through networks of family support that have been revitalized over the past decade.

To begin with, there is a strong degree of reciprocity and intergenerational trust, with the baby boomer generation playing a key role in supporting their children and grandchildren. This implies more responsibilities and burdens for pensioners, particularly women. According to a bank manager who has worked in different offices in Tarragona, the true crisis did not begin with people defaulting on their mortgages or having a hard time repaying their debts, but when pensioners began encountering trouble. All of a sudden, people who had attended to their savings and finances with the precision of a Swiss watch began to be late with their payments. This was directly related to the fact that the elderly were going the extra mile to support their offspring. Their support ranged from relatively small gifts (such as taking care of the grandchildren's lunch during school breaks, or simply their daily snacks) to more complicated and demanding arrangements. The most characteristic expression of the latter was the collective pooling of resources managed by the older generation, which I describe and analyze below.

The story of Lourdes and Juan's family is a case in point. Until 2010, the trajectory of this married couple was marked by intermittent yet gradual improvement. Both had humble origins, born into rural Andalusian landscapes of poverty and subordination. In the 1960s, they migrated with their parents to the poor neighborhood of Ponent in Tarragona, where they grew up in the midst of informal self-built homes and low-quality housing projects. After years of struggle, Lourdes had managed to open a small sewing shop while Juan led a fairly successful subcontracting construction firm. However, the great financial and real estate crisis that began in 2008 took a toll on their respective businesses, which they eventually had to shutter with outstanding debts. Lourdes applied for a meager pension, whilst Juan received a subsidy created by the government during the years of deep recession for the long-term unemployed. Their daughter, Laia, did not have it easy either; both she and her husband saw their incomes decline, until they became barely sufficient to pay the mortgage and cover their son's needs. Laia now works at a small beauty parlor managed by her older sister Sara, where she gets paid under the table as both sisters cannot have self-employed status. Nor can Laia become a waged worker; the parlor's revenues are so meager that it is impossible to pay Laia properly, with the attendant taxes and social security contributions. The sisters are painfully aware that their retirement pensions, if they get anything at all, will be as scant as their mother's.

During the first years of crisis, the two households, according to Lourdes, endured their respective crises with "indescribable anguish." Gradually, she and her husband Juan decided that they needed to change their way of looking at their problems. One Sunday, over family lunch, they invited their daughter to join their two—until then separate—household economies by pooling their resources. As Laia had lived in a different apartment with her husband and child since the day she had left her parents' home, this was a radical change for them. But forced by circumstances, the younger couple accepted.

The two households first placed their savings in joint bank accounts, which are currently managed by the grandmother of the family. In Lourdes' words, "we united the families"—which had until then managed their own finances independently, only occasionally helping each other with small items. Both Lourdes and Juan told me on different occasions that it is better to have a joint expense account than smaller, separate ones. When I pointed out that, living in different apartments, they must still pay their separate bills, Lourdes explained that the key difference is that she is better at economizing. This was something that other informants of her generation, including Paco and Mariela, insisted on. "Everything comes to me," Lourdes told me. All of the under-the-table money that Laia earns at the beauty parlor goes to Lourdes, who then deposits it in their joint bank account. More recently, Laia and Sara's rental of a laser machine has improved the fortunes of the small family business, allowing Laia to give approximately 800 euros each month to her mother.

The pooling of financial resources among different generations living in separate homes was by no means exceptional. Many people I met in Tarragona were doing the same thing. In some cases, the sharing of information about savings and expenses and entrusting the older generation to take care of their management preceded the current crisis. Several informants in their 60s and 70s traced the origin of this practice to the day they opened their children's first bank accounts. Paco and Laura, now retired, share three different bank accounts with their son Manuel, who lives in a separate apartment with his own wife and son. "We have always held everything collectively," said Paco. "All the money that has entered the house, it has always been in the name of the three... We get on quite well, quite well." The three of them are authorized to do anything with that money.

Lourdes buys the groceries and cooks the main meals for both households and prepares other things that they may need at home. She is the one who goes to the market and supermarket, buying in large quantities. The difference, according to the family members I spoke with, is that Lourdes knows how to buy fresh produce at much more affordable prices and cook it "wholesale" in order to save energy. Instead of cooking lentils for different mouths on different occasions, she cooks two kilos at a time. She then stores the food in two freezers in their suburban house, driving each week to the neighborhood where her daughter lives in Tarragona, to deliver Tupperware for the rest of the week. This, besides being a money-saver for Laia, liberates her from cooking so that she can focus on her job and son. Lourdes also saves the family money on things like soap: a do-it-yourself recipe for homemade soap, which she found on YouTube, takes her around 24 hours. She buys all the ingredients wholesale and prepares the soap in large quantities, for themselves and their kin.

Some of these practices are rooted in history. The very idea that the older generation knows how to economize, or how to economize better (cooking different recipes instead of buying fast food, growing vegetables, saving money more meticulously, etc.) has to do with this generation growing up in the post-Civil War years of the 1940s and 50s, and in the 60s, when saving and finding alternative household strategies to mainstream consumption remained central for poor immigrants from the south. This is the generation that grew up knowing the value of micro-solidarities, who built their houses and improved their neighborhoods through mutual aid. This experience remains relevant today, at a time when reciprocity and mutual aid are generally limited to one's nearest kin.

The hierarchy that situates the older generation as the better managers of money and resources is of course also ridden with tensions. Older parents often accuse their adult children of not understanding sacrifice, suggesting that they do not try hard enough to think of the future. Paco Trago, for instance, believes his son would not save any of the money he earns if it were not for him, and often complains that he goes on too many vacations. And when Manel actually goes on holiday or to a restaurant with his wife and son, he asks his mother not to tell his father: "don't tell papa, you know the way he is." Here, reciprocity overlaps with moral conflict among the generations.

The Articulation of Family Support with Finance and Property

It is impossible to understand these forms of revitalized kinship reciprocity without examining how they are entangled with finance and property. Investment in housing as a form of wealth, asset and transferrable inheritance (via credit/debt) plays a key role in kinship networks. Property is in fact the main form of wealth in the hands of families and Spain remains among the three European countries with the largest volume of household debt linked to housing. This remains the case even after this debt decreased by 21 percent between 2010 and 2017.

The home as an asset

To begin with, inheriting property obviously plays a major role in terms of its use-value: i.e. guaranteeing access to housing. During fieldwork, many of my informants spoke of their expectations of inheriting the parental home. Inheritance was often seen as salvation, as a way to ensure a roof over their heads as housing grows increasingly unaffordable and long-term income becomes increasingly precarious and unreliable.

But in the context of the crisis, the properties owned by the baby-boomer generation have also become enduring assets. On the one hand, they provide collateral for younger generations to access credit, either to get mortgages to buy their own apartments or loans to launch their own small businesses. For instance, Manel was able to buy a taxi driving license and a car thanks to the credit extended to his father, who used his home as collateral. Other families, such as Sara's, were financially enabled to start their own small businesses.

On the other hand, the home has increasingly become a rent-making asset, as was the case for Lourdes and Juan. In 2013, they moved into what had until that point been their secondary residence in a suburban area and began to sublet their main residence (in the immediate periphery of Tarragona, in the so-called working-class belt) for 450 euros per month. This practice is supported by the state which provides potential landlords with enormous fiscal incentives (only 40 percent of the income from this rent is taxed, unlike income from work which is fully taxed). The income they received from their tenants (a family of recent Moroccan immigrants) was immediately used for their own household expenses. Yet this became a source of tension when their tenants became unemployed in 2016 and were unable to pay rent for five months. Juan and Lourdes also tried to sublet the basement of their house in Mas del Plata, the apartment that Juan and his son-in-law used while they were building the house in the suburbs. While they managed to host a handful of foreign tourists, it amounted to little.

The home as a liability

The reverse of the scenario described above is when the mortgage becomes unpayable and the home becomes a liability. This was the case during the long decade of crisis in Spain (with over 700,000 foreclosures since 2007). However, my fieldwork in Tarragona revealed that among many working-class families, family reciprocity helped debtors to continue repaying their mortgages. Tere (Mariela's sister) and her husband Emilio were about to default on their loan after the demise of their plumbing company. When they received notice from the bank that it was foreclosing on their property—"I was about to lose it all, to have my home taken away from me"—her father and siblings pooled their resources and raised 20,000 euros so that they could slowly repay their mortgage. "We had to run and get all the money together, they were about to kick them out," Mariela told me. Such transfers between siblings were common among households under strain (particularly those linked to the construction sector) during the first years of the crisis.

The family thus turned an unrepayable debt to the bank into an informal debt among relatives. While the bank absorbs the resources of the extended family, monetary debt with kin can be turned into a gift or "forgiven." For Mariela, the loosely agreed upon plan was that Tere and her husband would sell the house in the future and repay their kin with a part of the proceeds. Mariela told me that "when they sell the house, if we the siblings want, we can charge them the debt, but we might forgive it as well. In my case, I've already forgiven it."

Property—when there is a network of support that can help to repay the mortgage—can become a source of capital for other ventures. But when credit becomes an untenable debt, the value of the property (compared to diminished income) can become a source of distress. What merits attention is that in both cases, formal balance sheets often come to be embedded in family arrangements and relations of reciprocity, especially in working-class households. Monetary transfers among relatives (intergenerational, or among siblings) that allow someone to repay a debt are often turned into a family debt or, more commonly, integrated into a system of reciprocity whereby they are seen as gifts or favors.

This chapter has sought to highlight the centrality of family assets and kinship reciprocity in the provision of welfare. Interestingly, this material transformation has been accompanied by a symbolic redefinition of some working-class families, where terms such as "tribe" or "commune" are used to express the process of micro-commoning or resource-pooling and of resorting to post-war methods of support. Conversely, the lack of "unity" or weak intergenerational support are generally frowned upon and talked about negatively, revealing the strength of these networks and the moral imperative of family solidarity. Moreover, ethnographic evidence from Tarragona suggests that this revamping of reciprocity has increased the burdens on pensioners and women. Increasingly, we see systems of kinship support where women take care of the home while also replacing the traditionally male breadwinner.

Nevertheless, the family is deeply interlinked with financialized and rentier capitalism. High debt linked to real estate implies that a lot of family energy, time and resources are channeled and absorbed by the financial system. A great deal of dispossession takes place through credit and property. This also means that people are actively or potentially engaged in rentier capitalism: the accumulation of property, its use as a source of access to other forms of credit and resources as well as a means of petty rent extraction. In other words, we are neither returning to a purely family-centered model of social reproduction nor to an asset-based one: the two dimensions are generally impossible to separate.

It is important to emphasize that these processes do not necessarily imply a rejection of the state's responsibilities. The existence of strong kinship arrangements wedded to real estate need not dampen struggles for a more redistributive state, for a stronger public system that guarantees universal rights. Many of my informants were politically active, in social movements as well as in progressive political parties.

The strength of these kinship/housing arrangements may also potentially explain why neoliberalism remains alive and kicking. Neoliberalism is often seen as a class project that puts welfare responsibilities in the hands of individuals and families, who are expected to behave entrepreneurially and compete amongst each other (Harvey 2005; Narotzky and Smith 2006). Part of the reason why this political program has survived the latest crisis has to do with the fact that its material foundations have not been challenged: the arrangements described in this chapter constitute highly atomized forms of kinship reciprocity embedded in asset-investment strategies, chiefly in the form of houses and rent. Paradoxically, these kinship networks are strong enough to prevent possibly millions of working-class people from becoming welfare recipients. While this may sound like good news, it means that the state has been freed of its responsibilities towards the majority of the population, allowing it to focus only on those at the very margins of the system, i.e. the completely destitute. The capacity to generate broader and more redistributive forms of solidarity that reach beyond the sphere of the home and the most immediate of kin, and to advance universal rights, will depend on people's ability to generate material and symbolic bonds at that level.

Notes

1. All names and locations are fictitious or purposefully vague in order to protect the anonymity of the people who willfully and with great generosity participated in the Greco Project.

References

Andreotti, A., M. García, A. Gómez, P. Hespanha, Y. Kazepov and E. Mingione. 2001. "Does a Southern European Model Exist?" *Journal of European Area Studies* 9(1): 44–62.
Bourdieu, P. and J.C. Passeron. 1964. *Les Héritiers: Les Étudiants et la Culture*. Paris: Éditions de Minuit.
Esping-Andersen, G. 1990. *The Three Worlds of Welfare Capitalism*. Cambridge: Polity Press.
Esping-Andersen, G. 1999. *Social Foundations of Postindustrial Economies*. Oxford: Oxford University Press.
Harvey, D. 2005. *A Brief History of Neoliberalism*. Oxford: Oxford University Press.
Katz, M. 1989. *The Undeserving Poor: America's Enduring Confrontation with Poverty: Fully Updated and Revised*. New York: Oxford University Press.
Kazepov, Y. 2010. *Rescaling Social Policies: Towards Multilevel Governance in Europe*. Surrey: Ashgate.
Laville, J-L. 2010. "The Solidarity Economy: An International Movement." *RCCS Annual Review* 2010(2): http://journals.openedition.org/rccsar/202 (last accessed July 2019).
Narotzky, S. 2002. "Reivindicación de la ambivalencia teórica: la reciprocidad como concepto clave." *Éndoxa: Series Filósoficas* 15: 15–29.
Narotzky, S. and G. Smith. 2006. *Immediate Struggles: People, Power and Place in Rural Spain*. Los Angeles: University of California Press.

Orlando, G. 2017. "Solidarity Economies in the Age of Brexit and Trump." *Palaver* 6(2): 165–78.

Palomera, J. 2014a. "How Did Finance Capital Infiltrate the Urban Poor? Homeownership and Social Fragmentation in a Spanish Neighborhood." *International Journal of Urban and Regional Research* 38(1): 218–35.

Palomera, J. 2014b. "Reciprocity, Poverty and Commodification in the Era of Financialization." *Current Anthropology* 55(9): S105–S115.

Rakopoulos, T. 2014. "The Crisis Seen from Below, Within, and Against: From Solidarity Economy to Food Distribution Cooperatives in Greece." *Dialectical Anthropology* 38(2): 189–207.

Wacquant, L. 2009. *Punishing the Poor: The Neoliberal Government of Social Insecurity*. Durham: Duke University Press.

8

Social Reproduction in Times of Crisis: Inter-Generational Tensions in Southern Europe

Susana Narotzky and Antonio Maria Pusceddu

Social Reproduction in Times of Crisis

Social reproduction can be defined as a form of continuity linking generations around household projects of making a living and enhancing future opportunity. It can also be defined as the continuity of social organization that distributes power and assets unequally. This chapter is about these two aspects of social reproduction and their articulation. In the process, inter-generational forms of care overlap with conflict and resentment at different scales. While obligations of solidarity weave everyday actions of support around parents and children, at a larger societal scale discourses of privilege regarding access to resources such as stable jobs, assets (home ownership) and income (retirement pensions) prevail. This configures a complex and contradictory map of responsibilities, and ultimately poses a question regarding the sustainability of the social system.

The economic crisis in Europe has created new practices and understandings of generational inter-dependencies reaching beyond family and household reproduction to the reproduction of society as a whole. Central to these reconfigurations are pension systems and the crystallization of savings into home ownership for the older generation. Younger generations working precarious jobs and unable to make ends meet must often return to their parental homes, relying on the savings, pension income and care work of older kin. At the same time, austerity governments and the media proclaim pensions to be "unsustainable"[1] and "unfair"—as a kind of privilege of the older generation.

The cases of Italy and Spain that we compare in this chapter have many similarities. Both countries began overhauling their pension systems in the 1990s, following EU recommendations to meet the public deficit criteria enshrined in the Maastricht Treaty. While the early reforms were controversial, those implemented following the 2008 financial crisis in a period of high youth unemployment and precarity revealed the importance of pensioners' incomes for the welfare of many extended households. At the same time, the alleged financial unsustainability of public pension schemes seemed to place younger and older generations in competition for scarce public funds.

The current crises point to an epochal breakdown of inter- and intra-generational expectations and strategies for making a living. At the micro level, investments in younger generations are being reconsidered as the labor market grows more fragmented, flexible and precarious. Mobility strategies, such as migration, often reveal increased dependency rather than autonomy between generations, while expectations of downward mobility for the young and longer lifespans for the elderly produce new anxieties and tensions within families as moral obligations unavoidably change. At the macro level, transformations in the political economic structure of capitalist societies over the last half century, including the neoliberal turn and the fall of the "socialist" model after 1989, have acquired a "generational" aspect that is often substituted for the previous "class" aspect of inequalities. This is an important cultural shift that presents inequalities in terms of moral responsibilities, i.e. a "moral economy," rather than in terms of the larger social structure of unequal distribution (Narotzky 2016).

Our case studies show how the transition from dependency to autonomy that framed the expectations of personal "growth," sustained transfers of income, and work and care practices under Fordism are now being overturned. Today's domestic moral economies entail prolonging the dependence of young adults, especially through their increased reliance on their parents' savings, care work and public pensions. At the same time, post-2008 structural adjustment policies and the alleged un-sustainability of the public pension system in the European social market model are expressed in policy documents as an unfair bargain between the baby boomer generation and their children (Bristow 2016). This inequity allegedly requires the radical transformation of intergenerational models of solidarity at the state level.

For younger generations, the shame of "depending" on older generations for such necessities as income, housing and childcare is compounded by the perplexity of being taxed to pay for the pensions of this older generation; at the same time, they are told by experts and policymakers that nothing similar awaits them in the future. The younger generations' failure to achieve recognition as autonomous adults and their inability to meet solidarity obligations through existing "pay-as-you-go" public pension systems predicated on continuous cycles of generalized reciprocity fuels the breakdown of expectations. In the meantime, the individually capitalized pension funds proposed by experts and policymakers as the solution to a sustainable pension system presuppose a growing economy, continuous employment and decent salaries. Indeed, the proposed pension schemes penalize precarious employment, which for many members of the younger generation is the only kind available. Short and long-term interests as well as domestic and civic moralities thus become highly ambivalent and often contradictory.

Gender inequalities are also salient as women and men have different opportunities to access resources and channel them across and within generations. Care—where the tension between love and money is always present—becomes a key resource for precariously employed young parents, with inter-generational claims and practices of care increasingly central to making a living (see Matos in this volume). Changing care practices within households and across generations are also informed by the insufficient or declining provision of care facilities and services by the state and their substitution by market services that result in care-giving and care-receiving processes of differentiation (Hochschild 2003; Yeates 2004; Parreñas 2001; Razavi 2007; Weber et al. 2003). At the same time, the inadequacy of many pensions and the lifecycle gaps between pre-retirement unemployment and the ability to claim a retirement pension present an altogether different picture of generational stress on the older—here mostly male—cohorts. We will address these transformations in the current economic and institutional crisis through a framework that views the moral aspects of economies as integral to the political economies of an industrial town in Spain and in a mid-size services and industrial town in southern Italy (see Pusceddu in this volume).

Moral Economy, Political Economy and Generations

The "moral economy" and "political economy" frameworks are often seen as mutually exclusive, with one historically following upon the other. The moral economy framework seeks to understand the mutual obligations and responsibilities that render differences acceptable and enable social continuity in a particular historical conjuncture (Moore 1978; Scott 1976; Thompson 1971, 1993). Meanwhile the political economy framework seeks to understand the structural processes that produce political and economic differentiations (Wolf 1982; Harvey 2003). By applying both to our ethnographic cases, we aim to highlight the ambiguous logic that sustains economic practice.[2]

In Thompson's original work (1971, 1993) the emergence of the "moral economy" concept is tied to a particular conjuncture of the expansion of market relations: "The breakthrough of the new political economy of the free market was also the breakdown of the old moral economy of provision" (Thompson 1971: 136). The analytical concept[3] of the moral economy thus cannot be separated from its concrete emergence as the expression of a clash of material forces and cultural constructs at a particular historical conjuncture of primitive accumulation. Today, the resurgence of the moral economy discourse in academic analyses parallels what some scholars have underscored as a new process of primitive accumulation (De Angelis 2007) with accumulation through dispossession recognized as central to capitalism (Harvey 2005). The "moral" aspect thus re-emerges in the concrete conjuncture of neoliberal capitalism, one that has shattered the moral economy framework based on Keynesian redistribution. Moral economy perspectives today stress how moral values, affects and emotions channel economic and political behavior (Edelman 2005; Brown 2009; Robbins 2009; Fassin 2009, 2012; Hann 2010; Sayer 2000; Fontaine 2008). Their particular force rests on the articulation of moral values and obligations with the politics of material provisioning and resource allocation.

In Chris Gregory's (2009) concept of the "domestic moral economy," domestic provisioning and moral economy appear as articulated dimensions that re-configure the concept of "householding" as a general process straddling the market/non-market divide and tied to diverse dimensions of value. As feminist voices have long emphasized (Elson 2001; Nelson 2006; Benería 2003; McDowell 2004; Razavi 2007; Lawson 2007), unpaid work and an ethics of care are key elements for understanding economic processes beyond their mainstream definition as the self-interested individual maximization of utility through rational choice. Diverse forms of providing support—often glossed over as "care"[4]—tend to fall outside of the range of recognized economic transactions. They nevertheless constitute non-marketable values crucial to the social reproduction of households and of the larger society (Picchio 1992). In contrast to the imagined autonomy of the individual in rational actor theory, relations of personal dependency and emotional value in this perspective are central to the capacity of the entire economic and political system to endure.

Household members also depend for their maintenance on income earned from formal or informal[5] market activities and relations, and on benefits or subsidies claimed from the state as citizenship entitlements. From a social reproduction perspective, market and non-market, private and public dimensions come together in the everyday practices and values that enable the continuity of social life. In turn, these practices and values contribute to create particular social relations and produce specific forms of life in common. In this process, relations and material transfers between generations, both at intimate and institutional levels, become the site for the reconfiguration of economic, political and moral obligations. The transformation of the channels of social reproduction becomes particularly visible and acute in the inter-generational arena, a site of solidarities, tensions and struggles. In the current climate of economic uncertainty for the young, the position and value of older generations, both male and female, have been radically transformed (Narotzky 2011; Pine 2007, 2009). On the one hand, the elderly are unable to pass on much in the way of either skills or assets, as their longevity devalues their knowledge and diminishes their savings. On the other hand, they often become the refuge of last resort for the young when employment, housing and income are scarce or volatile. But the old are also vulnerable as their health fails in the face of reduced institutional care, minimal pensions or delayed access to them, while real estate speculators prey on them by offering reverse mortgages that will provide lifetime income against the sale of the home. As precarity reconfigures relational aspects of personhood and social worth, examining both the political and moral economies in tandem can prove useful for understanding how material changes in the systems of inter- and intra-generation transmission transform the field of moral obligation, both at the household and at larger political scales.

The Transformation of Political Landscapes in Spain and Italy

Spain

Ferrol is an industrial town of some 70,000 inhabitants on the northwest coast of Spain. In the 1960s, two shipyards—one public (Bazán), one private (Astano)—provided living wages for almost every household. By the 1970s, some 20,000 people were working in the main shipyards or in auxiliary companies. The shipyard had a tradition of strong trade unions; employment stability and decent wages defined the employees as "privileged." Gendered responsibilities rendered the men the income providers; women were homemakers and mostly cared for the very young and old. Some women also worked in fish freezing factories; others were shopkeepers or sewed garments informally at home. Domestic responsibilities were structured around the expectation of job and income stability for adult men and care work for adult women. The expectation was that working adult households would be autonomous.

Following Spain's transition to democracy (1975–82), its first elected governments began restructuring all state industries, allegedly to prepare the country for its entry into the European Economic Community and the free market's "challenge of competitiveness." Complying with demands from Brussels, the shipyards were brutally downsized. From 1984 to 1987, thousands of jobs were lost; unemployment and early retirement became a generalized feature of the region. Although labor conflict increased during these years, the trade union leadership generally accepted the "need" to restructure what was admittedly an inefficient industrial system hindered by state intervention. Workers opposed the downsizing while simultaneously requesting better conditions for early retirement, retraining schemes and unemployment coverage as well as guarantees that new industries would be developed in the old industrial areas—requests that were supported by the availability of targeted EEC funds. The need to avoid confrontation in a fragile democracy and the fact that European institutions provided funds for restructuring led to many shipyard workers in Ferrol accepting early retirement. This trend has continued until the present, through various moments of restructuring and job losses in the 1990s and 2000s, thereby increasing the importance of the retirement pension income for many households. By 2009, the shipyard industry had both downsized and become extremely flexible, relying on a network of subcontracted auxiliary firms.

Parallel to this, small and medium enterprises sprang up mostly in apparel, logistics and services in the new industrial parks surrounding the town, providing volatile and unprotected jobs for women and younger people. Given the dearth of unionization in these sectors, individual strategizing and networking were the main instruments of social mobility. For most people, job precariousness and career instability rendered it difficult to make projects for the future. Moreover, the acquisition of housing and increased consumption that had accompanied the early 2000s expansionary moment fueled by easy credit in the wake of the Euro led to a heavily indebted younger generation. With the setting in of the crisis after 2008, precarity, unemployment and indebtedness made younger adults increasingly dependent on their parents, a generation that benefited from the early retirement subsidies of the restructuring years. Migration to national or international destinations has soared for young people in this region in recent years as they attempt to find better jobs elsewhere.

A major consequence of the crisis and subsequent structural adjustment measures in Spain was astronomical unemployment, which reached 23.9 percent, the highest in the EU after Greece. Among youth under 25, unemployment reached 53.5 percent, the highest in the EU.[6] By 2014, 62.7 percent of households in Galicia had at least one income coming from retirement or other state subsidies (mostly unemployment) while 61.3 percent of those under 34 lived with their parents, although 38.4 percent of them earned some kind of income from work. In Ferrol, subsidies provided more than two-thirds of the total income for 44.3 percent of households.[7] Industrial restructuring and early retirement created a long-term pattern of households dependent on subsidies, mostly retirement pensions. These pensions are now increasingly used to support young people, whether they are unemployed or work in precarious jobs, are single or have families, are resident or non-resident in their parents' households. As a result, forms of moral obligation have been transformed as older retired parents continue to feel materially responsible for the well-being of their children well into adulthood, increasingly providing shelter, food and money and taking care of the grandchildren.

Italy

Brindisi, a port city on the Adriatic Sea with 88,000 inhabitants, owes much of its historical development to its strategic geographical position. Since the late nineteenth century, the port, railways and later the airport have played central roles in the capitalist development of inland agriculture (especially wine production) and petty industrialization.

In Italy, the post-World War Two industrial boom was also linked to the state's institutional regulation of macro-regional differences through labor movement regulations, salary zones and plans to industrialize the South. In the 1960s, Brindisi, like other southern areas, was targeted by a state-driven process of heavy oil-based industrialization through a "growth pole" strategy which—according to the trickle-down logic—was supposed to spark the socio-economic transformation of the wider region (Ginsborg 1990: 229–31).

North–South dualism represents a long-standing and constitutive aspect of Italian history (Schneider 1998). Regional differentiation in Italy has often been explained through the role of the family in the country's uneven economic and social development. The "strong family" thus acquired different, even opposite, meanings depending on the region: "amoral familism" in the "backward" South (Banfield 1958) and a motor of entrepreneurial dynamism in the bustling economic development of SME economies in the central and northern parts of the country, the "Third Italy" (see Loperfido in this volume). The northern "family" with its cooperative virtues was the engine of prosperity and affluence; the southern "family" and its "self-interest" impeded cooperation beyond the family circle, thus preventing action for the common good (Gribaudi 1993).

On a more general level, "autonomy" (coupled with entrepreneurialism) and "dependence" (coupled with parasitism) remain the lens through which North–South dualism is perceived by "common sense." Although stereotypical to the extreme, these representations have penetrated the self-representation of southern "common sense" itself. Along these lines, the old story of the South "depending on the state" has been reframed within neoliberal discourses that celebrate the entrepreneurial value of individuals while holding them responsible for their economic and social failures. People must cope with this hegemonic discourse while struggling with the material constraints of their social reproduction. Household responsibilities have been structured around various sources of mostly male income provisioning and on the expectations of hard work, thriftiness and a life of sacrifice leading to household autonomy in one's adult years.

Neoliberal restructuring unfolded through the massive reorganization of industrial production with labor-saving technologies and corporate strategies of de-localization, resulting in the rapid decline of industrial employment. The rise of the service sector and the informalization of labor (Mingione 1983) were among its relevant effects, which also included the incipient networked structure of small and medium enterprises (ISTAT 2015). In a way, southern cities such as Brindisi leaped from a semi-rural to a post-industrial economy without fully developing the social and productive forces of an industrial economy. While a complex system of "complementary allocations" addressed deindustrialization in the South— introducing direct monetary transfers (e.g. disability pensions) to families, providing the basis for a "social income" dispensed through the logic of welfare clientelism (Vercellone 1996)—this began to unravel in the 1990s when policies to curb public debt led to nation-wide public expenditure cuts and the definitive end of "special policies" for Italy's southern regions.

Despite its industrial history tied to the public petro-chemical energy complex, industrial employment itself only accounted for a modest share of the occupational structure, with the rapid expansion of the service sector creating largely precarious and low-skilled jobs (cf. Mingione 1988).[8] Nowadays, despite the presence of extremely profitable capital intensive and manufacturing industries from chemicals to aeronautics— the peripheral articulations of multinational corporations—Brindisi faces gradual but steady deindustrialization and the legacy of industrial wastelands and social impoverishment.[9] Unemployment in Brindisi is among the highest in Italy, while internal migration to Italy's northern regions continues apace (Biagi et al. 2011).

The Domestic Moral Economy of Precarity: Changing Expectations and Obligations

Spain

It was a hot afternoon in May 2012 and Susana had been invited to a meeting of a women's group, part of a self-defined socialist cultural association. The conversation almost immediately turned to "the crisis" and to the anxieties pervading the everyday lives of young people, their inability to forge autonomous lives and support their new families, their feelings of impotence and lack of instruments for struggle. The older women extended this anxiety to their own situations, revealing the transformation of lifecycle expectations in the present conjuncture.

Carmen, a woman in her early sixties married to a retired shipyard worker and union activist, compared the present situation to the restructuring struggles of the 1980s that led to the loss of thousands of shipyard jobs. Those were hard times: her husband lost his job, people were destroyed, marriages ended, drugs came in. Carmen's nuclear family managed thanks to her parents' help until her husband found another job. Currently she thinks this past experience helps her deal with the present without panicking. In her view, inter-generational solidarity is crucial, and *the older generation has to support the younger generation*. Now, after a decade of being independent, her 36-year-old unemployed son has returned home; Carmen and her husband also help their daughter who works as a supermarket cashier. Transfers of money and care are continuous, draining their pension and strength. Three years later, in 2015, Carmen pointed to the constant conflicts created by cohabitation with her adult son: conflicts around household chores, autonomy, sexuality, pocket money, idleness. She added: "Nobody is happy with the situation; he is no longer happy living with us and we are no longer happy having him here. He suffers when he asks, and suffers when we give, knowing that we deprive ourselves on his behalf." With austerity pension cuts, resources are scarce; they also financially support their daughter who now has a small child. But mostly, Carmen is exhausted and anxious about the future, about what will happen to their son when they are no longer around to help. She imagines him homeless and relying on charity.

Today's domestic moral economy frames transfers between generations as a continuing gift of income and care between older and younger generations, transfers that reproduce dependency beyond what would have been expected in a functioning liberal economy. Parents feel the continuing responsibility of supporting their adult children and grandchildren, forgoing the disengagement that should come with adult children earning their own income. Moreover, the ability to take on this unexpected responsibility is mediated by the state through the public "pension" that expresses past work and collective intergenerational solidarity as an instituted right. But as the experience of the breakdown during the restructuring years reminds these older women, the current situation which inverts the expected cycle of domestic responsibilities is not altogether new.

Nevertheless, there is widespread uneasiness with the awkward inversion of the general lifecycle of responsibilities that were previously the norm in the domestic moral economies of a stable industrial environment: adults in their prime can no longer support their families and elderly parents or fight for their rights because they are afraid to lose their precarious jobs; retired people cannot rest and enjoy their pension but must keep struggling for a generation that has become permanently dependent on them and incapable of assuming full adult autonomy. In the past, transfers and obligations within the household and kinship networks were highly gendered, established around the long-term conjuncture (1950–1980) of stable, male industrial work providing income and the right to a contributive pension after retirement. Moreover, economic and demographic parameters favored a particular cycle of income transfer and care: the proportion of the active to the retired population was higher, unemployment was low, and life expectancy shorter. Obligations were also established around the housewife who took care successively or simultaneously of her husband, her children, and later in life, her parents or her husband's parents. The household and lifecycles then were tied to the transfers and moral obligations of money and care. Employed children residing in their parents' homes generally gave part of their wages to their mothers as a contribution to household expenses and kept another part as savings towards their future household or for pocket money. Likewise, the pensions of older parents were used to cover household expenses when they co-resided. The stable occupational structure also enabled this generation to transform part of their income into homeownership.

The stability of male industrial employment that contributed to this domestic moral economy began to break down in the 1980s with the first restructuring and job losses in the shipyards. Male unemployment and early retirement became widespread, forcing the reconfiguration of previous moral obligations within households. Income provisioning—although still strongly gendered as it depended on previous industrial employment—became increasingly tied to state subsidies—unemployment and retirement pensions—as well as to female wages in the service sector and other precarious employment. For the younger generation, the horizon of permanent restructuring to increase competitiveness became their only expectation.

Gendered patterns of work were transformed with the demise of local industry. Women entered the labor force for multiple reasons in the late 1980s and 1990s (aspirations of autonomy, new consumption patterns, improving household economies), but mostly because the labor market had transformed, closing industrial opportunities for male workers and opening opportunities for female jobs in the service sector and garment manufacturing. The latter were mostly unskilled and lower income occupations, often with temporary contracts. While their parents were reaching forced retirement at an early age, younger couples were captured in an unstable labor environment that favored female income opportunities. In any case, care obligations were redefined not only between couples—with nominally growing male responsibilities—but between generations, with grandparents increasingly taking care of grandchildren, often before switching to caring for their elderly parents. Although these continued to be mostly women's responsibilities, early retired men often participated in caring and housework tasks.

During the housing-bubble upturn of the early 2000s, new employment opportunities led to double income households acquiring mortgages to buy homes and to consume household appliances, cars and general leisure services on credit. But this was to be short lived. The economic crisis that began in 2008 has yet again reconfigured the domestic moral economies in town. Unemployment, mortgage foreclosures, indebtedness and general lack of income opportunities for the younger generation have deprived them of the material possibilities to assume most of the obligations that once came with adulthood. It is in this conjuncture that many of these responsibilities for income provisioning and care have shifted to the older generations who have their pensions as a source of income, who were able to capitalize their wages in the form of homeownership (free of mortgage) and are in relative good health and autonomous. Filial obligation no longer follows the industrial model of life- and household cycles that previously distributed obligations among kinship networks and household members in light of their capacities during their active adulthood years. Instead, the precarity model of obligations that began in the 1990s has intensified, based on the older generation's provision of income, housing and care. Many young families now move to their parental homes when they can no longer meet their mortgage payments; their irregular working hours while job hopping and job seeking make caring for the children increasingly difficult. The current situation inverts the expectations of autonomy of active adults, prolonging their dependence on the previous generation whose members must maintain their positions of responsibility past their nominally active years.

Italy

During his fieldwork in 2015, Antonio joined a day trip to Bari organized by a group of parishioners from a peripheral neighborhood, built in the 1960s to accommodate the fast-growing population of Brindisi. Among the organizers of the day trip were Elena (58) and Paolo (61), a leading couple in local charity activities.

Elena and Paolo are married and have three children. Their daughter, Silvia, lives near her parents' home with her partner—both have temporary jobs in a church-related high school—while their little child is cared for by Elena. Both sons, Daniele (30) and Mario (21), lack stable employment and live with their parents. Daniele had unsuccessfully tried searching for a job in northern Italy, where they have kin; his last temporary job was in a private cooperative contracted to provide catering services for the center for asylum seekers. His partner Laura, after losing her job as a shop assistant, applied to a national civil service scheme for "voluntary work," which provided her with a little stipend to work in a charity. Mario is also a casual worker, working as a waiter and in construction; he was planning to join a cousin in Australia. Daniele and Laura were also planning to search for jobs elsewhere, in northern Italy or perhaps abroad, to fulfil their project of a life together—something they cannot yet afford.

Paolo's career path was very different. He had been an apprentice in local workshops until he mastered the skills to set up a workshop with his brothers. But he gave up on self-employment when he obtained a position as a firefighter. After an initial period of living in a council house, and thanks to a public employees housing program, his family was entitled to rent a flat in a recently built apartment building on the outskirts of the neighborhood. They will have to vacate the flat when Paolo retires unless they are given the opportunity to buy it. In the meantime, they wonder whether it would be better to take a mortgage and buy a new house, even if this means slightly higher monthly installments than their current rent. While their life savings might enable them to do so, the unstable and precarious situation of their adult children hinders their investment decisions.

For the generation raised in the 1950s and 1960s, the lack of similar opportunities for their children fuels ambivalent feelings. On the one hand, they clearly acknowledge today's difficulties in making a living due to unemployment, low wages and the precarization of labor. On the other hand, they complain about the younger generation's lost work ethic and "spirit of sacrifice"—the "qualities" that sustained their own achievements. As a result, relations between parents and children who cannot become autonomous are marked by a mix of protection, disappointment and pressure that creates tensions, tempered nonetheless by a strong sense of parental responsibility.

Although they are well aware of the difficulties experienced by their children and the necessity of their material support, Paolo and Elena proudly claim to have taught their children the proper work ethic—to never give up searching for whatever job is available and to persevere with dignity. The moralization that suffuses discourses of one's work ethic as fundamental to achieving autonomy may prod children towards the only realistic option they can foresee: emigration. But migration of the younger generation is also the result of individual and household social mobility projects that make heavy demands on family budgets, often with uncertain success, when higher education is pursued far from home in distant and expensive places. At the same time, the financial commitment of the household can generate disquieting feelings. The lifelong project of responsible caregiving and resource allocation to the younger generation can fail, and parents are aware of the class-related differences underlying the value of an education as an investment for the future. The majority of those who leave for higher education never return—although this does not mean the project of social mobility has succeeded.

Despite parents' awareness (and hidden desire) that their sons would not return to Brindisi—as they understood that their goals could only be achieved by moving away from the city—the phenomenon of return has recently grown. Nichi Vendola's leftwing government in Puglia (2005–15) called for the return of highly educated young people and raised expectations and, overall, provided resources (from EU funds) either for further training or for small entrepreneurial activities. Many of the young returnee migrants Antonio met had decided "to bet" (*scomettere*) on trying to make a living at home. But if the regional government's call created the climate and provided the resources for returning, the real personal reasons often had to do with the astronomical rents and cost of living in cities such as Milan while working in precarious and casual jobs. Some also saw their return as temporary and were ready to depart again; having long-term expectations would be too painful if unfulfilled.

The above cases show how parental household resources support the next generation. Especially the new patterns of migration from southern Italy reveal important inversions in terms of relations of dependency and support. Young emigrants no longer provide economic benefits to their hometowns or families through remittances or investments in local real estate. Instead, they drain local resources (mostly those of their families) which are invested elsewhere (mostly in central-northern Italy), underscoring the spatial dimension of household aspirations of upward mobility. And when they return, it is often to remain dependent on their parents' resources, increasingly on their pensions.

The new patterns of moral obligation that we have presented for Spain and Italy are based on material premises that make their long-term viability very uncertain. First, demographic and economic forecasts for Europe, alongside the fiscal practices of structural adjustment, underline the unsustainability of present distributive, pay-as-you-go public pension systems (Van Parijs 1996; Artus and Virard 2006; for a critique, see Navarro and Torres López 2013; Etxezarreta et al. 2010). Many of the provisions which have been instituted in one European country after another—Spain and Italy have been trying to introduce such changes since 1996 but especially since 2011—require longer contribution periods (from 35 to 37 years) and are indexed to a "sustainability factor" that controls for life expectancy at the time of official retirement. It is obvious to those working today in an increasingly precarious occupational environment that their pensions will pale in comparison to their parents', and will also be insufficient to support a similar precarity model of domestic moral economy. Second, precarity inhibits forms of asset capitalization such as home ownership. Finally, the increasing privatization of higher education with its exponentially higher fees renders investing in the human capital of children (something that the expansion of public higher education in the 1980s and 1990s enabled their parents to do) much more difficult. Indeed, obligations, transfers of income and care, and autonomy and dependency in the domestic moral economy are mediated by the structure of the labor market and by the welfare structure of the state.

Sustainable Pensions: The Argument of Inter-Generational (In)Equity

Following the European Commission (2010, 2012), the Spanish and Italian governments have been warning about the unsustainability of their public pension schemes. They cite the growing population of people aged above 65, increased life expectancy and declining contributions to the social security pension fund due to the economic crisis and unemployment (Hernández de Cos et al. 2017). But unsustainability is also very much related to the growth of unstable forms of employment, to the extension of education and training periods for the young, and lower wages and thus social security contributions from younger workers. Moreover, growing unemployment means that social benefits for working age people compete with benefits for the retired generation, including those provided through the public healthcare system. This, compounded by structural adjustment measures responding to the fiscal crisis of the state, has produced a discourse warning against unsustainable distributive public pension schemes and the "inequitable" (i.e. unfair) aspects of the system.[10]

In policy and expert papers, inter-generational equity is defined by an actuarial approach to the state's pension obligations in terms such as these:

> Intergenerational equity is attained when the total expendable income per retiree (resulting from public pension schemes, from private pension funds, from personal savings) and the total expendable income per active person are comparable, including leisure utility (the absence

of work) for the retiree and the length of the periods of work and retirement (Artus and Virard 2006: 40).

Although the insurance approach to social security has been part of the European tradition, especially in Germany (Van Parijs 1996), recent policies have privileged the individualizing of investments and risks rather than the social pooling of resources geared to resolving intra- and inter-generational downturns in livelihood, an approach that was hegemonic in the interwar and immediate postwar period (Beveridge 1942). The current approach differs from the classic definition of intergenerational equity developed at the turn of the twentieth century. As it was defined then (and this was the model set in place after World War Two in most of Europe) intergenerational equity was not seen as a competition for scarce resources among contemporary age cohorts, but as a continuous chain of dependencies linking generations through time to the social reproduction of a particular collective community. In the French version—which became the model for welfare obligations for most Southern European countries—the state's role was seen as institutionalizing "natural solidarity." In this model, every individual was tied in a "quasi-contract" to all past and present generations that had enabled the continuing existence of society (Bourgeois 1896). Although this was a legal fiction enabling transfers between individuals in society, what is relevant here is the moral argument the quasi-contract sustained: that of a social debt endlessly reproduced through the individual use of collectively produced assets which needs to be endlessly cancelled, an obligation that the state must regulate: "[T]he only proposition that we need to establish here is the following: positive law can secure through imperative sanctions the cancelling of the social debt, the fulfillment of the obligation that results for every human being from his condition of debtor to all" (Bourgeois 1896: 57).

This argument sets the framework for an idea whereby solidarity is the basis for social continuity, the consequence of collective interactions resulting in a social good, the nation, with the state as the guarantor of its continuity. This idea can be observed as it develops in various European countries through their social security systems after World War Two. Even in a dictatorship such as Francoist Spain, the piecemeal consolidation of the social security system was based on an idea of "national" solidarity, here with an emphasis on the corporative nature of the nation.

The present-day injunctions of experts and policymakers have a completely different ring to them, based as they are on neoliberal individualized tenets of life-long self-responsibility and the economistic accounting of obligations between generations (Le Lann 2010; Le Lann and Lemoine 2012; White 2013). It is ironic that the term "sustainable" is used in this context to refer to a financial balance of accounts instead of its original reference to humanity's commitment to social reproduction, an injunction to ensure "the needs of the present without compromising the ability of future generations to meet their own needs" (Brundtland 1987). For the sustainability of public pension schemes, the actuarial perspective is framed in terms of financial accountability and viability, with the collective aspect being substituted by the aggregation of contributors and recipients in each age group. The state's moral responsibility as guarantor of the social reproduction of the nation, a transcendent and imagined community of citizens (Anderson 1991), is replaced by the managerial task of accounting that transfers the entire responsibility for social reproduction to each individual person. This can be seen in European governments favoring pension funds capitalized throughout individual careers, tied to investment in financial assets and to self-responsibility for future individual well-being (Devesa et al. 2012a, 2012b). Solidarity public pension schemes that socialized and redistributed national wealth between productively active and passive generations are being transformed into a patrimonial understanding of retirement pensions as tied to individual contributions (Le Lann 2010). Notional accounts systems for defined benefits pensions and "mixed-pillar" systems where individual savings in occupational and private pension plans are central and where financial and demographic "risks" are shared between the individual and the state are being introduced with the argument of inter-generational equity (European Commission 2010; Eichhorst et al. 2011).

Spain

While the changes first implemented in the late 1990s were met with resistance, economists and government agents turned to the media to trumpet the alleged inequity of the existing distributive public pension system, entailing the "unfair" transfer of resources from an active age cohort to a numerically growing passive age cohort. It was argued that the older generation was dispossessing the younger one, while prospects for these transfers continuing into the future were bleak given demographic and economic realities. In 2011 an agreement was reached between the "social actors" (state, unions, business) that was later fixed in a legal decree (BOE 2-08-2011; Frades 2011) that progressively replaces the existing system with a structurally flexible one that stresses long careers and extends the wage basis for calculating the pension. Younger generations reportedly considered this agreement an attack on their future rights as it preserved the old system for those over 50, the larger portion of union membership. Given the increased precarity that the latest labor reform legislation supports (BOE 11-02-2012; Fundación 1º de Mayo 2012), young people are aware that they will probably not have the accumulated career years nor the cumulated wage levels to access adequate pensions. Neither will they have the resources to access private pension funds nor other assets such as home equity. The reform of the pension system is presented in the media as the breakdown of intergenerational solidarity because the "older" union-represented generation has sought to consolidate its present privileges, which the "younger" generation is paying for through their taxable income—thereby being deprived of its use—with no prospect for future reciprocity. A generational confrontation is represented at the level of the wider responsibilities of social reproduction for the entire national community, as it is mediated by institutional stakeholders—the state, the unions and the business associations.[11] The 2013 reform of the public pension system decoupled pensions from the consumer price index, negatively affecting pensioners' purchasing power.[12] In September 2018, the new social democratic government returned to indexation, provoking severe admonitions from Brussels and conservative-liberal parties.[13]

The failure of the system of social reproduction is acutely felt by downwardly mobile households where pensions often support extended family networks. It explains the growing mobilization (since 2013, and especially in 2016 and 2017) of pensioners in defense of the public pension system and against austerity cuts to pensions. In response to the accusation that they are defending their own selfish interests, they answer: "To defend pensions today is to defend our children and our grandchildren's future."

Italy

The history of pension reform in Italy is chronologically similar to Spain and most other European pension system reforms. The first important reforms were implemented in 1992–3 (*Riforma Amato*) and 1995 (*Riforma Dini*). The *Riforma Amato* sought to reduce the public deficit in order to fulfill the Maastricht criteria.[14] Both reforms introduced important changes which were gradually developed in subsequent reforms until the apex of the Fornero reform in 2011, including the "three pillars system" that added private "defined contributions" supplementary schemes to the public "defined benefit" ones. In addition to reducing public expenditures, these reforms transformed the public pension system into a notional defined contribution (NDC) system.[15] Actuarial logics were introduced for the calculation of pension benefits for all categories of workers while the age of retirement was set between 57 and 65 years (depending on years of contribution). The introduction of the NDC system was negotiated with the union confederations, which initially protected the older generation of workers, defined as "guaranteed workers," from the new system. Workers who had contributed for 18 years in 1995 were exempted; their pensions continued to be calculated under the old system, on the basis of their earnings over the last ten years.

Reforms of the Italian pension system accelerated following the 2008 crisis, with the technocratic Monti government extending the NDC system to those workers who had been exempted in 1995. The age of retirement was pushed up to 67 with immediate effect for men (starting in 2021 for women) and certain categories of workers (e.g. the self-employed) who saw their contributions go up. The pension reform was part of a broader decree emphatically called "Safe Italy" (*Decreto Salva Italia*) that proclaimed the "unsustainable" pension system required urgent and immediate action. The Fornero labor reform included in this decree caused a great deal of trouble for workers who had negotiated with their employers to retire before 67 and who now found themselves in limbo: without a job and unable to claim retirement until they reached 67 (these were the famous *esodati*). Although this was a transitional problem only affecting those who had made pre-agreements before the Fornero law, many older people descended into poverty. To remedy the situation, subsequent governments in 2017 and 2019 introduced measures to allow workers to retire *before* the age set by the Fornero reform. The 2017 *Anticipo Pensionistico* enabled affected workers to access a public loan to pay their interim contributions, to be repaid later with the pension benefit.[16] The Fornero reform was also unpopular because it decoupled pensions from the consumer price index, affecting the purchasing power of pensioners.

Conflicts over pension reforms—especially the first reforms in the 1990s—were shaped by the official argument of "intergenerational inequity" whereby unions were blamed for protecting the older generation of "guaranteed" workers at the expense of younger generations of precarious workers. The generational dimension of the *precari vs. garantiti* argument was instrumentally mobilized by technocratic elites and political reformers alike to lambast the never-ending reforms to the Italian pension system. Compared to earlier reforms, the Fornero reform of 2011 was considered more impartial as it treated all workers equally under the austerity premise that cuts will eventually result in general economic improvement.

Neoliberal reforms in Italy have been supported by a discourse which highlights the "privileges" of certain categories of workers while insisting on "equal" opportunities for all as individuals, a discourse—which our interlocutors were skeptical of—that consistently hides the class dimension and insists on the relevance of individual merit (*meritocrazia*). In the case of pensions, the "privilege" of the older generation was presented as responsible for the grim prospects of future generations. The previous distributive pension system was based on a lifecycle "solidarity" principle whereby younger workers' contributions paid for retirement pensions in a generalized reciprocity of inter-generational responsibilities. In contrast, the new system made providing for one's old age an individual responsibility, increasingly shifting from public, *defined benefit* pensions to *defined contribution* pension funds, whether public or private. This was described in actuarial terms as more equitable as precarious young workers were not obliged to pay for privileged old pensioners, but could now "invest" *in their own* pensions. Young and old were thus placed in a "competitive" struggle for the distribution of benefits and pensions from a state budget under austerity. At the same time, allegedly "privileged" pensioners have been taking over responsibilities for the informal welfare (e.g. childcare, housing and provisioning) necessary for social reproduction.

Moral Economies between Household and State

We highlight two main issues in our concluding remarks. The first is the tension between dependence and autonomy the breakdown of expectations has brought to active adult cohorts. The second is the contradiction between the transformations in the everyday domestic moral economy and the political economic changes affecting the larger responsibilities of the state towards social reproduction. Structurally related, they fuel ambivalence and anxiety in people's everyday lives.

Younger generations who must depend on their retired parents for income, housing and care[17] are barred from what was previously expected to be the road to autonomy in adult life, where being employed and raising a family created new responsibilities detached from one's family of origin, with men mostly being the providers and women the care-givers. This reversed their expected position in the flow of transfers from recipients to givers where to achieve adult personhood was to achieve autonomy from the previous generation, the main watershed in one's lifecycle.

The new situation makes these obligations increasingly difficult to fulfil, for both men and women alike. Conversely, retired persons who once expected their obligations to diminish and to eventually be taken care of by their children, see instead their filial obligations continue for as long as they can physically bear them. For these older generations, the new domestic moral economy of precarity appears as an extension of their initial obligations of caring for the next generations; for the younger generations, it is a complete reversal of their expectations of adult responsibility. Although they may have their own families, and possibly some kind of employment and income, they must now depend on their parents' care, assets and pensions. This creates an ambivalent situation and a permanent feeling of inadequacy towards their domestic obligations and their personal worth. And while society increasingly privileges individualized forms of autonomy, expressed through consumption, over family-centered versions of independence, the young active generation is unable to achieve it.

This has resulted in various forms of anxiety that produce intimate forms of conflict. While young adults may be grateful to their parents for supporting them, they are reluctant to remain dependent on them. For the national economy, the prolonged dependence of active generations on state subsidies—often on the pensions of their retired parents—enables an "internal devaluation," i.e. the reduction of labor costs, the objective of southern European governments to enhance competitiveness in the Euro crisis conjuncture. This largely represents a form of transfer from labor to capital through the mediation of the state.

Recent structural adjustment policies in Europe, as they affect public pension schemes, underscore a different set of issues. Here, the state's reconfiguration of its moral responsibility towards the nation's social reproduction into a form of actuarial management of risk and accounting has resulted in a trade-off between the pension rights of older and younger generations. This has in turn resulted in competition between generations at the abstract level of their entitlements as part of the national community. The expectation of a morality of solidarity and redistribution mediated by the state has broken down, and has been replaced by the neoliberal emphasis on individual responsibility for future welfare. But younger active adults perplexed by the older generation's self-centeredness—

expressed in union support for the Italian 1995 Dini Reform or the Spanish 2011 Pension Agreement, abandoning the well-being of future generations for the protection of their own present gains—are hard pressed to square this with their lived experiences at home. While the willingness of parents to share their pensions and offer everyday support is a lifesaver, gratitude towards parents at home gets entangled with misgivings about what they see as an older generation's privileges on the level of policy. Nevertheless, their parents are also ready to struggle by their side in defense of a shared domestic morality of social reproduction. Although the discourse of sustainability (increasingly conceived in financial terms) that has replaced the discourse of solidarity at the level of the moral economy of the state is cloaked in the words of intergenerational equity, it has encouraged competition for scarce resources between generations. Here, the breakdown of the "national moral economy" underscores the transformation of political objectives for the "common good," which are now completely submissive to capital.

Spanish and Italian societies today have largely bought into a neoliberal ideology that values individual autonomy, entrepreneurship, wealth and conspicuous consumption. Within this ideology, autonomy and responsibility are linked because freedom from obligation is the basis of individual contractual freedom, the foundation of law and of the citizen as a meaningful and entitled agent in a state-of-law. It is difficult, then, to be considered responsible without being recognized as an autonomous individual (Guyer 2012: 499; Hyland 2012: 19, 35–6). As detailed in this chapter, precarity keeps the young active adult generation in a position of prolonged dependency on their parents and state subsidies—an obstacle to the social recognition of their worth as responsible adults (through familial autonomy) and as successful individuals (through consumption). The recognition they receive, expressed through the transfers and care of kin and state, is a statement of their failure to achieve what is valued in this kind of society: freedom from dependency.

As feminists have repeatedly underlined, interdependency is always present as the shadow side of freedom. While nobody is free from social ties, some have the power to appear as free agents of their own will, able to freely enter into and respond to commitments, while others cannot emerge from the shadow of dependency. The growing mismatch between precarious livelihoods, prolonged dependency and limited opportunities to realize self-worth on the one hand, and the dominant neoliberal ideology of individual autonomy and successful entrepreneurship on the other, may help create a precarious working class devoid of self-respect and the capacity to struggle. Or it may create the basis for moral outrage at the terms being imposed for the social reproduction of a capitalist society (Bourdieu 2003). The breakdown of social reproduction as it is expressed in the reconfigured obligations between generations in Spain and Italy points to the ambivalence of inter-generational solidarity at various scales and to the instability, anxiety and vulnerability of future generations.

Notes

1. This concerns the fiscal crisis of the state, largely due to the abandoning of Keynesian welfare systems of progressive taxation, the reduction of corporate taxation and the dismantling of job security and wages through global outsourcing.
2. See Sayer (2000) for another attempt to articulate radical political economy and moral economy.
3. We do not refer to the interest in morality present in many historical works on economic activities, but to the emergence of an analytical concept that has become a synthetic tool for understanding conflicts around the distribution of resources.
4. Care in practice and as a domain of observation straddles domestic, market, state and voluntary sectors in what has been defined as the "care diamond" (Razavi 2007).
5. We use the formal/informal divide because the pressure of regulatory frameworks creates real differences in labor market opportunities. These concepts do not describe a bounded reality but an entangled continuum of differently regulated labor relations.
6. In 2017, total unemployment was 16.7 percent and youth unemployment 38.2 percent. Spain continues to have the highest unemployment rates in Europe after Greece (Eurostat news release, 30 November 2017). We use 2015 statistics as they refer to our period of fieldwork (2012–15). Eurostat news release, 7 January 2015: http://ec.europa.eu/eurostat/documents/2995521/6454659/3-07012015-AP-EN.pdf (last accessed March 2015).
7. Instituto Galego de Estadística https://tinyurl.com/rjh875r; https://tinyurl.com/yx5pvwfy https://tinyurl.com/u2bnrb6; https://tinyurl.com/rjvzhq4 (last accessed June 2016). For 2016, the last year for which figures are available, 63.8 percent of people under 34 lived with their parents. Meanwhile 26.9 percent of those 25–34 and 56.5 percent of those 18–24 had no income. 35.8 percent of households in Galicia received more than 75 percent of their income from benefits. In Ferrol, 43.4 percent of household income comes from benefits. Instituto Galego de Estadística: https://tinyurl.com/trmd9ax (last accessed July 2018).
8. In 1961, workers in the industrial sector (including construction) accounted for 31 percent of the employed population. This peaked at 34.1 percent in 1971 and has since been declining (29.5 percent in 1981 and 23.2 percent in the

last national census (ISTAT). The service sector has been growing steadily, accounting for 42.7 percent of the employed population in 1961, 58.7 percent in 1981, and 70.1 percent in 2011. Whereas service sector growth is in line with national and international trends, in Brindisi it is more linked to the expansion of services in the public administration than to the growth of high-tech services—a common feature in southern Italy. The latter reflects the peripheral and subordinate position of Brindisian plants in the broader geography of corporate strategies and interests. For regional comparison, see Pasetto et al. 2002.

9. "The labour market situation in Puglia is currently rather sluggish. The average unemployment rate stands at 19.3% (in the 18-32 age group it exceeds 45.5%, while female unemployment stands at 52.1%). People in employment are mostly men and aged over 30. The out-migration flow is growing significantly, and concerns all groups... [T]he region's employment is mainly in services, including public employment, which accounts for 66% of workers, while the numbers are lower for industry (25.4%) and agriculture (8.5%). About 19% of work is irregular" (EURES brief for 2018). ,https://tinyurl.com/ukva3np (last accessed July 2019).

10. Although the public pension fund in Spain is part of that for social security, a reserve pension fund was created in 1995 to protect pensions from possible deficits. These protected funds, popularly known as the "pension's piggy bank," have been depleted since 2012. Cinco Días: https://cincodias.elpais.com/cincodias/2015/08/07/economia/1438971113_586899.html El Diario.es: https://www.eldiario.es/economia/pensiones_0_713928942.html (last accessed June 2018).

11. "Percepciones sobre el futuro de las pensiones: un experimento toledano," Antonio Baylos, Facultad de Ciencias Jurídicas de Toledo, n.d.

12. Cinco Días: https://cincodias.elpais.com/cincodias/2013/12/12/economia/1386840999_548351.html (last accessed June 2018).

13. https://tinyurl.com/va7gp6f https://www.expansion.com/economia/2018/03/08/5aa0efe6268e3e27728b4663.html (last accessed July 2019).

14. "Convergence criteria (or "Maastricht criteria") are criteria, based on economic indicators, that European Union (EU) member states must fulfill to enter the eurozone. These criteria were established during the Maastricht treaty, and were signed by the members of the European Union on February 7 1992. The four criteria are defined in article 121 of the treaty establishing the European Community. They impose control over inflation, public debt and the public deficit, exchange rate stability and the convergence of interest rates." In addition, "the annual government deficit must not exceed 3 percent of GDP [and] Government debt must not exceed 60 percent of GDP." INSEE: https://www.insee.fr/en/metadonnees/definition/c1348 (last accessed July 2019).

15. "Like traditional social insurance schemes, they are publicly provided. However, the pension formula differs somewhat from the 'traditional' earnings related model, with the benefit based on the accumulation in one's account at the time of retirement. Pension accounts in this system are called 'notional' because there is no pot of pension fund money, just a series of individual

claims on the future public budget. They are pay-as-you-go financed—current contributions pay for current benefits—just like most defined-benefit public schemes... Linking individual pension benefits more closely with individual contributions is a central motivation for reforms based on notional accounts. This enhances the 'actuarial fairness' of pay-as-you-go pension systems." http://siteresources.worldbank.org/INTPENSIONS/Resources/395443-112 1194657824/PRPNoteNotionalAccts.pdf (last accessed July 2019).
16. The current Salvini government has introduced a further measure (Quota 100) that should allow workers with at least 38 years of contribution and who are at least 62 years old to apply for early retirement under certain conditions.
17. For Spain, see Pérez-Diaz and Rodríguez 2007.

References

Anderson, B. 1991. *Imagined Communities: Reflections on the Origin and Spread of Nationalism*. London: Verso.
Artus, P. and M-P. Virard. 2006. *Comment nous avons ruiné nos enfants*. Paris: La Découverte.
Banfield, E.C. with L.F. Banfield. 1958. *The Moral Basis of a Backward Society*. Glencoe: Free Press.
Benería, L. 2003. *Gender, Development and Globalization*. London: Routledge.
Beveridge, W. 1942. *Social Insurance and Allied Services*. London: H.M. Stationary Office.
Biagi, B., A. Faggian and Ph. McCann. 2011. "Long and Short Distance Migration in Italy: The Role of Economic, Social and Environmental Characteristics." *Spatial Economic Analysis* 6(1): 111–31.
BOE. 30-12-1963. Ley 193/1963, de 28 de diciembre, sobre Bases de la Seguridad Social.
BOE. 2-08-2011. Ley 27/2011, de 1 de agosto, sobre actualización, adecuación y modernización del sistema de Seguridad Social.
BOE. 11-02-2012. Real Decreto-ley 3/2012, de 10 de febrero, de medidas urgentes para la reforma del mercado laboral.
Bourgeois, L. 1896. *Solidarité*. Paris: Armand Colin. http://classiques.uqac.ca/classiques/bourgeois_leon/solidarite/solidarite.html (last accessed July 2018).
Bourdieu, P. 2003. *Méditations pascaliennes*. Édition revue et corrigée. Paris: Seuil.
Brown, K.E. 2009. "Economics and Morality: Introduction." In K.E. Browne and B.L. Milgram, eds. *Economics and Morality: Anthropological Approaches*. Lanham: Altamira Press.
Bristow, J. 2016. "The Making of 'Boomergeddon': The Construction of the Baby Boomer Generation as a Social Problem in Britain." *The British Journal of Sociology* 67(4): 575–91.
Brundtland, G.H. 1987. *Report of the World Commission on Environment and Development: Our Common Future*. Oxford: Oxford University Press.
De Angelis, M. 2007. *The Beginning of History: Value Struggles and Global Capital*. London: Pluto Press.

Devesa, J.E., M. Devesa, I. Domínguez, B. Encinas, R. Meneu and A. Nagore. 2012a. "Sobre las inequidades del sistema contributivo de pensiones de jubilación en España: ¿Se han impuesto los ideólogos a los actuarios?" *Economía Española y Protección Social* 2012(4): 21–58.

Devesa, J.E., M. Devesa, R. Meneu, A. Nagore, I. Domínguez and B. Encinas. 2012b. "Equidad y sostenibilidad como objetivos ante la reforma del sistema contributivo de pensiones de jubilación." *Hacienda Pública Española / Review of Public Economics* 2012(2): 9–38.

Edelman, M. 2005. "Bringing the Moral Economy Back in... to the Study of 21st-Century Transnational Peasant Movements." *American Anthropologist* 107(3): 331–45.

Elson, D. 2001. "For an Emancipatory Socio-Economics." Draft paper for UNRISD meeting, *Need to Rethink Development Economics*, 7–8 September, Cape Town.

Etxezarreta, M., E. Idoate, J. Iglesias Fernandez and J. Junyent Tarrida. 2010. *Qué pensiones, qué futuro*. Barcelona: Icaria.

European Commission. 2010. *Green Paper: Towards Adequate, Sustainable and Safe European Pension Systems*, July 7. http://ec.europa.eu/social/main.jsp?langId=en&catId=89&newsId=839&furtherNews=yes (last accessed July 2019).

European Commission. 2012. *White Paper: An Agenda for Adequate, Safe and Sustainable Pensions*, February 16. http://eur-lex.europa.eu/LexUriServ/LexUriServ.do?uri=COM:2012:0055:FIN:EN:PDF (last accessed July 2019).

Fassin, D. 2009. "Les économies morales revisitées." *Annales. Histoire, Sciences Sociales* 2009(6): 1237–66.

Fassin, D., ed. 2012. *A Companion to Moral Anthropology*. Oxford: Wiley-Blackwell.

Fontaine, L. 2008. *L'économie morale. Pauvreté, crédit et confiance dans l'Europe pré-industrielle*. Paris: Gallimard.

Frades, J., ed. 2011. *El Sistema Público de Pensiones de Jubilación. Desafíos y respuestas*. Madrid: Fundación Francisco Largo Caballero.

Fraser, N. 1995. "From Redistribution to Recognition? Dilemmas of Justice in a 'Postsocialist' Age." *New Left Review* 212: 68–93.

Fundación 1º de Mayo. 2012. *Las reformas laborales en España y su repercusión en materia de contratación y empleo*. Madrid: Fundación 1º de Mayo.

Ginsborg, P. 1990. *A History of Contemporary Italy: 1943-1980*. London: Penguin.

Gregory, C. 2009. "Whatever Happened to Householding?" In C. Hann and K. Hart, eds. *Market and Society: The Great Transformation Today*. Cambridge: Cambridge University Press.

Gribaudi, G. 1993. "Familismo e famiglia a Napoli e nel Mezzogiorno." *Meridiana* 17: 13–43.

Guyer, J. 2012. "Obligation, Binding, Debt and Responsibility: Provocations about Temporality from Two New Sources." *Social Anthropology* 20(4): 491–501.

Hann, C. 2010. "Moral Economy." In K. Hart, J-L. Laville and A.D. Cattani, eds. *The Human Economy*. Oxford: Polity.

Harvey, D. 2003. *The New Imperialism*. Oxford: Oxford University Press.

Harvey, D. 2005. *A Brief History of Neoliberalism*. Oxford: Oxford University Press.

Hernández de Cos, P., J.F. Jimeno and R. Ramos. 2017. *El sistema público de pensiones en España: situación actual, retos y alternativas de reforma*. Documentos Ocasionales, N.º 1701. Madrid: Banco de España.

Hochschild, A.R. 2003. *Commercialization of Intimate Life: Notes from Home and Work*. Berkeley: University of California Press.

Hyland, R. 2009. *Gifts: A Study in Comparative Law*. New York: Oxford University Press.

ISTAT. 2015. *Attraverso la crisi. Occupazione e reti di imprese in Puglia*. Rome: ISTAT.

Lawson, V. 2007. "Geographies of Care and Responsibility." *Annals of the Association of American Geographers* 97(1): 1–11.

Le Lann, Y. 2010. "La retraite, un patrimoine?" *Genèses* 80: 70–89.

Le Lann, Y. and Lemoine, B. 2012. "Les comptes des générations. Les valeurs du futur et la transformation de l'État social." *Actes de la recherche en sciences sociales* 194: 62–77.

McDowell, L. 2004. "Work, Workfare, Work/Life Balance and an Ethic of Care." *Progress in Human Geography* 28(2): 145–63.

Mingione, E. 1983. Informalization, Restructuring and the Survival Strategies of the Working Class. *International Journal of Urban and Regional Research* 7(3): 311–39.

Mingione, E. 1988. "Work and Informal Activities in Urban Southern Italy." In R.E. Pahl, ed. *On Work: Historical, Comparative and Theoretical Approaches*. New York: Basil Blackwell.

Moore, B. 1978. *Injustice: The Social Bases of Obedience and Revolt*. New York: Macmillan.

Narotzky, S. 2011. "Memories of Conflict and Present-Day Struggles in Europe: New Tensions Between Corporatism, Class, and Social Movements." *Identities* 18(2): 97–112.

Narotzky, S. 2016. "Between Inequality and Injustice: Dignity as a Motive for Mobilization During the Crisis." *History and Anthropology* 27(1): 74–92.

Narotzky, S. and N. Besnier. 2014. "Crisis, Value, Hope: Rethinking the Economy." *Current Anthropology* 55(S9): 4–16.

Navarro, V. and J. Torres López. 2013. *Lo que debes saber para que no te roben la pensión*. Barcelona: Espasa.

Nelson, J. 2006. *Economics for Humans*. Chicago: University of Chicago Press.

Parreñas, R.S. 2001. *Servants of Globalization: Women, Migration and Domestic Work*. Stanford: Stanford University Press.

Pasetto, A. and S. Sylos Labini. 2002. *Occupazione e specializzazione commerciale dell'industria manifatturiera in Italia e nelle regioni dal 1951 al 1996*. Rome: Quaderni di Informazione SVIMEZ 14.

Pérez-Diaz, V. and J-C. Rodríguez. 2007. *La generación de la transición entre el trabajo y la jubilación*. Barcelona: Servicio de Estudios La Caixa.

Picchio, A. 1992. *Social Reproduction. The Political Economy of the Labour Market*. Cambridge: Cambridge University Press.

Pine, F. 2007. "Memories of Movement and the Stillness of Place: Kinship and Migration in the Polish Mountains." In J. Carsten, ed. *Ghosts of Memory*. Oxford: Blackwell.

Pine, F. 2009. "Lost Generations? Kinship, Unemployment and The Failure of Reproduction." Paper at the Canadian Association of Social and Cultural Anthropologists Annual Meeting, Vancouver.

Razavi, S. 2007. *The Political and Social Economy of Care in a Development Context.* Geneva: UNRISD.

Robbins, J. 2009. "Rethinking Gifts and Commodities: Reciprocity, Recognition, and the Morality of Exchange." In K.E. Browne and B.L. Milgram, eds. *Economics and Morality: Anthropological Approaches.* Lanham: Altamira Press.

Sayer, A. 2000. "Moral Economy and Political Economy." *Studies in Political Economy* 61: 79–103.

Schneider, J., ed. 1998. *Italy's "Southern Question":Orientalism in One Country.* London: Berg.

Scott, J.C. 1976. *The Moral Economy of the Peasant: Rebellion and Subsistence in Southeast Asia.* New Haven: Yale University Press.

Smith, G. 2011. "Selective Hegemony and Beyond-Populations with "No Productive Function": A Framework for Enquiry." *Identities* 18(1): 2–38.

Sykes, K. 2010. "Adopting an Obligation: Moral Reasoning about the Duty to Provide Bougainvillean Children with Access to Social Services in New Ireland." *Revue du MAUSS* 36(2): 223–37.

Thompson, E.P. 1971. "The Moral Economy of the English Crowd in the Eighteenth Century." *Past and Present* 50: 76–136.

Thompson, E.P. 1993. "The Moral Economy Reviewed." In *Customs in Common.* New York: New Press.

Van Parijs, Ph. 1996. *Refonder la solidarité.* Paris: Les Éditions du Cerf.

Vercellone, C. 1996. "The Anomaly and Exemplariness of the Italian Welfare State." In P. Virno and M. Hardt, eds. *Radical Thought in Italy.* Minneapolis: University of Minnesota Press.

Weber, F., S. Gojard and A. Gramain, eds. 2003. *Charges de famille. Dépendance et parenté dans la France contemporaine.* Paris: La Découverte.

White, J. 2013. "Thinking Generations." *The British Journal of Sociology* 64(2): 216–47.

Wolf, E.R. 1982. *Europe and the People Without History.* Berkeley: University of California Press.

Yeates, N. 2004. "Global Care Chains." *International Feminist Journal of Politics* 6(3): 369–91.

PART III

EXPERIENCING AND EMBODYING AUSTERITY

9
The Entrepreneur's Other: Small Entrepreneurial Identity and the Collapse of Life Structures in the "Third Italy"

Giacomo Loperfido

Introduction

The currently much maligned economies of southern Europe had their moment in the sun in the 1980s and 90s when rising growth and the expansion of tourism, construction and production by Small and Medium Enterprises (SMEs) fueled hopes that alternative policies promoting "development from below" had the potential to diffuse growth throughout the less industrialized parts of the continent. It was a brief moment of optimism when a set of negative stereotypes commonly used to stigmatize these countries magically turned positive. Several southern European regions with an existing historical structure of SMEs, putting out systems and family agricultural enterprises—from the famous Third Italy to the Valencia region in Spain and some areas of northern Portugal and coastal Greece[1]—suddenly found themselves at the center of debates about the end of Fordism and a new model of capitalism (Becattini 1992; Piore and Sabel 1983, 1984; Sabel 1989).

Within this general excitement, old critiques of the almost proverbial "burdens" carried by southern European economies began to be transformed into a celebratory narrative around the discovery of unforeseen possibilities for economic and social development, where the "moral bases of backward societies" suddenly became assets for overcoming this very backwardness. Southern "familism" (Banfield 1958) now became the secret for the harmonious development of family-based enterprises and local reciprocity networks; "provincialism" transfigured into "localism" and "economic embeddedness" as the "local" became the site for healthy, endogenous economic forces to proliferate. Personal leverage that had once been defined as "clientelism" became "social capital," while unequal topographies of social relations relying on "favor" became the flagship for reciprocity-based economic networks allegedly built on "mutual trust relations" (Putnam 1993; for critique see Hadjimichalis and Hudson 2004; Narotzky 2007, 2009; Narotzky and Smith 2006).

This thread of economic modeling, which for the sake of simplicity I will call the "New Regionalism," was informed by earlier theorizations of the unforeseen development of a flourishing SME economy in northeastern Italy since the 1960s, or what was termed the "Third Italy" (Bagnasco 1977).[2] The Third Italy generated a great deal of interest in how it seemed to materialize possibilities for rural–urban economic interaction in semi-peripheral, semi-urban locales, which appeared to better fit contemporary forms of accumulation. Networks or clusters of SMEs, later re-categorized through the Marshallian notion of "industrial districts," could germinate from local assemblages of rural family production units. Relying on household labor and resources, they benefited from particular histories of local social ties and mutual responsibility which fostered trust among the various segments of the production chain.

This chapter challenges this optimistic view by placing it against the backdrop of the epidemic of entrepreneurial suicides that has been taking place in Veneto since the unfolding of the economic crisis in 2008–9. In what follows, I use ethnography at (and with) the InOltre help desk, a service organized by the Venetian regional government to counter the suicide epidemic, to show how these suicides are the product of the collapse of entrepreneurialism as *both* an economic project and a symbolic space of identification. Indeed, my ethnography shows how it is precisely the conflation of economic and non-economic aspects celebrated by the new regionalist literature that has become, in the current economic slump, central in pushing entrepreneurs to take their own lives.

Through the life histories of Anna (an entrepreneur who, after verging on suicide, was helped by the InOltre service) and her husband Marco,[3] I will show how economic actors resorting to non-economic institutions—the community, the family, the so-called "social capital" of bonds of friendship and trust between patrons and clients, etc.—has "personalized" relations of production (Narotzky 2001), that initially proved highly functional for SMEs (Blim 1990; Ghezzi 2003; Narotzky and Smith 2006; Yanagisako 2002). But as Anna and Marco's case exemplifies, enthusiasm about the early accomplishments of this scheme were often misleading. Many of the cases seen by the InOltre service show that grassroots, expert and institutional sensationalism surrounding the New Regionalist formula had persuaded entrepreneurs to expand their businesses through financial speculation and indebtedness. But a crude and very different reality emerged with the popping of the economic bubble, revealing power imbalances in the subcontracting chain, unequal risk burdens in accessing credit and unequal treatment of insolvency by the state. It is within this new conjuncture, I argue, that the overlapping and mutual entanglement of economic and personal relations, representations and the organization of life spaces becomes an insurmountable obstacle in the effort to sustain one's self-representation.

The first section of this chapter briefly illustrates the contemporary collapse of the entrepreneur as a space of identity. In the second section, I use Anna's entrepreneurial and existential trajectory to show how this space was constituted through historical processes that relied both on individual initiative and the systemic transformations and institutional actions that made individual initiative possible. The third and final section analyzes the functional parameters of this identity field while pointing to the weaknesses that made it collapse under the pressure of economic turmoil.

The Rough Wake up Call for Small Entrepreneurship

Entering the classroom at Padova University, she looks down at the points of her shoes. Her steps seem uncertain and she's clearly emotional. She looks shy and appears even smaller when the professor, a tall, strong man in his early 50s, starts introducing the event, loud and self-assured. Viewing them together, something seems off. He's standing and she's sitting. His voice is loud; he hardly needs the microphone yet keeps it close to his mouth so that his words clearly reach the end of the hall. He gesticulates with his left arm, occupying all the physical space available and even more. She, on the other hand, almost seems to be shrinking as she sits at his side. When she starts to talk, she is tentative, shy, stumbles on her words and apologizes. The professor interrupts her at will to clarify to his students what she is saying. She begins her talk with a sentence that strikes me: "I am here to talk as an 'expert' on the SME sector, but I never wanted to be one. They forced me into becoming an expert."

Those who are unfamiliar with Veneto and the specific set of ideologies that emerged there in the last half century may not appreciate the surprise of hearing a sentence like this coming from the mouth of an entrepreneur. Since production began to take off in the 1960s and further accelerated in the 70s, 80s and 90s, this once poor peasant society has undergone massive transformations. Over the past four decades, an abundant literature has addressed material changes such as the emergence of Veneto as the archetype of a new economic model (Lanaro 1984; Roverato 1996; Zanin 1987), social change and its political implementation (Messina 2001; Riccamboni 1997; Stella 2000) and the radical transformation of the landscape (Fregolent 2014; Lironi 2011; Vallerani and Varotto 2005). But much less has been written about the non-material changes that have taken place in this short period of time. In just a few decades, Veneto was so deeply affected by its own economic success that a thorough recategorization of the surrounding world, its axioms and functioning principles, became necessary to cope with the changes and sustain representations of self and society. Individualism, drives towards competition, autarchic ideologies of independence, self-reliance and self-made-manship all emerged due to grassroots economic expansion. The figure of the entrepreneur[4]—as both the origin and the expression of the industrial districts—became the cornerstone of this new cosmology.

We need to pause here to examine the local gradations of meaning which the concept of entrepreneurship—and its embodied equivalent, the entrepreneur—acquired during Venetian expansion. Unlike the Shumpeterian notion of entrepreneurship, which mainly revolves around creativity and the courage and ability to innovate both economically and socially, Venetian understandings rested upon more individualistic notions of the self-reliance, autonomy and independence of the businessperson who is equipped with entrepreneurial good will. Rather than a risk-taking, economic innovator, the Venetian entrepreneur is an autonomous man, extraordinarily capable of fending for himself and his family. This understanding bears the legacy of a still very recent past of rural poverty, when the only resource available to Venetians was one's own labor power and that of one's family, most often working as a factory hand or in domestic service. With the hardships of poverty and rural life still clearly in mind, Venetians created the myth of the local entrepreneur as a demiurge who, thanks to his relentless ability to work, was able to emancipate himself, his family and his people by transforming, in Yanagisako's (2018) words, labor into capital. This is exemplified in the saying *Faso tuto mi* (I'm doing it all by myself), a mantra that Venetians repeat all the time, conjuring the glorification of individual independence/self-reliance and the idea that this can only be obtained through practice, action and real work (as opposed to intellectual work and theorizing, which tend to be denigrated). This is why Anna's apparent shyness, passivity, loneliness and presentation of herself as "forced into being something she didn't want to be" sounded so absurdly far from the locally established idea of the almighty entrepreneur, the only master of her/his own destiny.

The event I described took place in the Department of Psychology at the University of Padova (one of Veneto's largest cities as well as one of its industrial cores) during the fall of 2016. Anna had been invited there to tell her story as a struggling entrepreneur who had been "rescued from suicide" by the InOltre service, a public help desk for Venetian entrepreneurs under duress, which the regional government had funded and the professor had helped create back in 2012. At the time of Anna's talk, I had been observing the InOltre service for several months, where I became acquainted with Anna and her story as well as those of several others who were in similar situations.

The InOltre service itself is a good illustration of the collapse of the identity space of the small entrepreneur. Between 2013 and 2015, Veneto was the Italian region with by far the highest number of suicides related to the economic crisis (119 suicides, equating to 18.6 percent of the national total).[5] The larger economic area of northeast Italy witnessed 170 suicides, or 26.6 percent of the Italian total (also the highest figures nationally).[6] In light of this disconcerting series of events, the regional government (Regione Veneto) launched InOltre in June 2012, which became known colloquially as "the anti-suicide help-desk." InOltre consisted of a phone number, open 24/7, for "bankrupting entrepreneurs" in distress. Anna's story is one of many that I collected through the help desk.

The Entrepreneur's Other: Passive, Lonely and Dependent

From approximately the early 1970s, Veneto, the poor region where Anna was born, seemed to be enjoying a widening window of opportunities for profit, especially for the many rural households pursuing a mixture of agriculture and commerce. The proliferation of small and medium family firms soon developed into what has famously been described as "industrial districts" (Becattini 1992; Locke 1995; Piore and Sabel 1984)—complex networks of specialized firms engaged in one or two phases of the manufacturing process and linked to one another in dispersed production chains that were not vertically integrated, allowing for greater flexibility and lower production costs.

As was the case for many others,[7] Anna's entrepreneurial history was embedded in networks of "highly specialised but flexible firms that were rooted in kinship, friendship, and local community relations" (Yanagisako 2018: 49)—the kinds of firms celebrated in the Regionalist literature of the 1990s. Veneto, and Third Italy more generally, became a paradigm for new patterns of economic development, a picture in which social conflict seemingly had no place: "The most important trait of the local community is its relatively homogenous system of values and views, which is an expression of the ethic of work and activity, of the family, of reciprocity, and of change" (Becattini 1992: 38). In this unproblematized rendering, existing *personal* relations of kinship, friendship and mutual trust were seen to be constitutive of—and conducive to—non-conflictual relations of production, thus enhancing flexibility, efficacy and business viability.

The entanglement and mutual constitution of love, friendship and community feelings with market transactions and relations of production was indeed a foundational aspect of regional economies. The resort to non-economic institutions—kin, community and local political connections—for economic purposes allowed the exploitation of unpaid or underpaid family labor, high levels of trust and cooperation among firms, and easier access to both formal and informal credit. For Anna (and for that matter, for all of my informants in the industrial district compound), experiences of work, family, friendship and personhood were inextricably enmeshed. But what the regional economy literature failed to grasp was that this "organic" and "cultural" understanding of the relations of production was repressing, on a massive scale, conflicts and tensions that naturally arise in the sphere of production by confining them to the intimate domains of the family, the household and the self (Ghezzi 2003; Hadjimichalis 2006; Narotzky 2001; Narotzky and Smith 2006).

Anna (45) grew up in the hangar behind the family house, the shop floor of her father's enterprise. She played there with her sisters as a child, until, at age 14, she stopped playing and started using the hangar as a worker. Although she earned a salary, she didn't receive it directly; it was kept aside "for her" by her father until she got married (after which her savings were administered by her husband, who eventually used them without telling her in a desperate attempt to cover the debts of his own business). When she married Marco at the age of 26, Anna left her father's business to become a housewife (like her mother before her) as her first pregnancy had complications which did not allow her to work.

Like his wife, Marco is the eldest child of an entrepreneur; he inherited his father's packaging business not by succession but due to bankruptcy. A common scheme in the district, Marco's parents declared bankruptcy and moved abroad, letting their son start a new enterprise with the old facilities and machinery. Starting the enterprise anew was a common practice among insolvent entrepreneurs since pre-existing debts rest on the official owner of the bankrupted business. The strategy works well as an economic side-stepping trick as it allows the firm to erase its debts and start working again. Socially, however, it is hardly sustainable in the long run, especially in the industrial district kind of arrangement where, as one of the InOltre psychologists put it, "they [insolvent entrepreneurs] never face the fact that the creditors they let down are the same people they will find the next day at the street corner café" (Letizia, Sant'Orso, interview).

When Marco took over his father's business in the mid-1990s, the economic conjuncture remained favorable. Venetian industrial districts were enjoying an unforeseen abundance of capital investments, the flow of business was steady, and the financialization of markets was easing access to credit through mortgages and bank credit for those courageous entrepreneurs willing to expand. Anna did not report any problems following her in-law's foreclosure; in any case, Marco's business was going well. They had their third child and Marco, ever the optimist, opened another (smaller) firm with his friend. However, unbeknownst to Anna, he used their house as collateral to get a loan.

Anna's eyes still glowed when she talked of her husband's "old self" in the early days of his entrepreneurial adventure: "he was a force of nature: ... operating the machines, negotiating with buyers, sellers, always getting the best prices, he would do it all!" When asked where Marco had acquired all these skills, her explanations echoed the naturalizing narratives found in the New Regionalism literature: "We're all entrepreneurs!! The entrepreneurial ability is tied to the cultural evolution in the history of our provinces: you have areas bound to rural cultures of entrepreneurship like Rovigo, other ones [like ours], have a vocation to new forms of entrepreneurship: quick, innovative ... we're like this."[8]

Unfortunately, the entrepreneurial enthusiasm did not last. In 2004, the workflow of their main enterprise was suddenly hit by their largest client ceasing to pay for orders that had already been delivered. In this instance, the client—above Marco in the subcontracting chain—was "institutionally protected" by the state. The Marzano Law of 2003 had been designed to protect large enterprises and their employees from failure and unemployment. Following the requirements of this law, the debts of the failing enterprise were frozen, and a commissioner was named to begin restructuring the firm. The law, which has the merit of saving the numerous jobs in the larger enterprise, overlooks the chain reaction of events for smaller entrepreneurs who depend on the larger firm's payments to keep production going. Without the liquidity made available by the payments of their larger client, small downstream firms cannot pay their own suppliers. This in turn has further dramatic effects: (1) the small firms cannot provide raw materials to fulfil new orders that would keep them afloat, and (2) they will likely trigger a domino effect in the district.[9] When the large firm subcontracting Marco invoked the Marzano law, Anna and Marco realized that the "small is beautiful" motto everyone was touting during the miracle years no longer applied when the drying up of liquidity forced choosing "whom to save."

The last 15 years had been a nightmare. Marco's main enterprise went bankrupt in 2009. This was when Anna discovered that her husband had not only consumed all of her and their savings to repay his debts and to try to avoid foreclosure, but that there was also a mortgage on their house. As with his father before him, Marco's business foreclosed out of indebtedness, and he asked Anna to re-open it under her name. The "friends" they had in local banks now treated them with disdain and refused to give her credit. Kin once again emerged as the cushion to absorb economic stress, with Anna eventually managing to borrow enough from a relative to restart the business. Yet, her life had become impossible. She fought a lot with Marco, while people from the bank called her constantly, up to 20 times a day—"on Friday nights, and at times even on Saturdays"—to remind her that she owes money and that they will seize the house. They even asked her about her grocery shopping and made her feel guilty if she bought meat for her kids. She felt that she was suffocating, that she no longer had a private life.

Anna told me that she and Marco had split up, that they had filed for separation in court but continued to live under the same roof. The bank, believing they did this to avoid the seizure of the house since the mortgage was on Marco's name, hired private inspectors to ascertain their story. Anna was summoned by the court, where she was shown pictures of herself, Marco, her parents and especially her kids, taken from outside the children's schools. Both she and Marco work constantly, trying to make

Anna's firm survive; both have found part-time jobs. The ability to work relentlessly, once a proud trademark of this territory, has now turned into a trap, leaving them no space for life. Paradoxically, the business is not going too badly: there is still demand, but since they have no access to credit, it is impossible to buy material to complete the orders. Marco "is not himself anymore," she says: "he used to be very happy, he was an aggressive, charismatic entrepreneur, had a lot of will to do things, and then you see now he is annihilated, he is nothing now."

Anna claimed that she had been thinking for a while about taking her own life: "you think about it all the time, you think: 'at least I won't have to wake up anymore, at least I won't feel anything, I am tired of feeling.'" It was only an opportune call from her eldest son, Luca, which stopped her from swallowing the pills which would have taken her life. Interpreting Luca's call as a sign, she called InOltre the following day; its staff has been helping her to cope ever since. To this day, Anna, Marco and their three children continue living in their family home, which remains under the threat of seizure. Anna stated that if the bank repossesses the house, she will burn it down with her own hands.

The Small Entrepreneurial Identity

> *If you labor the land properly, you know it will pay you back*
> *time passes slowly, one season after the other, and the land is your life companion*
> *oh farmer in your farmstead, hope is a prayer,*
> *Tradition and technology, with the help of our good Lord*
> *Together with you, with us, Maschio Gaspardo gives strength to your work*
> *Together with you, with us, Maschio Gaspardo, united we are stronger, you know that united we win*
> *To protect your harvests, your strong arms won't be enough, farmer, pull out your hand!*
> *We are your wheat bank*
> *Making agriculture better is our true passion*
> *Tradition and technology, with the help of our good Lord*
> *Together with you, with us, Maschio Gaspardo, in any land of this world*
> *Together with you, with us, Maschio Gaspardo, united we are stronger, you know that united we win.*
>
> —"Maschio Gaspardo's Ode to Joy",
> anthem of the Maschio Gaspardo S.p.A.

I have tried to show through Anna's life history how the (assumed) organic relations between personalized trust networks and business viability ceased to hold once they were no longer sustained by the availability of capital and economic success. I now turn to the structures, dynamics and processes through which the specific field of identification of "the small entrepreneur" was configured in order to make sense of its collapse—as witnessed in Veneto's epidemic of entrepreneurial suicides.

Identity formation is a complex process, grounded in the direct material experience of social relations but also dependent on the non-material processes through which they are condensed—or in psychoanalytic terms, sublimated—into metaphors and symbols (Friedman 1994, 2005). The symbolic configurations that emerge through this process may subsequently be totally or partly instituted in society through collective liturgies, rituals and mythologies (Kertzer 1989). The process is never linear, univocal or unidirectional, but results from a diachronic set of repeated (and often dialectical) interactions (both at the material and symbolic level) between institutionally promoted actions and models on the one hand and grassroots practices, paradigms and interpretations on the other (Narotzky and Smith 2006; Smith and Narotzky 2005). In this sense, models, metaphors and symbols elaborated in everyday life are likely to be absorbed, transformed and condensed into analytical models by experts and intellectuals. As I have tried to show in the previous section, these models can be re-distributed locally and re-appropriated by grassroots actors via scientific literature, media information and (even more effectively) via the various scales of policymaking and funding strategies that structure political economic reality (Lovering 1999). While this may all sound banal, it does help to illustrate how the identity space of "the small entrepreneur" has taken shape within the tensions and contradictions between the diversely situated and dynamically circulating set of actions and representations set in motion by the sudden success of regional economies in the late 1970s.

Take the short text above—the lyrics, advertised online, of the anthem of Maschio Gaspardo's enterprise. Egidio Maschio, founder with his brother Giorgio of this once small enterprise, was one of the many entrepreneurial suicides that shattered the myth of the small Venetian entrepreneur. A few years after the crisis broke out, debts to banks, other enterprises and creditors of various kinds amounting to millions of euros apparently pushed Egidio to commit suicide.[10] The Maschio brothers' trajectory—"from the staple to the economic empire"[11]—represents the typical foundation myth of the "Venetian miracle" and its aura of organic metaphors. Egidio and Giorgio had gathered funds and used the family staple to start a small workshop producing milling machines, which over several decades had grown into a multinational enterprise, a world leader in agricultural machinery with 19 production sites in Italy and around the world.

One only has to search online for the video in order to appreciate the theatricality and the well-coded liturgies with which the anthem was sung: Egidio in his elegant suit, holding the microphone and leading his uniformed workers in song, in front of the table where they would all eat lunch together. One after the other, Egidio brings the mic to his standing employees to sing the enterprise anthem. Quite apart from the fact that an anthem, by definition, is a unifying symbol, the lyrics present a harmony and cohesion that suppresses or suspends the classed, gendered and ethnic diversities of socio-economic life, offering in its stead an overriding symbolic unity of elements that are usually opposed. The proverbially excruciating relationship between the land and its laborers—which Venetians, being former peasants, know only too well—is reconfigured as one of harmonious interaction where the land almost becomes a spouse, a "life companion." Another oppositional dichotomy the anthem rhetorically resolves is that between tradition and technology, with their patent contradiction dissolved "with the help of our good God." The unity, the togetherness, of workers, owner and clients is based on an organic solidarity that is transfigured into a sort of life force that allows everybody to work (hard work inevitably being one of the tenets of the ideology that sustains the small entrepreneurial self in labor-intensive SME economies). Passion, joy, unity, hope and the love of God—such are the affects that nurture "the life" of the firm.

Susana Narotzky notes how some of the categories that emerged in the New Regionalism literature made use of classical social anthropological concepts such as "embeddedness" and "reciprocity" which carried with them notions of organic solidarity as the key element underlying social cohesion. She notes how the label of "Third Italy"—a development model that became a global paradigm for regional economies—evokes historical attempts to institute a "third way" between economic liberalism and communism, generally shaped by the idea of overcoming the conflicts and tensions underlying the structure of social reproduction. Third way experiments, Narotzky (2007: 406) argues, "all aim at maintaining capitalist market-led relations of production while solving 'the social question' that is, the social unrest created by the necessary differentiation those very relations produce." Organicism thus becomes a key metaphorical field representing usually opposed elements of the social structure as different parts, segments or functions of a single mechanism, or rather organism, which operates for its own good—the good of the whole being equated with the good of the parts as well.[12]

Powerful organic metaphors thus structure the representations that seemingly animate the small entrepreneur identity field. These appear to proliferate from within the lived experience of overlapping shop floors and households, kin and labor relations, patriarchy and industrial paternalism. This conflation of usually separate categories is not merely the work of top-down ideologies but is grounded in the actual routines and interactions that structure our interlocutors' everyday lives. Like Anna and Marco, many people I talked to had inherited their father's enterprise and could not separate their memories of playing in the warehouse as kids, or of their love life with a partner that almost always was hired in (or already part of) the enterprise, from the actual economic destiny of the business.

In this way, the enterprise was often naturalized—by extension—as "a family." The firm was often said to be the person's "life," and when the firm is in risk of going under, "you feel like dying." Suffice it to quote this excerpt from the letter Egidio's former employees read at his funeral:

> Your life was the firm, your breath us workers … with your example you've been our model, you made us feel like a family of families, and we always saw in you our point of reference: you knew us all one by one, you loved being there on the shop floor, and you would go visit every office. … Help us realize your dream, because we see ourselves as part of it. Andrea, Mirko [his sons]: we have the same faith in you that we had in your father: just know us workers will always be by your side, to bring along the great project [of our firm]. Good bye Gigi, Good bye boss.[13]

A symbolic configuration that appears to be central to these constructions revolves around the house(hold) in its multi-faceted articulations to the epiphenomenal realities of lived experience. For small investors, the house often becomes the asset from which everything else begins, as it allows one to access credit for one's initial investment. In many cases, the house(hold) is also the site of both production and social reproduction. The house(hold) thus becomes the potent symbolic archetype of unity, the metaphor allowing for the conflation of labor and affective relations, of productive and reproductive work, incorporating webs of complex, unequal and hierarchical, affect-laden relations of production into a grand organic narrative of efficient, dynamic, non-conflictual economic organization.

This synthesis, or rather fusion, and subsequent annihilation of old oppositional dichotomies (labor vs. affective relations, production vs. social reproduction, favors vs. contractually regulated transactions, etc.) appears to reproduce itself at the level of personal identity. But if labor relations and market transactions on the one hand, and friendship, love and community feelings on the other are conflated in the constitution of the entrepreneurial self, the failure of one part inevitably implies the sinking of the other, and for that matter, of the subject as a whole. More specifically, the progressive disintegration of the economic foundations of this identity—the availability of cash, credit and opportunities to expand production—or rather, of the material basis for the possibility of identifying with this identity field, are likely to drag entrepreneurial selves into an unbearable bind. The Venetian entrepreneurs who had managed to constitute themselves as *self-reliant, autonomous* subjects who derived their vital and economic force from their families, acquaintances and communities, only to give it back to them, now found themselves: (1) betrayed by their *dependency* on creditors, court decisions and state regulations, and (2) betray-*ing* precisely the families, acquaintances and communities, unity with whom had become one of the most basic foundations of their personhood as well as its social recognition.

Conclusion

This chapter has sought to make sense of the epidemic of entrepreneurial suicides in Veneto by focusing on the relationships between processes of identity formation and transformation at the grassroots level, the circulation of economic ideologies in the European Union and the larger processes of material transformation related to changes in the global system of accumulation.

Since the mid-1970s, the decline of growth in old industrial centers has channeled capital investments to new regions. For several decades, some medium-sized southern European towns found themselves at the center of the new routes of capital investment in production, mainly in their peri-urban areas. Several factors were at the roots of this geographical shift: the existence of cheap labor, the unlikeliness of social unrest and existing socio-cultural structures that facilitated the development of flexible production, which in turn allowed small firms to quickly respond to the vagaries of increasingly volatile markets.

Sensational claims advanced by experts on the early successes of (some of) these emerging economies were often nurtured by comparing them to the established socio-economic stigmatization of southern European countries (Piore and Sabel 1983, 1984). This effective representational strategy produced a plethora of enthusiastic scholarly models as well as media narratives about the figure of the small entrepreneur, the family enterprise and regional economies—a thaumaturgic solution for the trailing regions of southern Europe. Furthermore, the translation of this enthusiasm at the grassroots level, combined with the expansion of financial markets in the 1990s, fueled the often-disproportionate debt-based expansion of existing businesses.

Through analyzing the ethnographic evidence, I have tried to show how these processes have resulted in the constitution of a field of identifications which revolved around the archetypical figure of the small entrepreneur. This field is characterized by symbols and metaphors (generally of the organic kind) pointing to the reassuring ideas of personal independency, social homogeneity, "natural" solidarity and unity across the divisions of class, gender and race. During the expansion of SME economies, these metaphors, symbols and ideas operated through the active concealment (at least at the etic level) of existing hierarchies, inequalities and established dynamics of exploitation. Yet the 2008 crisis has helped to shed light on how structures of inequality in the subcontracting chain are intensified by uneven risk burdens in the access to credit, the unequal regulation of debt and the exploitative integration of family businesses into vertical and often transnational subcontracting chains (Reinach 2019; Yanagisako 2013, 2018). The underlying inequalities in what were presented as homogenous structures of economic collaboration became most visible when it became clear that the state supported larger firms and multinational contractors while forgetting the smaller players (Vetta and Palomera, 2020 forthcoming).

With the advent of the crisis, what became visible was the displacement of production-related conflicts between capital and labor to the personal sphere that the small entrepreneurial identity had created. The conflicts that finally surfaced have become part of the affective space of intimacy, so powerfully symbolized by the household or—at an even smaller scale—by the person and her body, the site where tensions, conflicts and contradictions between capital and labor, ideology and actual life, the public and the private persona precipitate, at times in the most violent and self-destructive forms.

Notes

1. For Italy, see Bagnasco 1977; for Spain, Costa Campi 1988 and Buruaga 1983; for Portugal, de Oliviera 1983; and for Greece, Hadjimichalis and Vaiou 1990.
2. "Third Italy" is understood to be comprised of the northeastern part of the country: the regions of Emilia Romagna, Friuli, Marche and Veneto.
3. All names in this ethnography are pseudonyms.
4. In this text, I retain the emic use of the world "entrepreneur" in the masculine form, because it represents well both the overwhelmingly male composition of the Venetian business world, and how the former is locally understood and represented as such. It thus helps me to portray yet another aspect of Anna's loneliness and structural fragility.
5. Second was Campania, with 12.6 percent of national suicides, although the dominance of the illegal economy controlled by organized crime likely pushes the figure upwards. The third region, Lombardia, accounts for 9.4 percent of national suicides and has economic structures which are far more comparable to Veneto.
6. Statistical data provided by Link Lab, Rome.
7. In the rest of my ethnographic sample, seven out of the seven firms I researched in Vicenza's industrial districts were family firms, largely relying on the labor of family, kin and friends.
8. If it is true that Third Italy consolidated "a new orthodoxy" (Hadjimichalis 2006: 84) or even a "mythology" (Bianchini 1991; Hadjimichalis and Papamichos 1990) in economics and policy studies, the latter has certainly been diffused and implemented through the institutional embrace of Regionalist ideology (Lovering 1999). On how established economic paradigms become absorbed in grassroots models, narratives and patterns of behavior, see Narotzky 2007; Narotzky and Smith 2006; Smith and Narotzky 2005.
9. Italy's special insolvency regime for protecting large enterprises and their employees—unique in the Euro Zone—has been extensively debated. Prior to the Marzano law were the highly criticized *legge fallimentare* of 1942, followed by the so-called Prodi law (law n. 26 of 1979) and its reformed version known as Prodi bis (law n. 279 of 1999). The Marzano law was implemented in 2003 to address issues raised by the insolvency of the Parmalat group (e.g. Belhocine et al. 2018; Bianca 2001; Danovi 2010; Manganelli 2010; Oppo 1981). The perplexities about which so much ink has been spilt were the same as Anna's: while creditors play a passive role in the insolvency, they are in effect forced to absorb most of the bigger firm's losses.
10. "Siamo Senza Soldi, Sono Disperato." Maschio, l'Ultima Lettera. *Corriere del Veneto*, July 11, 2015.

11. Such was the title of the newspaper article through which I found notice of Maschio's suicide, just a couple of weeks into my fieldwork. *La Stampa*, June 24, 2015.
12. See for example Becattini's postulation of the existence of a "community-like superior interest, which becomes an inner principle for the people of the district *as a whole*" (1992: 39, my italics).
13. *Il Mattino di Padova*, June 27, 2015. http://mattinopadova.gelocal.it/padova/cronaca/2015/06/27/news/funerali-maschio-arrivato-il-feretro-coperto-di-rose-rosse-1.11685263 (last accessed May 2019).

References

Bagnasco, A. 1977. *Tre Italie: La Problematica Territoriale dello Sviluppo Italiano*. Bologna: Il Mulino.

Bagnasco, A. 1981. "Labour Market, Class Structure, and Regional Formations in Italy." *International Journal of Urban and Regional Research* 5(1): 40–44.

Banfield, E.C. 1958. *The Moral Basis of Backward Societies*. Glencoe: Free Press.

Becattini, G. 1992. "The Marshallian District as a Socio-Economic Notion." In F. Pyke, G. Becattini and W. Sengenberger, eds. *Industrial Districts and Inter-Firm Cooperation in Italy*. Geneva: International Institute for Labor Studies.

Belhocine, N., D. Garcia-Macia and J. Garrido. 2018. "The Insolvency Regime for Large Enterprises in Italy: An Economic and Legal Assessment." *IMF Working Paper No. 18/218*.

Bianca, M. 2001. *La Dichiarazione dello Stato di Insolvenza nella Amministrazione Straordinaria delle Grandi Imprese*. Trieste: Università degli Studi di Trieste Pubblicazioni della Facoltà di Giurisprudenza.

Bianchini, F. 1991. "The Third Italy: Model or Myth?" *Ekistiks* 58(350–51): 336–45.

Blim, M. 1990. *Made in Italy. Small Scale Industrialization and Its Consequences*. New York: Praeger.

Cooke, P. 2013. *Reframing Regional Development. Relatedness and Transversality in the Evolving Region*. London: Routledge.

Cooke, P. and A. da Rosa Pires. 1985. "Productive Decentralization in Three European Regions." *Environment and Planning A* 17: 527–54.

Corò, G. 2004. I sistemi produttivi locali dagli anni 90' al 2000. In G.L. Fontana, ed. *L'Industria Vicentina dal Medioevo ad Oggi*. Vicenza: Cleup.

Corò, G., G. Tattara and M. Volpe, eds. 2006. I processi di internazionalizzazione e frammentazione come strategia di riposizionamento competitivo. *Andarsene per continuare a crescere. La delocalizzazione internazionale come strategia competitive*. Rome: Carocci.

Costa Campi, M.T. 1988. "Descentramiento productivo y difusión industrial: el modelo de especialización flexible." *Papeles de Economía Española* 35: 251–76.

Danovi, A. 2010. "Managing Large Corporate Crisis in Italy: An Empirical Survey on Extraordinary Administration." *Journal of Global Strategic Management* 4(2): 61–7.

De Buruaga, G.S. 1983. "Towards A New Regional Policy in Spain." In D. Seers and K. Ostrom, eds. *The Crisis of European Regions*. London: Macmillan.

Duménil, G. and D. Lévy. 2004 [2000]. *Capital Resurgent*. Cambridge: Harvard University Press.
Friedman, J. and C. Chase-Dunn, eds. 2005. *Hegemonic Decline: Present and Past*. Boulder: Paradigm.
Friedman, J. 1994. *Cultural Identity and Global Process*. London: Sage.
Friedman, J. 2005. *La quotidianità del sistema globale*. Milan: Bruno Mondadori.
Fregolent, L., ed. 2014. *Conflitti e Territorio*. Milan: Franco Angeli.
Ghezzi, S. 2003. "Local Discourse and Global Competition: Production Experiences in Family Workshops of the Brianza." *Journal of Urban and Regional Research* 27(4): 781–92.
Hadjimichaelis, C. 1987. *Uneven Development and Regionalism. State, Territory and Class in Southern Europe*. London: Croom Helm.
Hadjimichalis, C. 2006. "The End of Third Italy as We Knew It?" *Antipode* 38(1): 82–106.
Hadjimichalis, C. and R. Hudson. 2004. "Reti, sviluppo regionale, e controllo democratico." *Meridiana* 49: 75–97.
Hadjimichalis, C. and N. Papamichos. 1990. "'Local' development in Southern Europe." *Antipode* 22(3): 181–210.
Hadjimichalis, C. and D. Vaiou. 1990. "Flexible Labour Market and Regional Development in Northern Greece." *International Journal of Urban and Regional Research* 14(1): 1–24.
Kertzer, D. 1989. *Ritual, Politics and Power*. New Haven: Yale University Press.
Lanaro, S. 1984. "Genealogia di un modello." In S., Lanaro, ed. *Storia d'Italia, Le Regioni dall'Unità ad Oggi. Il Veneto*. Turin: Einaudi.
Lironi, S. 2011. *Paesaggio e Consumo di suolo nel Veneto*. Padova: Legambiente Report.
Locke, R.M. 1995. *Remaking the Italian Economy*. Ithaca: Cornell University Press.
Lovering, J. 1999. "Theory, led by Policy: The Inadequacies of the 'New Regionalism' (Illustrated from the Case of Wales)." *International Journal of Urban and Regional Research* 23: 379–90.
Manganelli, P. 2010. "The Evolution of Italian and US Bankruptcy Regimes: A Comparative Analysis." *Journal of Business and Technology Law* 5(2): 237–62.
Messina, P. 2001. *Regolazione Politica dello Sviluppo Locale. Veneto ed Emilia Romagna a Confronto*. Turin: Utet.
Mingione, E. 1981. *Social Conflict and the City*. Oxford: Basil Blackwell.
Mingione, E. 1983. "Informalization, Restructuring, and the Survival Strategies of the Working Class." *International Journal of Urban and Regional Research* 7: 311–39.
Narotzky, S. 2001. "Un nouveau paternalisme industriel? Les liens affectifs dans les rapports de production des réseaux économiques locaux." *Anthropologie et Sociétés* 25(1): 117–40.
Narotzky, S. 2006. "Binding Labor and Capital: Moral Obligations and Forms of Regulations in a Regional Economy." *Etnográfica* 10(2): 2337–54.
Narotzky, S. 2007. "The Project in the Model: Reciprocity, Social Capital, and the Politics of Ethnographic Realism." *Current Anthropology* 48(3): 403–24.
Narotzky, S. 2009. "Regulation and Production in a Globalized World: What Ethnography Brings o Comparison." *Ethnology* 48(3): 175–93.

Narotzky, S. and G. Smith. 2006. *Immediate Struggles, People, Power, and Place in Rural Spain*. Berkeley: University of California Press.

de Oliviera, V. 1983. "Regional Development in Portugal." In D. Seers and K. Öström, eds. *The Crisis of European Regions*. London: Macmillan.

Oppo, G. 1981. "Profilo sistematico della amministrazione straordinaria della grandi imprese in crisi." *Rivista di Diritto Commerciale* 1: 233.

Palomera J. 2014. "How Did Finance Capital Infiltrate the World of the Urban Poor?" *International Journal of Urban and Regional Research* 38(1): 218–35.

Piore, M.J. and C. Sabel. 1983. "Italian Small Businesses Development: Lessons For US Industrial Policy." In J. Zysman and L. Tyson, eds. *American Industry in International Competition. Government Policies and Corporate Strategies*. Ithaca: Cornell University Press.

Piore, M.J. and C. Sabel. 1984. *The Second Industrial Divide*. New York: Basic Books.

Putnam, R. 1993. *Making Democracy Work: Civic Traditions in Modern Italy*. Princeton: Princeton University Press.

Reinach, S. S. 2019. "One Fashion, Two Nations: Italian-Chinese Collaborations." In L. Rofel and S. Yanagisako, eds. *Made in Translation: A Collaborative Ethnography of Italian-Chinese Global Fashion*. Durham: Duke University Press.

Riccamboni, G. 1997. "Ritorno al futuro? La transizione nell'ex subcultura "bianca"." In *Le Elezioni della Transizione*. Turin: Utet.

Ross, A. 2004. "Made in Italy, The Trouble with Craft Capitalism." *Antipode* 36(2): 209–16.

Roverato, G. 1996. *L'Industria nel Veneto, Storia Economica di un "Caso" Regionale*. Padova: Esedra.

Roverato, G. 1997. La crescita di una periferia industriale: il Vicentino nel caso Veneto. In G.L. Fontana, ed. *Le Vie dell'Industrializzazione Europea*. Bologna: Il Mulino.

Roverato, G. 2004. "L'industria Vicentina nel 900." In G.L. Fontana, ed. *L'Industria Vicentina dal Medioevo ad Oggi*. Vicenza: Cleup.

Roverato, G. 2005. *L'industrializzazione Diffusa. Storia dell'Economia Padovana 1923–2003*. Padova: Esedra.

Sabel, C. 1989. "Flexible Specialization and the Re-Emergence of Regional Economies." In P. Hirst and J. Zeitlin, eds. *Reversing Industrial Decline? Industrial Structure and Policy in Britain and Her Competitors*. Oxford: Berg.

Smith, G. and S. Narotzky. 2005. "Movers and Fixers: Historical Forms of Exploitation and the Marketing of a Regional Economy in Spain." In A. Smart and J. Smart, eds. *Petty Capitalists and Globalization: Flexibility, Entrepreneurship and Economic Development*. New York: SUNY Press.

Stella, G. 2000. *Schei. Dal Boom alla Rivolta: il Mitico Nordest*. Milan: Mondadori.

Vallerani, F. and M. Varotto, eds. 2005. *Oltre le Siepi, Geografie Smarrite e Racconti del Disagio in Veneto*. Portogruaro: Nuovadimensione.

Vetta, T. and J. Palomera. 2020 forthcoming. "Concrete Stories: Financialization and Inequalitiy in the Construction Chain." *Antipode* 52(3).

Yanagisako, S. 2002. *Producing Culture and Capital: Family Firms in Italy*. Princeton: Princeton University Press.

Yanagisako, S. 2013. "Transnational Family Capitalism." In S. McKinnon and F. Cannell, eds. *Vital Relations: Modernity and the Persistence of Kinship.* Santa Fe: SAR Press.

Yanagisako, S. 2018. "Reconfiguring Labour Value and the Capital/Labour Relation in Italian Global Fashion." *Journal of the Royal Anthropological Institute* 5: 47–60.

Zanin, G. 1987. *Dalla Bottega alla Fabbrica. La Fenomenologia Industriale nelle Provincie Venete tra 500 e 900.* Verona: Libreria Universitaria Editrice.

10

The Body Politics of Austerity in Portugal and Spain: Women, Dispossession and Agency

Diana Sarkis and Patricia Matos

Introduction

The implementation of austerity measures in the southern European periphery following the 2008 financial crash entailed the infliction of severe bodily injuries, resulting in an escalation of social suffering and the undermining of people's claim-making capabilities and sense of entitlement and dignity. Stuckler and Basu's (2013) work on the "body economic of austerity" reveals a direct causal relationship between the austerity project and growing mortality patterns, the spread of infectious diseases and mental health pathologies across large numbers of the population. Various national and supra-national reports have shown how austerity-led restructuring in social security and welfare, public health, education and employment are linked to increasing levels of food deprivation, health insecurity and work-related accidents.

In our comparative fieldwork in Portugal and Spain between 2015 and 2017,[1] the embodied dimensions of dispossession through austerity, and how they are expressed along the lines of class, gender and generation, figured prominently in how ordinary people experienced, perceived and acted upon the disruption to their life projects and means of livelihood. This was particularly the case among working-class women[2] of different age cohorts, whose life trajectories and working and living conditions we detail in this paper. In Setúbal, Portugal, it was common for working-class women to speak and make sense of austerity as a bodily tension between not doing enough to care, protect and nurture themselves and their household members, and feelings of exhaustion for having gone beyond their physical capacities to ensure the well-being of those around them.

In Vélez-Málaga, Spain, exhaustion and a sense of "being sunk/drowned" (*estar hundida*) were prominent structured feelings among dispossessed class women, who often resorted to embodied metaphors of physical violence, suffering and death to convey their reflexive experiences of austerity-led attacks on their living conditions.

In this chapter, we examine the relationships between the body, gendered dispossession and agency under conditions of austerity. We ask: how is austerity experienced and perceived with and through the body? How do gendered embodied dispositions become livelihood coping strategies within the crisis of social reproduction? How is human agency conditioned (or enabled) by bodily narratives used as models to justify and legitimate needs, claims and entitlements? We examine how concrete physical experiences and social anxieties framed working-class women's explanations of the crisis; the ways in which the body was mobilized as a metaphor to make sense of the disruption to their means of livelihood and reproduction; and how working-class women resorted to embodied practices, knowledge and moralities to provide for their families and to assert their rights, entitlements and aspirations. In this chapter, the body is our main point of entry from which to reflect on broader processes of reproductive crisis, class politics and social change within the current austerity conjuncture. We focus mainly on women's bodily experiences and embodied practices, knowledges and moralities, looking at how women's *bodily worlds* (Sutton 2007, 2010) illuminate the contested and negotiated nature of the austerity economic and political project.[3]

While presented separately, the chapter's two main sections on the Spanish and Portuguese case studies are guided by common themes and axes of analysis, addressing the most prominent forms through which our dispossessed female interlocutors experienced and made sense of the austerity crisis. We focus on how experience and explanation merge with and through the body, represented by concrete physical experiences and embodied metaphors of social anxiety tied to the exhaustion of women's laboring bodies as they grapple with the intensified demands of formal, informal, domestic and caring labor, inter-generational obligations of care, and cuts to the public provisioning of health, education and social security. We emphasize how the extraction of women's embodied resources and knowledges is central to ensuring household survival under conditions of austerity.[4] We also examine how particular bodily narratives (linked to valued models of working-class motherhood, morality and hard work) were mobilized to claim social worth and articulate possibilities for devising alternative future projects. In the conclusion, we argue that under the austerity-led crisis in reproduction, afflicted gendered bodies not only crystallize the violence of structural and institutional power but also signal the resourcefulness of coping dispositions while pointing to the strengths and limits of subaltern class struggles for producing and performing a politics of hope across generations.

Exhaustion, Hope and the Struggle for a Life Worth Living in Vélez-Málaga

In contrast to dominant historical narratives, dispossessed women in Vélez-Málaga have long worked in their own homes and those of others. Life and family histories reveal self-employed women working in small shops and as wage laborers, particularly in day-labor, domestic service, the textile industry and, more recently, in agro-processing and in all kinds of jobs in the public and private service sectors, for example as nurses, teachers and cleaners. The idea that through their hard work and tired, suffering bodies women remain the main pillars of the household was a recurrent theme in our interviews and informal conversations.

Austerity policies have re-actualized these historically embodied sedimentations by overburdening women's (paid and unpaid) work (Benería 2005; Collins and Mayer 2010; Federici 2013; for the Spanish context: Ezquerra 2012; Gálvez and Torres 2009; Pérez Orozco 2012). On the one hand, the growing precariousness of work in the private sector, the cutbacks to public services, the growing tax burden on the self-employed and increasing male unemployment (particularly in the aftermath of the construction crisis) have prolonged and intensified women's working hours. In some cases, women sought *extra income* on top of their jobs, doing handicrafts, transforming agricultural products into petty-commodities, or renting rooms in their own homes (sometimes including meals and cleaning). This privatization and housewifization of social reproduction (Ezquerra 2012; Mies 1986) has become intertwined with a crisis in intergenerational responsibilities for care, with younger generations continuing to depend on their elders (particularly their mothers) and middle-aged women often having to take care of both their elderly parents and grandchildren. As the welfare state retreats, women have also continued to remain primarily responsible for housework and care work.

Physical pain, stress and exhaustion were the everyday outcomes of this space/time compression of work and life. The everyday life of Tania

(Diana Sarkis' landlady)[5] crystallized the silent violence at the basis of the reproduction of working-class households attacked by the austerity regime, even when households are not labeled as "poor or at risk of exclusion." Her testimony underlined the crucial role of gender and generation in the configuration of particular experiences of this class conflict.

When Diana lived with her, Tania (50) had a formal job as a kitchen assistant (although she worked as a cook) at a public primary school in the city of Vélez. She had divorced years ago and now lived with her 18-year-old single son. Since 2010, she rented rooms in her house—from one room in 2010 to three rooms (out of four) in 2016–17, including meals and cleaning—to complement her monthly salary of 1,100 euros to meet her rising living expenses.[6] On top of this, her responsibilities in the school kitchen had grown since 2015 due to cutbacks, with public institutions no longer filling vacant posts following retirements and short, medium or even long-term medical leaves. The following description registered in Diana's field notes illustrates her everyday embodied feelings of overburden, pain and exhaustion:

> As every day from Monday to Friday, Tania arrives at home at five o'clock after nine hours at the school kitchen. She stops at the kitchen where I meet her; looks at me with an explicit grimace of pain, and exclaims, "I am dead tired" (*estoy muerta*). Then she does one household chore after another: puts the Tupperware that she brings from the school in the fridge and arranges some other food brought from the supermarket; starts the washing machine and washing the dishes that her son and the other housemate have stacked since last night. While doing these tasks, she describes the situation at the school kitchen as "killing her little by little": she can no longer stand the back pain and feels that her knee is going to give out at any moment while carrying the extremely heavy pots they use for cooking for three hundred kids! "Three workers cannot work for five! This is something inhuman!" she says. Then she adds: "You see, it [work] never ends. I come here [home] and…" She stops suddenly and asks me if I would like some potato omelet for dinner because she is going to prepare one for her son, the other housemate and herself. I decline the invitation and say, "you have to rest." Tania nods her head and responds that she will sleep for an hour after finishing the kitchen. "I am dead tired," (*estoy muerta*) she repeats, and adds: "I will do Domingo's bedroom afterwards. I am sure that he didn't do it before going to the gym!" (February 2016)

Cutbacks to public services, the devaluation of her real salary which forced her to rent out rooms in her flat, her son's lack of responsibility for his basic maintenance, not to mention taking care of his mother—all materialized in her exhausted and painful body: a detached bladder, a crushed meniscus,[7] back contractions and a racing mind "unable to stop" (*le cuesta pararse*), even when she went to sleep at night. Although in medical terms these problems were traced to the continuous heavy loads she carried, no institution recognized them as occupational illnesses. Tania's physical burden also had moral, emotional and political dimensions. Alongside the heavy school kitchenware and utensils, water jugs and bags full of food for her son and lodgers, she carried the responsibility of feeding 300 school children with fresh meals in a clean kitchen even if there were only three workers instead of five. She carried the responsibility of feeding her son and the rest of the housemates and maintaining the shared 90 square meter apartment. She also carried the entire burden of assuring the well-being of her small (in her terms) family.

To be exhausted or *estar muerta* (to be dead) was a common expression among working-class women to describe their embodied experiences of the austerity-led crisis of social reproduction. This metaphor of bodily devastation encompasses physical exhaustion—in Tania's terms, pushing the body to "inhuman" limits—as well as the psychological and emotional toll of being overburdened by responsibilities. As Jimena (aged around 60) conveyed during a focus group:[8]

> I have suffered the three crises: public health cutbacks killed my husband last year… The crisis of my small business. I have been forced to work in our shop day and night for it to get ahead, but it didn't. And all of this has led me to a deep personal crisis [later she explains that she is trying to overcome depression]. I feel that tiredness. I am sick to death of everything. As you were saying [Diana Sarkis had raised these issues]… I feel very, very tired of carrying everything on my shoulders (*de cargar todo sobre mi espalda*). In the end, I can't manage it all. Because women, we know, we burden ourselves with everything! Now, I also take care of my mother who is 90 years old. What a shame! They have refused [our application for] *la dependencia* [social benefit for caring for people with specific degrees of disability] because of the cutbacks. And me… I… you know, we women have to manage everything. My brothers come to visit her every day, but they don't even give her a pill… I have been absolutely destroyed and sunk (*muy, muy hundida*), only now I start to

recover, to feel that I am not the only person in the world who has these problems and feelings. That it is not my fault or incapacity. We must continue to struggle. It is not only for our children and us, but particularly for our grandchildren.

A new bodily metaphor appeared in Jimena's discourse about her lived experiences of the current crisis of social reproduction: she felt tired of *cargar todo sobre la espalda*. The Spanish expression, not far from the English *carrying the world on one's shoulders*, literally means *carrying everything on one's back*, carrying a burden that brings pain, crushes the back and annihilates the person. The exhausting burden of "managing everything"—as Jimena put it—is well known among women. From their point of view, income, care and housework are part of the same "whole," that of supporting the well-being of their families and keeping the hope for a better future alive, even if it entails the devastation of their bodies and spirits, their drowning. Feminist thought has long dealt with the questions surrounding the construction of the female body as "a body for others" and of how the female self is forced to disappear in the tide of others' needs and desires (Beauvoir 1949; Guillaumin 2007; Izquierdo 1998; Sutton 2007). This loss of the sense of self appears in Jimena's discourse as the impossibility of forming the sentence "And... me... I..." Some women in the field explained that sometimes, particularly at the end of their day, they felt that "my body is not mine, as if I have borrowed it" (*Siento que mi cuerpo no es mío, como si me lo hubieran prestado*). Under the current austerity regime, it involves taking on their individual shoulders the violent accumulated effects of the restructuring of capital's domination over labor—in other words, managing the unmanageable.

Mariana (55) had worked in agriculture until 2011 when her mother and mother-in-law were respectively struck by cancer and dementia and she was forced "to give up everything," "to give up her life" in order to take care of them. It was a hard decision, taken at the crossroads of different dimensions of the austerity-led reproductive crisis at the household level. On the one hand, her decision was forced by her household's meager agricultural income, the lack of other monetary resources and the absence of any public alternative for the care of dependent elders. On the other hand, her relinquishing of agricultural work both in the shared plot managed by her husband and as a day laborer for landowners offered an employment opportunity for her son (37) who used to work in construction, was unemployed, and now returned to his parents' house to start working with his father. When Diana Sarkis met her in June 2015, the two old women Mariana had been caring for had passed away some months ago, while her older daughter (35) had moved back into the parental house after separating from her husband and renting out the marital flat in order to pay the mortgage on her own. Mariana made artisanal detergents and soap from olive oil and manufactured clothes, hand-made bags and other handicrafts to sell to neighbors and acquaintances in order to earn some extra income, necessary to cover her rising living expenses and to compensate for the reduction of her husband's working hours. In 2015, the landowners for whom he worked, arguing that "they were in crisis," reduced his hours to three days a week, although as a self-employed farmer he still had to pay his own social contributions.

Mariana's everyday discourse and life story interviews emphasized feelings of bodily damage, self-estrangement, anxiety and depression—feelings which she explicitly associated with the urgency of caring for others under the austerity regime:

> I have been imprisoned at home for more than three years, without even going out to visit neighbors… You know the state is cutting back, not giving new social benefits [*ayudas*]… The last times at the [public] Vélez hospital were horrendous! It's like you have one doctor for everything instead of three… I have developed anxiety and depression. He [her son] is fine, here with us, but it is not easy. He has developed a difficult character… To work and live with his father is not easy… particularly for me! And I feel awful [with this situation]… Such are the lives of women. From children to parents to grandchildren. To care for someone is the question. Now, with my daughter here it is also hard. She is also depressed… the worst is this anxiety. The anxiety for their [her children's] future. As my husband says: "The rich want to see the poor sink more and more" [*los ricos quieren ver a los pobres cada vez más hundíos*]. (August 2015, Almayate)

Working-class women's bodies are at the core of this "politics of drowning,"[9] not only as suffering subjects but as resisting and struggling agents. Their bodies are the primary instruments of the everyday politics of work and care that support their reproduction and that of their loved ones, despite and against the current and historical class-based politics of devaluation and domination:

Mariana: My life? Work. My life has been very hard. I was very, very poor. Without electricity, or tap water, I used to wash clothes by hand, working in day-labor [a jornal]... and with three children playing around me. My daughter makes fun of me and calls me *cateta* [backwards-rural-informally educated woman]! She wants me to do my hair and take care of my body. She says that I am only 54, and look 70 years old. But work is unforgiving! I take it very well, given the burden I have to carry! Thank God I have gotten ahead with my house and my family. How I have struggled. I know how to live with little; I have never had holidays in 54 years. How many buckets of water I have carried in order to maintain the house! My one-room house was always cleaner than the Falcon Crest [a CBS soap of a rich San Francisco family popular in Spain in the 1980s] villa of the landowners... They don't even let us breathe. Working? No, they don't do anything, but the old man (*el viejo*, the landowner) came to the land only to control us, to put pressure and to ensure that we worked like mules. They have their Falcon Crest mansion, but they don't want us to live with dignity. They want more and more... and they don't understand that agriculture is not stable... They see you drown and want you to drown more and more in order for them to live better (August 2015, Marcela, 79, retired agricultural day-worker/share-cropper, accompanied us during the interview).

Damaged dark skin, particularly hands, are bodily marks of exploitation, but also of women's power to ensure the worthy living of their households through hard work. They also signal their class pride and self-valuation, in stark contrast to the lazy and incapable bodies of the rich. In Vélez-Málaga, the *apañá* and the *escapá* are the gendered feminine versions of the *good* person within the working-class moral economy of hard work, honesty and modesty. Both concepts stress the working bodies of women as key sources of familial-collective well-being, valorizing their skills and capacity to work and connecting them to other valued, embodied dispositions such as always being ready (*estar dispuesta*) to help and collaborate with others, having a modest attitude (*no se le caen los anillos*) and being able to ensure a modicum of good living for their households under constricted conditions. In contrast to the attitude of some young adults (e.g. Mariana's daughter), other women and men commended the historical value of, in their terms, "poor or modest people"—their creative power to give birth, to struggle as mothers, and to work and care for others. Nevertheless, very few consciously rejected the individualized forms of responsibility and struggle that reinforce capital's exploitation of overburdened working-class bodies.

This individual power to "get by" (*apañárselas*), despite the structural crisis of social reproduction, crystallizes the strength and limits of working-class women's current forms of agency. In the absence of prospects for a collective struggle that would reshape their particular fight for a worthy livelihood and a better future into a general framework for social transformation, the power of these women for *tirar pa alante* (pulling ahead or getting by) collapses in their physically, emotionally and morally exhausted bodies. Individualized forms of responsibility and struggle are hard-pressed to build a politics of hope across generations other than by the reproduction of volatile and precarious forms of coping sustained by the continuous transfer of work and resources (from past work) from older to younger generations.

Bodies of and against Austerity in Setúbal

It was primarily through their bodies that working-class women in Setúbal experienced and made sense of the changes brought by austerity in Portugal following the 2011–14 IMF-sponsored structural adjustment program.[10] In contrast to middle or upper-class women, working-class women had no property, no accumulated wealth, no retirement funds or prospects for acquiring a family inheritance. For most of the working-class women Patricia Matos talked to during fieldwork, their body was the first and last instrument and resource for mediating, confronting and coping with the violence inflicted by austerity. Most prominently, they reported experiencing intensified feelings of physical vulnerability, a constant fear for one's integrity and that of their loved ones linked to food insecurity, reduced income, the lack of jobs and social protection; the exhaustion of their laboring bodies due to the intensified burdens of formal, informal, domestic and care work; the somatization of their inability to access adequate healthcare or to counter the spread of diseases, physical stress, mental disorders and the embodiment of pain in others; and feelings of being socially devalued and unworthy due to their inability to meet normative expectations of female public self-presentation, given their lack of money to visit the hairdresser and to buy cosmetics and new clothes. Maria's experiences illustrate all of these dimensions.

Maria (53) was born in the district of Setúbal and had split her childhood and teenage years between the north and south of Portugal, living respectively with her mother or father, who had separated before she was born. She returned to Setúbal in 1985 with her then-husband and two daughters (at the time aged 5 and 1). Since the 1960s, Setúbal had been the destination for many agricultural landless workers hoping to build a better life for themselves and the next generation; this was also Maria's hope. But her arrival in Setúbal coincided with a severe economic and social crisis fueled by de-industrialization, entailing mass lay-offs in car assembly factories, electronics factories and metallurgic workshops. During the 1980s, Setúbal was portrayed in the national media as the "district of hunger."

From the mid-1990s until 2008, Maria worked in a furniture and decoration shop in the city center and was able to buy a refurbished three-bedroom flat in a lower-middle-class neighborhood in the city center with a bank mortgage. She had separated from her first husband and was the primary provider of the household and her daughters' education. In mid-2008, Maria's employers informed her that due to problems of liquidity, they would need to temporarily place her in a part-time position, which lasted for more than one year. After this period, she was fired. "I found myself with an unemployment subsidy of 230 euros, and I had to put my hand forward and beg."

After missing the payment on three monthly instalments, Maria went to the bank to renegotiate the terms of her mortgage: "I had to decide what was more important, to have food on the table or to keep paying the loan. It is very painful to go to bed knowing that you do not have food to give to your children the next day." Maria went to the bank twice. The first time she waited for more than an hour to be received by her account manager, who finally sent a message informing her that the meeting was postponed. The second time, Maria was more careful with her appearance and clothing. She was immediately received and was able to renegotiate her mortgage. In 2009, through a personal connection, Maria started working as a care-provider in the private household of a retired old lady, combining this (informally) earned income with unemployment benefits. But earning very little, Maria had, for the first time, to ask for food in one of the local branches of the *Banco Alimentar* (national food bank), coordinated by *Caritas*.[11] She felt humiliated; her movements and behaviors were under constant surveillance, with social security public servants and *Caritas* technicians regularly coming to her house to assess her level of poverty and destitution. Maria described how she "lost face" when the social security services obliged her daughters to be present at an interview for the alleged goal of corroborating their mother's lack of work and income. Failure to attend the interview would result in losing access to *Banco Alimentar*.

Maria remained unemployed until 2012 and was only able to make ends meet with the help of neighbors and friends. Through a personal connection, Maria got a (formal) job post in the refectory of a charity organization, working from 7 am to 3 pm preparing vegetables, cooking and cleaning. She then continued working (informally) as a domestic private cleaner and care-provider, from 4 pm to 8 pm. She spoke extensively about her feelings of physical exhaustion and emotional strain: "I leave the house when it is still night and return home at night again." In the refectory, work was always done standing, cutting vegetables for long hours, carrying heavy industrial pots and pans, and using industrial detergents that were particularly damaging to the skin. She showed Patricia her hands and arms when narrating her refectory work, including a burn mark on one of her hands. She added: "it is tough, and then you arrive at the end of the month and receive less than 500 euros after paying taxes and social security contributions."

Maria noticed the limits of her bodily capacities when she began having difficulties sleeping at night, a somatization of her constant stress which would express itself in agitation, tiredness, tremors and a perpetual irritability towards others, including her daughters. Her doctor told her she was displaying symptoms of depression and should be medicated in order to cope with the demands of everyday life. Maria tried to follow this course of medication but found herself with no energy and decided to stop, "also because it was an extra expense which I could not take on." Maria would often remember the days when she had a stable job and enough income to go on holidays, to see other countries and take photographs. She would show Patricia pictures of herself, her partners and daughters, remarking that travelling made her feel good and gave her a "happier face." She would note how she had looked different in the past. But now her skin was ageing, and her hair was not dyed; she could not remember the last time she had visited the hairdresser, bought some skin cream for herself, gone shopping for a new blouse, or gone for dinner with friends in a restaurant. Maria would emphasize how difficult it was to perform for others in public, with a "knot in the stomach" from having to invent excuses for not participating in shared outside activities that involved spending money.

In 2015, the majority of Patricia Matos' working-class female interlocutors in Setúbal, aged between their mid-30s and mid-60s, were formally or informally employed in similar types of work, often involving cleaning, cooking, serving or caring for others. Most had not always worked in such jobs. Some had been former factory workers or had their own small businesses; others had been clerical workers in the public or private sectors. Following the austerity adjustment program, many of these women lost their jobs, including permanent posts, and had to struggle to maintain their households without regular access to the job market, often with the additional pressure of their husbands or partners being unemployed. The impact of austerity policies on the labor market and social protection turned back the clock on women's entry into many sectors of the economy, consigning many working-class women to jobs associated with naturalized and devalued feminine skills such as cleaning, cooking, serving and caring. While the austerity regime did not equally impact women belonging to different class strata, for most working-class women in Setúbal of different generations and age cohorts, the body that works, nurtures, cleans and cares became the main instrument and site for survival and struggle. They were thus increasingly subjected to the contradiction between reverting to the historically and culturally constituted female body that sacrifices itself for others, and the body that acts, does, claims and demands entitlements and moral worth.

Women recurrently expressed this contradiction as a bodily tension between not doing enough to care, protect and nurture themselves and their household members, and feelings of exhaustion for having gone beyond their physical capacities to ensure the well-being of those around them. This tension between wanting to do more and doing more than what is humanly possible mirrors Marion Young's (1990) analysis of the central contradictions pervading feminine bodily existence, in particular that between aim and enactment, between the body that acts with the purpose "I can" which is confronted with the structural constraints of "I cannot." Young's understanding of feminine bodily existence is rooted in the idea of women's "inhibited intentionality"—an intentionality constrained by broader structures pertaining to the history, context and culture in which their bodies are simultaneously experienced as things and as capacity.

In the austerity-led crisis of reproduction, the bodies of working-class women in Setúbal were increasingly subject to various forms of extraction, expressed, for instance, in the intensification of dislocations in the public sphere resulting from women's bodily investments in the production, allocation and distribution of livelihood resources. The public and private intensification of the extraction of the energy, capacities and creative resources of women's bodies intensified feelings of constraint and the lack of freedom associated with the embodiment of "I can" and "I cannot." At the same time, women's bodies provided a privileged site from which to articulate demands, with working-class women responding to the intensified extraction of their embodied resources by articulating claims and entitlements grounded in the values and moralities underpinning their bodily activities across the realms of motherhood, work and class. Julia and Teresa's stories below illustrate this double argument of bodies of and against austerity.

When Patricia met her in 2015, Julia was in her mid-40s and married. Her 24-year-old son and only child was studying at the university. Until 2008, Julia had a small business sewing and painting various kinds of fabrics, which she had to close; it left her with a debt to the bank that she and her husband are still paying today. When Julia's husband became unemployed, he moved to Scotland to work in a frozen fish factory. Julia began working as a cleaner in a private home in the mornings and in a commercial office in the afternoons. To afford her accumulated debt payments (including the mortgage) and her household's everyday living costs, Julia continued sewing and cooking sweets and salty pastries to sell. Her day began early. She was up at 6 am, doing the laundry and planning the meals for the day or week before leaving the house. Her morning job began at 9 am, in the house of her first employer, a local public servant living with her husband and parents. Julia had to vacuum, iron, clean the bathrooms, and tend to the garden and the dogs. She often told Patricia that she felt under surveillance by her boss' parents, who were constantly checking whether she had taken an apple or eaten a chocolate bar. She did not understand how people who had so much had so little generosity towards others. She said she would clean the floor and people would walk on it without being aware of her work, "as if I don't exist."

Julia was diagnosed with lupus[12] many years ago; her lack of money contributed to inconsistent medical follow-up and treatment. She would sadly remark that before the disease she was an entirely different person; now, she was physically exhausted by lunchtime. Nevertheless, during her lunch hours she had to go to the bank to deposit the mortgage payment, pay the utility bills, visit the various "one euro shops" in the city center comparing the prices of fabrics and sewing materials, and deliver her sewing work to people's homes and collect the payment. In between places, Julia would sometimes run into one of her husband's friends, a neighbor, a member of the extended family, or a friend of her son's. Such encounters were moments of exchanging small talk and information about daily discounts in the supermarkets, news of someone about to give birth who might become a potential client or a factory in the region hiring people, or arranging for a baby's initials to be sewn onto a set of bed linen. This exchange of information during lunch hour was a necessary part of Julia's privatized livelihood. She had to play the part, talking, socializing and calibrating her bodily performances depending on who she encountered, all in an effort to secure access to resources to meet her needs and those of her household. After lunch, Julia went to her second cleaning job in the tourist office where she could work alone. Returning home always involved waiting at the bus stop with female neighbors, some of them coming from the supermarket or the fish market. Their conversations were often about their exhaustion accumulated during the day, or the things left to do before arriving home. This could be picking up grandsons at the school, getting bread for dinner, or picking up vegetables or fish from a neighbor working at the fish market.

Julia's story shows how the energies, capacities and corporeal resources of working-class women were essential to ensuring the survival of many working-class households in Setúbal. Working-class women combined various forms of formal and informal money-earning activities, working at home and engaging in neighborhood networks of mutual help and solidarity. Their hard work was particularly visible in public spaces such as supermarkets, public transportation and gardens, and welfare, utility and post offices where the transfer of resources from the public to the private spheres takes place. As Julia once remarked while explaining the value of her work at home "it was this little work of mine which many times saved the day."

Working-class woman in Setúbal also mobilized particular bodily narratives to underline the moral and social legitimacy of making specific claims, demanding entitlements and securing the satisfaction of their needs, thereby contributing to broader processes of social change. Teresa (in her early 40s) lived with her partner and her 19-year-old son. She had been working for the past 15 years on the assembly line of an electronics factory. In this, Teresa had followed in the footsteps of her parents. Her father had been a factory worker in a reputed car assembly factory; her mother had worked in a cannery. Teresa had grown up hearing her father talk about politics and his membership in the Portuguese Communist Party (PCP), and her mother's involvement in various strikes and demonstrations to demand better working conditions. Teresa was a member of the PCP and had joined her sector's union five years ago; she was recently elected to its decision-making body. Despite visible middle-class aspirations in her clothing and in her choices for entertainment, Teresa often mobilized her working-class background and its ethic of hard physical labor as a way to emphasize, in contrast to white-collar workers, the value of "doing something with her hands."

Teresa proudly recounted her mother's demanding physical labor in the cannery, standing for more than twelve hours a day, waking up in the middle of the night to go to work when she heard the sound of boats arriving in the port, and walking many kilometers each day from home to the factory and back again. Teresa often remarked that working in the assembly line meant "the work rhythm was dictated by the machine." Her narrative of her working-class background and her work experience was a way to criticize the social devaluation of manual labor and claim dignity and worth for the female bodies in the assembly line, a way to reclaim for herself the value of physical endurance, strength and resistance.

Most working-class women in Setúbal responded to the social inequalities intensified by austerity by emphasizing the value and morality of the embodied experiences of motherhood, class and hard work. When working-class women remarked ironically that the local female mayor "always looked like she came right from the hairdresser," they were implicitly articulating a class critique and claiming for themselves a value and worth beyond superficial appearances. To varying degrees, working-class women compared the degradation and injuries to their bodily looks with the superior moral value of how they cared for their loved ones, their hard embodied work in doing so, and the honesty and generosity with which they treated strangers, neighbors and friends. Julia, mentioned earlier in this section, could not understand why the parents of her "morning boss" could not even share a piece of fruit with her, remarking that one should be generous with others "because we harvest what we plant."

Conclusion

This chapter has addressed the most prominent embodied experiences of austerity among working-class women in two particular locations—part of a topography of dispossessed, gendered and generationally differentiated historical experiences (Katz 2001). In Setúbal and Vélez-Málaga, austerity policies and their ongoing effects have reinforced bodily feelings of exhaustion, insecurity, vulnerability, anxiety, exploitation and dispossession. These structured feelings are simultaneously the embodied products and the agents of an economic configuration where ubiquitous paid and unpaid, domestic and non-domestic work expresses the subaltern struggle for a *life worth living* (Narotzky and Besnier 2014). Individuals, and particularly *women as mothers*, were burdened with the entire responsibility of creating social well-being. We have shown how our interlocutors became increasingly subjected to the extraction of their energies, capacities and corporeal resources as a way to enable the *worth* and survival of their households.

The similarity of female embodied dispossession in Portugal and Spain—in contexts with contrasting economic structures, the former industrial and the latter agricultural—suggests that the economic and political project of austerity tends towards the production of converging forms of gendered exploitation. We argue that this happens due to the role played by historical legacies of classed and gendered dispossession in the making of austerity regimes. Portugal and Spain are countries historically shaped by a family welfare model, unequal gendered patterns of domestic labor, and the devaluation of feminized skills within and beyond the household. These historical patterns have returned in the austerity conjuncture, leading critics to speak of the "re-familiarization of care" (Ferreira and Monteiro 2015) and the "re-housewifization of social reproduction" (Ezquerra 2012).

Nevertheless, working-class women's bodies have become privileged instruments and sites of struggle within the austerity-led attack on livelihoods and means of reproduction, with their exhausted bodies expressing the politics of capital's hegemony over labor as well as the reproductive and moral struggles of dispossessed people (Harvey 1998). As feminist economist Pérez Orozco (2012) notes, households—not isolated individuals—are the primary sites of the structural adjustment of capital/labor relations, producing gendered and generationally differentiated consequences for working-class people. On the one hand, austerity policies dismantling the welfare state, the lack of formal jobs and the crisis in male-centered sectors (e.g. construction) have fueled women's overwork and reinforced their historical, embodied social roles as the primary agents responsible for the reproduction and care of the household and its members. On the other hand, under the privatization of social reproduction, women's struggles for a *worthy* present and a better future are materially (as well as ideologically) ever more dependent on their capacity to *do their best* under harsh social conditions. The growing dispossession of working-class people from their means of livelihood and well-being, the deterioration of their bodies, and the devastation of their livelihood expectations and hopes converges in women's bodies as they struggle to produce the conditions for worthy living in the face of powerful structural and institutional barriers.

Until the 1970s, the body was primarily viewed as a natural entity, dominated by unruly and irrational passions and desires. Women's reproductive roles and functions linked them to the "natural" realm of existence and were used to justify their confinement to the private sphere of the household and their exclusion as citizens from the public sphere (Coole 2013). Feminist scholars played key roles in re-introducing the material and physical dimensions of the body into discussions about gender-laden structures of power, hegemony and inequality, and possibilities for resistance, agency and social change. In the early 1980s, Fernández-Kelly's (1983) study of the *maquiladoras* (assembly plants) on the Mexican-US border highlighted the link between the exploitation and devaluation of women's embodied resources in the factory and in the household within a culturally-bound idiom that considered female wage labor as supplementary to family income—a cultural and social stereotype which women draw on in their efforts to make ends meet. In the mid-1980s, Emily Martin (1987) examined how biomedical metaphors of female biological reproduction in the US were underpinned by a notion of the female body as a machine, which intensified women's feelings of bodily alienation. In the same year, Ong (1987) addressed how industrial discipline and capitalist proletarianization were simultaneously internalized and contested by young female factory workers in Malaysia through recurrent spirit possessions on the shop-floor, an embodied idiom of protest and accommodation. More recently, Han's (2012) study of socially, economically, morally and personally indebted existence in neoliberal Chile has revealed the contiguity between bodies, economic forms and precariousness in the context of people's caring strategies and struggles to mitigate everyday violence and achieve a dignified life through distinct relational modes along the lines of kin, friends and neighbors.

While this literature shows the relevance of attending to the contradictory potentials of the body—as both a marker of subordination and resistance—the female body as a site of agency and political struggle is still a source of controversy and debate among feminist scholars. This is partly because, as Fraser (1992: 17) notes:

we have often opted for theories that emphasise the constraining power of gender structures and norms while downplaying the resisting capacities of individuals and groups. On the other hand, feminists have also sought to inspire women's activism by recovering lost or socially invisible traditions of resistance in the past and present. The net result of these conflicting tendencies is the following dilemma: *either* we limit the structural constraints of gender so well that we deny women any agency *or* we portray women's agency so glowingly that the power of subordination evaporates. Either way, what we often seem to lack is a coherent, integrated, balanced conception of agency, a conception that can *accommodate both the power of social constraints and the capacity to act situatedly against them* [our emphasis].

Our broader aim in this chapter has been to contribute to a "more coherent, integrated, balanced conception of agency" by highlighting the relevance of attending to embodied forms of agency and political engagement under conditions of austerity. We argue that embodied forms of agency capture the mutual constitution of impersonal structures and experience, oppression and resistance, livelihood projects of being and becoming. In our comparative fieldwork, the visible intensification of forces targeting the extraction of women's bodily resources and knowledge paralleled women's bodily deployment of particular practices and moralities through which they claimed value and self-worth. Working-class women in Setúbal and Vélez-Málaga articulated critiques of social and material inequality with and through their bodies—bodily critiques that entailed class resentment but also class pride. Although aware that theirs were bodies of necessity, work and care, women in many mundane encounters and situations mobilized their bodies to claim social recognition, value and worth—for themselves and for those around them. Dispossessed women in both locations emphasized the moral value of sacrificing themselves for the household, the qualities of generosity, mutual help and modesty, as well as the value of doing (in opposition to speaking about) and producing well-being for others, both inside and outside the home.

We suggest that in conditions of reproductive crisis, working-class women's self-valuation of socially devalued feminized skills is not only a way to reproduce a subordinated bodily *hexis* (Bourdieu 2000).[13] It is also, and perhaps more importantly, an expression of how embodied dispositions configure a form of agency which aims to intervene and shape livelihood conditions for oneself and for the household, the material space through and within which the next generation is reproduced. In both of our field sites, the embodied livelihood pursuits of dispossessed women were shaped by their immediate needs and projects for an alternative future, as well as by the dynamics of kinship, generation and class. Bodies that comply are also bodies that demand, torn between anticipation and expectation, of and against austerity. This remains the case even when the absence of clear horizons for collective resistance in support of a radically different future society limits the possibilities to reshape their particular fights into a general framework of social transformation.

Notes

1. Matos' fieldwork was undertaken in Setúbal, a mid-sized post-industrial city 50km south of the Portuguese capital. A national symbol of the rise and decline of heavy industry, Setúbal has experienced recurrent cycles of prosperity and crisis in the twentieth and twenty-first centuries. Sarkis' fieldwork was in two localities of the municipality of Vélez-Málaga in Andalusia, Spain: Vélez-Málaga and Almayate. Agriculture was traditionally prominent in the household economies of Vélez-Málaga; since the 1990s, the area has also witnessed booms in construction and tourism. With one of the highest rates of unemployment in the country (30 percent), it is the main center of the agro-export industry of subtropical crops in Europe.
2. We use the concepts of working and dispossessed class interchangeably. We understand wage workers as a dispossessed group of people forced to enter into exploitative relations with capital in order to make a living. At the same time, we also consider that for many millions of people, the hegemony of capital simply devastates their livelihood possibilities (Marx 2007 [1867], particularly chapter IV; Narotzky 2004; Federici 2013).
3. We understand the austerity project as a set of economic policies, broadly grounded on measures of internal devaluation to tackle government debt (Blyth 2013), and as a political framework to reshape capital/labor relations through the rescaling of the welfare state and the unmaking of social reproduction expectations, entitlements and claims (Bear 2015; Knight 2015; Knight and Stewart 2016). It follows the structural adjustment policies applied in many countries in Latin America, Asia and Africa since the 1980s (Hadjimichallis and Hudson 2014).
4. Feminist scholarship shows that women very often bear the human and social costs of structural adjustment (e.g. Benería 2005; Benería and Feldman 1992; Sparr 1994).
5. Diana Sarkis lived with Tania in her mortgaged flat in the Barrio Nuevo de Vélez while conducting fieldwork between September 2015 and July 2016.
6. According to the ILO (OXFAM 2016), real salaries in Spain dropped by 25 percent between 2007 and 2015. Among the rising expenses eating into household budgets during my fieldwork were monthly mortgage payments

and property taxes, bills for electricity and other essential supplies, food, medicines, indirect and direct taxation and social security contributions.
7. The *meniscus* is a piece of cartilage in the knee that cushions and stabilizes the joint.
8. This focus group on the grassroots meanings and lived experiences of austerity took place at the headquarters of the Social and Community Services of Vélez-Málaga in May 2016.
9. See Sarkis and Amarianakis in this volume.
10. Following the 2008 financial crisis, Portugal signed a four-year structural adjustment agreement with the Troika (the IMF, the European Central Bank and the EU) in May 2011, resulting in a 78,000,000,000 euro bailout on the condition of severe cuts to state spending. Under a right-wing coalition government, it was implemented through harsh tax increases, spending cuts, and the reduction of welfare benefits. Like other countries on the indebted periphery of the Eurozone, Portuguese policies of austerity centered on measures of internal devaluation including wage repression, precarious employment, labor devaluation and mass unemployment.
11. *Caritas* is a confederation of Catholic relief, development and social service organizations operating worldwide.
12. Lupus is an autoimmune disease in which the body's immune system attacks healthy tissue in various parts of the body. Symptoms may include painful and swollen joints, fever, tiredness and red rashes.
13. The notion of bodily *hexis* derives from Bourdieu's notion of *habitus*, which may be defined as the set of structured, incorporated dispositions through which social agents apprehend, understand and act upon the world. The habitus makes the "world endowed with sense and value, in which it is worth investing one's energy" (Bourdieu and Wacquant 1992: 127–8). Although the notion of habitus proved useful in reinserting the body into discussions of power and inequality following the discursive turn, it has also been mobilized as a way to justify perennial exclusions and subordinations grounded on incorporated and non-reflexive bodily habits, orientations and dispositions (Alcoff 2006).

References

Alcoff, L. 2006. *Visible Bodies, Race, Gender, and the Self*. London: Oxford University Press.
Bear, L. 2015. *Navigating Austerity: Currents of Debt along a South Asian River*. Stanford: Stanford University Press.
Beauvoir, S. 1949. *Le Deuxième Sexe*. Paris: Gallimard.
Benería, L. 2005. "Paid/Unpaid Work and the Globalization of Reproduction." *International Working Group on Gender, Macroeconomics and International Economics. IWG-GEM Working Paper*.
Benería, L. and S. Feldman, eds. 1992. *Unequal Burden: Economic Crisis, Persistent Poverty, and Women's Work*. Boulder, NC: Westview.

Blyth, M. 2013. *Austerity: The History of a Dangerous Idea*. Oxford: Oxford University Press.

Bourdieu, P. 2000. *Pascalian Meditations*. Stanford: Stanford University Press.

Bourdieu, P. and L. Wacquant. 1992. *An Invitation to Reflexive Sociology*. Cambridge: Polity Press.

Collins, J. and V. Meyer. 2010. *Both Hands Tied: Welfare Reform and the Race to the Bottom of the Low-Wage Labour Market*. Chicago: University of Chicago Press.

Coole, D. 2013. "The Body and Politics." In G. Waylen, K. Celis, J. Kantola and L.S. Weldon, eds. *The Oxford Handbook of Gender and Politics*. New York: Oxford University Press.

Ezquerra, S. 2012. "Acumulación por desposesión, Género y Crisis en el Estado Español." *Revista de Economía Crítica* 14: 124–47.

Federici, S. 2013. *Revolución en punto cero. Trabajo doméstico, reproducción y luchas feministas*. Madrid: Traficantes de sueños.

Fernández-Kelly, P. 1983. *For We Are Sold, I and My People: Women and Industry in Mexico's Frontier*. New York: SUNY Press.

Ferreira, V. and R. Monteiro. 2015. "Austeridade, emprego e regime de bem-estar em Portugal: em processo de refamilização?" *Ex Aequo—Revista da Associação Portuguesa de Estudos sobre as Mulheres* 32: 49–67.

Fraser, N. 1992. "Introduction." In N. Fraser and S.L. Bartky, eds. *Revaluing French Feminism: Critical Essays on Difference, Agency and Culture*. Bloomington, IN: Indiana University Press.

Gálvez, L. and J. Torres. 2009. "La crisis económica y sus alternativas: una perspectiva de género." In L. Galvéz et al. *Feminismo ante la crisis*. Madrid: Fórum de Política Feminista.

Guillaumin, C. 2007 [1990]. *Sexe, race et pratique du pouvoir. L'idée de nature*. Paris: Coté Femmes & Indigo.

Hadjjimichallis, C. and R. Hudson. 2014. "Contemporary Crisis Across Europe and the Crisis of Regional Development Theories." *Regional Studies* 48(1): 208–18.

Han, C. 2012. *Life in Debt: Times of Care and Violence in Neoliberal Chile*. Berkeley, CA: University of California Press.

Harvey, D. 1998. "The Body as an Accumulation Strategy." *Environment and Planning D: Society and Space* 16: 401–21.

Izquierdo, M.J. 1998. *El malestar en la desigualdad*. Madrid: Cátedra.

Katz, C. 2001. "On the Grounds of Globalization: A Topography for Feminist Political Engagement." *Signs: Journal of Women in Culture and Society* 26(4): 1213–34.

Knight, D. 2015. *History, Time, and Economic Crisis in Central Greece*. London: Palgrave Macmillan.

Knight, D. and C. Stewart. 2016. "Ethnographies of Austerity: Temporality, Crisis, and Affect in Southern Europe." *History and Anthropology* 27(1): 1–18.

Martin, E. 1987. *The Women in the Body: A Cultural Analysis of Reproduction*. Boston: Beacon Press.

Marx, K. 2007 [1867]. *El Capital. Libro I. Tomo I-III*. Madrid: Akal.

Mies, M. 1986. *Patriarchy and Accumulation on a World Scale*. London: Zed Books.

Narotzky, S. 2004. *Antropología económica. Nuevas tendencias*. Barcelona: Melusina.

Narotzky, S. and N. Besnier. 2014. "Crisis, Value and Hope: Rethinking the Economy: An Introduction to Supplement 9." *Current Anthropology* 55(59): S4–S16.

Ong, A. 1987. *Spirits of Resistance and Capitalist Discipline: Factory Women in Malaysia*. New York: SUNY Press.

OXFAM. 2016. *Bajan los salarios, crece la desigualdad. Informe de Oxfam-Intermón.* https://oxfamintermon.s3.amazonaws.com/sites/default/files/documentos/files/bajan-salarios-crece-desigualdad.pdf. 05/2019 (last accessed April 2019).

Pérez Orozco, A. 2012 "Crisis multidimensional y sostenibilidad de la vida." *Investigaciones Feministas* 1: 29–53.

Sparr, P., ed. 1994. *Mortgaging Women's Lives: Feminist Critiques of Structural Adjustment*. Chicago: University of Chicago Press.

Stuckler, D. and S. Basu. 2013. *The Body Economic: Why Austerity Kills*. New York: Basic Books.

Sutton, B. 2007. "Poner el cuerpo: Women's Embodiment and Political Resistance in Argentina." *Latin American Politics & Society* 46(3): 129–62.

Sutton, B. 2010. *Bodies in Crisis: Culture, Violence and Women's Resistance in Neoliberal Argentina*. New Brunswick: Rutgers University Press.

Young, M. 1990. *On Female Body Experience: "Throwing Like a Girl" and Other Essays*. Oxford: Oxford University Press.

11

Austerity from Below: Class, Temporality and Scale in Grassroots Analyses of Crisis

Diana Sarkis and Stamatis Amarianakis

Introduction

Since the beginning of the so-called financial crisis in 2008, mainstream economists, politicians, journalists and other "experts" from across Europe have employed organic and corporatist images of southern Europe in crisis. Three core ideas shape this discourse. First, the crisis is a (class-blind) state of disruption that affects the entire social body. Second, national entities share responsibility for forcing the economic bust through their collective *bad southern* behavior (resulting from corruption, conspicuous consumption and lack of an *ethos* of hard work). Finally, the discourse praises austerity as the "cure" for crisis and the regeneration of the social body (Hadjimichalis 2017; Mylonas 2014; Narotzky 2012; Raudon and Shore 2018).

Along the Mediterranean basin, ordinary people have in different ways reproduced, resignified and contested these hegemonic discourses and made sense of the decade-long crisis of livelihoods, hopes and expectations in their *own* words. Dispossessed people[1] tend to place the current economic and social turmoil *on a continuum* with other recent episodes of social upheaval, including those of the 1980s and 90s when, driven by the process of *European convergence*, industrial and agricultural restructuring led to massive layoffs and over 10 percent unemployment in Europe as a whole with peaks of over 20 percent in Spain. Nevertheless, the extent of the latest iteration of crisis—including cuts to public spending, over-taxation and sovereign debt—atop memories of previous restructurings have reinforced doubts about the trade-off of sacrifice against European full membership and convergence (Narotzky 2016).

This chapter draws on ethnographic material collected between 2015 and 2017 in Vélez-Málaga in Spain and Chalkida in Greece[2] to study the ambivalent meanings and explanations of crisis held by ordinary working people. On the one hand, we examine their uneasy fit with "expert" discourses and how they are grounded in gendered and generationally differentiated lived experiences of "losing ground." On the other, we explore their ties to particular historical topographies (Katz 2001) and memories of domination.

The Gramscian concept of "common sense" helps us to understand differences and tensions within subaltern models of crisis as part of a fragmented consciousness that both reproduces and challenges hegemonic models. On the one hand, this contradictory conception of the world reflects tensions between material experience (practical activity) and hegemonic ideology (explicit language); on the other, it reworks the cumulative sedimentation of past tensions and struggles in relation to the present conjuncture (Gramsci 1977, 1997, 2010; Crehan 2011; Hall and Massey 2010; Narotzky and Smith 2010; Roseberry 1989, 1994; Sapkus 2001). Methodologically, this focus on common sense orients us towards the shared everyday experiences and discourses of dispossessed women and men, despite their differences in voting or formal political positioning. Our comparative framework also allows us to evaluate the significance of place—of dynamic configurations of *glocal*[3] history in shaping the particular grassroots languages of a common crisis in social reproduction (Knight 2015; Knight and Stewart 2016).

The chapter first outlines how grassroots explanatory models of crisis reworked mainstream corporatist discourses in Vélez-Málaga and Chalkida. It then examines the metaphors used by working people to dispute hegemonic meanings and explanations of crisis. Through the images of "the rich sinking/drowning the poor" in Spain and of "a neocolonial economic war" in Greece, the dispossessed understood the austerity regime as a politics of privilege and violence, both cyclical and conjunctural in nature. The conclusion highlights the diverse, overlapping and conflicting models of crisis as differently positioned social actors analyze and explain the causes and remedies for both addressing failed expectations and providing new ones. It also reflects on how grassroots explanatory models in Vélez-Málaga and Chalkida address issues of class and scalar orders of power, and how conflicting interpretations and narratives of previous conflicts form a backdrop for making sense of the ongoing rescaling and adjustment of capital/labor relations.[4] Rather than supporting expert analyses and narratives of crisis that underscore discontinuity and failure in an otherwise functioning system, the analyses of crisis we found in the field stressed structural continuity within the new forms of breakdown in social reproduction.

Grassroots Predicaments of Crisis Across Spain and Greece

In sharing everyday life with dispossessed women and men in Vélez-Málaga and Chalkida, one thing immediately became clear. Ordinary people used the term "crisis" to talk about the breakdown in their conditions of living, hopes and expectations (Narotzky and Besnier 2014). For some, this breakdown was due to unemployment caused by the collapse of construction and the shuttering of industries (particularly in Chalkida, where about 3,000 industrial workers were laid off between 2009 and 2015).[5] For others, the breakdown was tied to the contraction of the public sector (Martínez Matute and Pérez 2017) and the demise of small firms (Ministerio de Economía, Industria y Competitividad 2018; Giannitsis and Zografakis 2018). In Vélez-Málaga, the expansion of subtropical agriculture (OALDIM 2010; Yus and Torres 2010) partially offset this crisis in construction, providing precarious jobs in agriculture, agro-industries and logistics.[6] In both field sites, the decline of formal employment was tied to the expansion of informal waged work (agricultural day-work, cleaning, temporary work in services), smuggling and other *illegal* activities (from the growing of vegetables or fishing without permission to activities related to the drugs economy).

With falling demand, tightening credit and the increasing pressure of taxation, people trying to set up or maintain a small business (e.g. retailers, service providers and petty agricultural producers) were among the hardest hit by the crisis.[7] Even for people who retained steady jobs, the understaffing that followed widespread cuts devalued their labor; they were burdened with additional responsibilities and hidden overtime while their salaries were in most cases reduced. As we argue elsewhere (Sarkis and Matos in this volume), crisis goes well beyond unemployment—which was around 30 percent in both places in 2016—and includes the growing precariousness of remunerated work and income-measured poverty.[8] In addition, crisis fuels forced migration, the deterioration of physical and emotional/mental health and increased interdependence between generations through extended family co-residence, care of dependent family members and the transfer of resources and labor, particularly from older to younger generations (Tsekeris et al. 2015; Apostolidou 2018). The dismantling of public services and other mechanisms of redistribution played a key role in the deterioration of working-class livelihoods. Although this holistic dimension of crisis was highlighted in everyday discourse by women and men of different generations, this *continuum* was most apparent in the discourses of women. Following gendered divisions of responsibility for the household's reproduction, women particularly focused on state cutbacks while men tended to focus on the lack of remunerated work and other sources of income.

Working-class young adults contested the exceptionality of the "crisis" in terms of unemployment and increasingly precarious work: as they put it, "in this sense we have always been in crisis." But they agreed with other age groups in emphasizing other aspects of the term (deteriorating public services and emotional and physical health, growing and problematic dependence on family members, etc.). Moreover, they attributed particular meanings to the dimension of "crisis" related to hopes and expectations. Some regretted having to live with their parents as they were unable to set up and/or maintain their own households. Younger couples postponed having children, while others had ambivalent feelings of both anxiety and hope when they considered the prospect of having to emigrate. "Being lost" (*estar perdido*) or "doomed,"[9] "being unable to imagine any future," "feeling thrown out of society," "being deprived of self-worth and dignity" (*ehoume hasei tin aksioprepia mas*) and "feeling stuck, incapable and stagnant" (*sentirse parado, no servir para nada; eimaste animporoi na kanoume to otidipote*) were common expressions of the embodied structures of feeling emerging from crisis in both places. The collapse of social advancement through education and public employment was a key aspect of the crisis of social reproduction experienced by the working class.

Older people (aged 60 and above) emphasized the absence of expectations and hopes for the future as the most acute dimension of the current crisis. They felt that previous patterns of livelihood improvement had broken down and saw the sacrifices and hardships they had endured to assure a better future for younger generations come to naught. This painful process was captured in Vélez-Málaga with the widespread expression "we face a very dark future" (*tenemos un futuro muy negro*"). In Chalkida, a 79-year-old pensioner explained that while his generation may not have enjoyed abundance, they had hope that their situation was constantly improving, while now it was only going from bad to worse: "we have not reached the bottom of the barrel yet, and still, we do not know whether the barrel has a bottom at all."

These embodied grassroots experiences and understandings contested experts' views of the crisis as one of stagnant growth. Ordinary people thus challenged the dominant capitalo-centric definition with their own crisis of social reproduction. Some dispossessed people flatly refused to countenance the existence of an organic crisis of the social body, arguing instead that "they [rich people, politicians, bankers, in sum, powerful people] weren't experiencing any crisis." Likewise, they argued that the idea of "a common crisis" was a rhetorical weapon to legitimize "cut-backs" (an inclusive term for austerity measures). The idea that (at some level) the "crisis was a lie" was common in both Vélez-Málaga and Chalkida, with both women and men explaining the crisis as a planned attack on "poor people" (in Vélez-Málaga) or on "subordinate countries" and "protectorates" (in Chalkida).[10]

Their rejection of an organic crisis as proclaimed by governments and mainstream economists, however, was ambiguous. While it was sometimes argued that "the rich were not in crisis," at other times, "it was *their* crisis" that they had transferred to the common people—an ambivalence that makes sense when we distinguish between people's crisis of reproduction and capital's crisis of accumulation. Roman (82), a pensioner from Vélez who had worked as an agricultural day-laborer in the municipality and as a construction worker in Switzerland between 1963 and 1973, put it in these terms:

> It is their crisis: the crisis of the banks and of the powerful people who want to gain more and more money. At the beginning, it was not our crisis as they pretend. But government, all governments, the former PSOE and the later PP ones, had transformed *their* problem into ours when they gave 40,000,000,000 euros to the banks.[11] They gave them our money, people's money, the money of the poor who had worked all their lives. It has been a robbery (*ha sido un robo*) ... The problem in Spain is that the rich are not going to let the poor live as human beings (*vivir como personas*).

In Chalkida, austerity policies were seen by working people who used to have relatively stable and secure incomes—as industrial workers, pensioners, civil servants, small firm owners and self-employed—as a direct attack on what they described as "middle class" livelihoods. From their perspective, the "crisis" was a fabricated, controlled phenomenon employed by national and international elites to extract more profits and establish a new regime of political and economic power. Crisis had been planned in order to enforce Greek governments to accept bailout agreements under predatory and punitive terms that shifted the burden onto the Greek middle class. On top of cuts to public provisions, middle-class households had cumulatively lost, on average, more than 50 percent of their pre-crisis income. Alongside declining purchasing power, the so-called neoliberal rolling back and rolling out of the state (Peck and Tickell 2002) pushed Greek households back to where they were in the 1970s, before the country joined the European Economic Community and social-democratic (PASOK) governments developed the welfare state. Ntina, a 58-year-old retailer and owner of a small clothes shop, argued that "it is their crisis, yet we are paying the bill." She pointed out that the loans were going to be repaid by the Greek people, overburdened with taxes and special contributions such as the "solidarity" contribution and the special tax on home ownership.[12] Over-taxation alongside declining social services had fueled social unrest and undermined the legitimacy of political institutions and elites in both of our field sites. Feelings of dispossession and the idea that crisis was in fact robbery were widely shared by working people in both Vélez-Málaga and Chalkida, who disputed mainstream celebrations of austerity policies as the solution to the crisis, instead portraying them as part of projects of domination.

Explanations of crisis in terms of a politics of privilege and violence co-existed, articulated and sometimes overlapped alongside an imaginary of crisis as the product of moral-national failure (Mylonas 2014), even in the discourse of the same person. From this perspective, crisis was the outcome of a degenerate economic model of quick growth and "empty" money (epitomized by the construction crisis) embraced by a corrupt social body. Although these grassroots models in some ways reproduced mainstream discourses, they also reworked them as critique rooted in working-class moral economy. They disputed mainstream schemas of responsibility by blaming politicians and bankers as well as people (*la gente, to lao*) for following corrupt political elites and abandoning the historic working-class ethic of hard work and consumption limited to one's real means.

The Rich Are Drowning the Poor: The Austerity Regime as Class Struggle in Vélez-Málaga

The first time Diana Sarkis heard the idea that "the rich were drowning the poor" was from Marcela (79), a pensioner who had worked all her life as an agricultural day-laborer and sharecropper. Diana and Marcela were returning from interviewing Roman (see above) and Marcela was commenting on the situation of her friend and his wife. She felt sorry that they were depleting their meager savings by supporting the households of their unemployed son (42) and daughter (40) who worked informally doing small repairs and cleaning private homes. Marcela put it as follows: "They are not going to stop until they drown all of us (*nos hundan a todos*). Because in the end: who do you think are the beneficiaries of all this? Those who have the money. Those who rule. The rich. Those who have ruined Spain, in order to become richer and richer."

Diana heard many different versions of the *drowning* metaphor to represent the current structural adjustment of capital/labor relations as a politics of class, particularly from those above 50. The idea that "the rich were drowning the poor in order to live better" (*los ricos quieren hundir a los pobres para vivir ellos mejor*) was a common explanation of crisis among friends, neighbors and other informants. With this framework, dispossessed women and men made sense of their embodied experiences of disposability (Li 2010; Smith 2011), dispossession (Federici 2013; Harvey 2005; Mylonas 2014) and exploitation (Collins and Mayer 2010; Kasmir and Carbonella 2014; Narotzky 2016) under the austerity regime. They stressed that public cut-backs (particularly to healthcare), higher taxes and declining purchasing power were part of a planned project to annihilate redundant *poor people* (common expressions registered during fieldwork were: "they want to kill us, the poor" and "we are redundant, so they prefer to annihilate us"). At other times, they emphasized the economic functions—rent extraction, primitive accumulation, devaluation of labor—of this politics of drowning. They argued that the so-called polices "against the crisis" (austerity policies) were in fact instruments for stealing public assets (privatizations), extracting working-class wealth through taxation, pension vulnerability, depletion of savings and the forced loss of small property as well as forcing working people to accept lower wages and growing precariousness in working and living conditions by neutralizing social struggle through fear.

This dialectical model of the rich and the poor suggests not only "descriptive" stratification but a recognition of the mutual historical determination of both social categories, thus placing the austerity regime within the history of a never-ending class conflict. José (65), a pensioner who was previously a temporary restaurant worker, explained during a focus group:

> This society is divided into strata and those from above make their living from those from below (*los de arriba viven de los de abajo*). What dominates everything here is "money" [in English in the original discourse]. It has always been like this: poor and rich have always existed (*eso ha habido siempre: pobres y ricos*) ... the rich have always tried to eat the poor (*el rico siempre ha intentado comerse al pobre*).[13]

Several studies have emphasized the historical wisdom of this binary language of class relations for other regions of the Andalusian countryside (and other areas in Spain), associating it with an oligarchic regime of power where the class fracture between the poor and rich was enormous and power took dramatic forms of omnipotence, despotism and forced compliance (Costa 1982 [1846–1911]; Collier 1997; Frigolé 2005; Martínez-Allier 1968). In contrast to other parts of Andalusia, *caciquismo* (the Spanish term for this social configuration) in Vélez-Málaga was not strictly related to a longstanding *latifundia* system and a preponderance of landless day-laborers. Until the beginning of the twentieth century, much of the land in this area was in the hands of petty and medium farmers (Montoro 2009; Yus and Torres 2010). Nevertheless, the appropriation of agricultural value by commercial and financial capital was historically assured through the mechanisms of unequal exchange, debt and control over other means of production (e.g. mills), forcing small farmers, alongside working their own plots, to work as day-laborers and sharecroppers to make a living. The early 1900s witnessed a process of land hoarding by commercial-financial (and in some cases, industrial) capitalist families. Particularly important was the Larios family, which arrived in Málaga from La Rioja in northern Spain at the beginning of the nineteenth century. The Larios invested in multiple agricultural (sugar cane, vineyard), industrial (sugar,[14] oil, soap, textile) and financial enterprises (providing local loans and opening the Bank of Málaga in 1856). At the turn of the century, the Larios expanded their control over land through the usurious mechanisms of credit/debt (Montoro 2009) and established a *colonato* system by leasing lands in the irrigated regions of the Vega that continues to define this part of the agricultural landscape until today.

Although Sarkis' fieldwork revealed a partial displacement in the subaltern languages of class across generations,[15] the force of these historical configurations and embodied historical experiences often returned in understandings of the ongoing restructuring of class relations among all age groups. My interlocutors used the concept of day-laborism (*jornalerismo*) to capture current forms of precarious work and compared (and even equated) the mortgage crisis and other forms of enclosure (e.g. banks' control of public assets through privatizations) with the old process of usurious land hoarding by the Larios.

Alongside this cyclical perspective, dispossessed women and men attributed to "crisis" a kind of *double reversed temporality*. On the one hand, they described it as a form of "going back" or "returning" (*volver para atrás*) to old forms of social suffering (for the Greek case, see below and Knight 2016) and previous periods of harsher class conflict. On the other hand, they distinguished between previous cyclical experiences of crisis where the poor at least kept their expectations of the future and the present conjuncture of "crisis without a future."

Ordinary people in Vélez-Málaga underlined the breakdown of their living conditions (*cada vez estamos peor*) by comparing their current situation to their previous experience of relative—and in part ideologically constructed—prosperity (cf. Knight and Stewart 2016). They described breakdowns in their access to formal education and healthcare and in their credit-led consumption patterns for housing, clothing, car ownership and holidays which in previous decades *seemed* to have erased class frontiers. Jaime (62), previously employed in construction but now unemployed, described how the economic turmoil has both uncovered the eternal conflict between the poor and the rich (cyclical temporality) and thrown them back in history (reversed temporality):

> Before the crisis we lived in an epoch where everyone believed himself to be "middle-class" (*se creía clase media*).[16] They wasted money without limits. They believed they were no longer poor (*se creían que habían salido de pobres*) because they had a credit card. They thought that it was not going to have an end, but I saw the end very clearly. Now the poor are poor again and the rich are richer than ever (*ahora el pobre vuelve a ser pobre y el rico más rico que nunca*).

The second type of reversed temporality entailed the collapse of dispossessed women and men's hopes and expectations for the future.[17] Some made sense of this collapse in terms of changing class relations. An old fisherman (75) compared his own experience of inhumane (in his terms) exploitation and exhaustion as a waged worker in bottom-trawling fishing with his son's situation. The son (40) had worked with his father until 2009 when he was fired due to the European regulatory-led crisis in the sector.[18] He then worked in informal trawling until 2013 when the state started to systematically persecute this *illegal* activity. When Diana met them in 2017, the son was unemployed and living with his parents, working only sporadically as an assistant mechanic. In the old fisherman's words: "We are now returning back to the past. These children don't have any future. We are facing more than exploitation. We are victims.... The poor, we are no longer of use to anybody."[19]

Embodied reflexive experiences of crisis re-worked grassroots historical representations of class conflict while eliding the international dimension of these transformations (e.g. European fishing polices and the relocation of European fishing industries to Africa, or the Memorandum of Understanding signed by Spain and the Troika in 2012 and its implications for Spanish tax policies and cuts to public spending).[20] In contrast, grassroots explanatory models of "crisis" in Greece, which we turn to below, focused on the European and international scales of the austerity regime, often obscuring the class cleavages that divide this *subjugated nation*.

Neo-Colonial Economic War: Grassroots Explanations of Crisis in Chalkida

One of the first things that drew Stamatis Amarianakis' attention upon arrival in Chalkida in May 2015 was the struggle of the cement factory workers who had been laid off after the factory's closure. The loss of their jobs had dispossessed them of their identity as industrial workers, which had been tightly knit in Chalkida's socio-economic web. The factory was owned by Lafarge, a French multinational cement giant, that had since 2007 wanted to limit the union's negotiating power and cut wages, claiming that the Greek labor market should align with global free-market standards. Back then, when management threatened to close the factory—a move characterized by the workers as "neocolonial"— the workers and the union had declared a strike. But the high national demand for cement at the time—driven by the housing bubble—led to a compromise between the union and management. By 2013, the national demand for cement had reached a historic low.[21] On 26 March 2013, management seized the opportunity to close the factory and fire the "troublesome Gauls,"[22] making use of the austerity legislation enabling mass lay-offs included in the second memorandum (Dedoussopoulos et al. 2013). The trade union has been struggling to reverse the lay-offs and reopen the factory ever since, and the struggle continues to this day, six years after the plant's closure. The union claims that Lafarge imposed its terms directly to the former prime minister, Antonis Samaras, when he met with the heads of 13 multinational companies to discuss how to enhance the competitiveness of the Greek economy in 2012.[23] All participants in a group interview of cement factory workers agreed when one person took the initiative to speak:

> We [the Greek nation] used to produce cars and electric appliances. Greece had a growing industrial sector which was dismantled to serve the demands of the Germans. They wanted to make us dependent on imports and credit, and that is how they achieved control over us. They gave us funds to dismantle both our industrial and agricultural production and made us dependent on them, and many Greeks believed this money was for free [see Gkintidis 2018]. Now with this crisis they are buying us cheap and they make the workers easy prey for the multinationals.

The critical situation for the factory had begun in 1995 when, in the context of the financialization of Greek industry, it was sold to foreign investors. Subsequent reforms only accelerated the accumulation of capital by transnational firms which, in times of crisis, often acquire structural power, the power to make structures act on their behalf (Wettstein 2009; Bourdieu 2005). Large firms exploited the national economic crisis to accelerate neoliberal restructuring and labor market deregulation, thereby undercutting the hard-won rights of Greek working people. Impugning the dignity of Greek workers, their struggle was framed as one of national resistance to the re-invasion of foreign capital. In an interview in a mainstream newspaper,[24] the CEO of Lafarge explained that the factory in Chalkida was closed due to broader plans to restructure cement production in Greece, a move that favored two of their other Greek factories. But the structural violence against the laid-off workers' livelihoods resonated nationally and fed into the image of the whole of Greek society being attacked by neoliberal austerity. At the same time, laid-off workers blamed Greek governments for selling the nation to multinationals and being unable to defend its citizens, who in the midst of deep economic crisis struggled to defend the national interests of labor (Giannitsis and Zografakis 2015).

The massive closure of big industries in Chalkida, along with cuts to pensions and civil servant wages, had a domino effect on local markets. As in other places in Greece,[25] the lack of wage labor opportunities in the city's public and private sectors (Tsoucalas 1986a, 1986b) pushed people to pursue other livelihoods through self-employment. While self-employment, particularly since the 1980s, had provided opportunities for laid-off industrial workers (Parker 2004) as well as for many women, the ongoing economic turmoil undermined small businesses. Small shop owners whom Stamatis met criticized European Union funds to boost entrepreneurship, arguing that the problem for small entrepreneurs was not their competitiveness but the declining purchasing power produced by the austerity regime: "If people have no money to pay me, what difference does it make if I renovated my shop and upgraded my equipment?" a 49-year-old general store owner wondered. A highly skilled 36-year-old, pointing out that the initiatives funded by the state and the EU in the area of Chalkida consisted of traditional shops and taverns, asked rhetorically, "How is it that you boost the productivity of the national economy by funding someone to open a tavern?" The mainstream solutions to the persisting crisis were not only criticized as unjust and inhumane but as irrational. For the vast majority of ordinary people Stamatis interacted with, the economic crisis they had been experiencing for the past decade was the *outcome* of austerity. To the extent that austerity policies promoted the interests of non-human, foreign companies at the expense of real, suffering, working middle class people, they were deemed inhumane.

Ntina, a 58-year-old "entrepreneur" who had owned a small clothes shop for the past 27 years, was squeezed between the contracting demand for clothing and over-taxation. In her view, the crisis was fabricated to further dispossess the working middle classes in Greece, with the increased unemployment created by austerity policies producing a docile labor force amenable to exploitation by large multinational firms. Ntina discerned that multinational firms accumulate the locally/nationally produced wealth abroad, further dispossessing local/national society: "when you shop at a local business, the money circulates in Chalkida. You tell me what happens if you shop at a multinational firm." The latter had penetrated Greek markets not only by exploiting labor, but through new patterns of consumption. During the crisis years, numerous small shops and retailers in Chalkida were forced to close, out-competed by large, foreign-owned department stores which could take advantage of economies of scale to provide cheaper products to cash-strapped customers. This created another source of public deficits as many firms could no longer pay their taxes and social insurance contributions and became indebted to the state.

Dispossessed women and men also pointed out that the crisis enabled foreign investment funds to buy up depreciated public assets. The mineral resources of Greece (Sutton 2018) and the renewable energy resources of the sun (Knight 2014) and wind were targeted by French and German energy companies. One popular belief was that the "crisis" had been implanted in Greece because of the country's oil reserves in the Aegean, Ionian and Libyan Seas—fabricated in order to force Greece to sell cheap its natural resources (see Engdahl 2013; Sutton 2018).

Many cement factory workers portrayed the crisis as a retrograde move towards the past. They spoke of de-unionization and authoritarian restructuring as belonging to a past era when workers did not have official negotiating power, and of the re-emergence of extended family co-residence and generational interdependence as a return to peasant forms of livelihood. More literally, many laid-off factory workers had to turn to agricultural labor for their livelihood which suggested a return to the past. The crisis ushered in a new period of resource scarcity and economic failure, often characterized as a national catastrophe triggered by foreign "fingers" (Hertzfeld 2016) taking advantage of Greek state weakness. The state had not only rolled back its welfare provisions but acted against the interests of its own citizens. As in previous crises, the current crisis was understood in national terms, often as a new type of war led by the Germans who aspired to re-occupy Greece.

Public indebtedness had previously been used to exercise economic and political control over Greece (Tsoulfidis and Zouboulakis 2016). Michael Hertzfeld (2002) defines the relationship of modern Greece to the hegemonic cultural and economic models of the West as one of "crypto-colonialism." The outburst of the crisis and subordination of Greek governments to foreign control led working people to realize that Greece, throughout its modern history, had not been an independent nation but a debt colony, a subordinate nation serving the demands of the world's superpowers.[26] The crisis revealed to a wider public the covert crypto-colonial relationships between Greece and the West (Hertzfeld 2002).

Amarianakis' interlocutors in Greece viewed crisis and austerity as a neo-colonial economic war led by foreign capital to subjugate the Greek nation/society to the global neoliberal project. Ntina believed that "we have crisis because they say so, I do not know who 'they' are. They call them 'the markets.' I cannot understand how Greece, a small country, poses a threat to the world economy and (yet) they are doing this to us, this is a new type of war." In a similar vein, Katerina (65), a hard-working housewife, said that "what the Germans did not manage to get with weapons in World War Two, they are getting it now with the crisis. Greece is the best plot of land in Europe, we have the sea and the sun and all the northerners envy us... they want us to transform into a nation of underpaid waiters to serve tourists."

Conclusion: Class, History and Scale in Subaltern Explanations of Crisis

This chapter has examined how dispossessed women and men in Vélez-Málaga in Spain and Chalkida in Greece reworked and disputed mainstream capitalo-centric definitions of crisis and their celebration of austerity policies as the solution to economic downturn, social convulsion and suffering. "Common sense" not only rewrote expert discourses but re-actualized past experiences and social memories to provide an alternative, critical explanation of the austerity regime. In Chalkida, working people underlined the international dimension of austerity as a project of "neocolonial" domination (materialized in the figures of the Troika, the German state, a "Germanized" European Union, international banks and companies, and at times the "German people" and "the northerners"). In Vélez-Málaga, working people stressed the national and particularly local scale of crisis, one that crystallized around the never-ending conflict between the poor and the rich.

Although their voices reflected differences in gender, age and glocal histories and were at times ambivalent, grassroots understandings of crisis contested the idea of "exceptionality" that pervades the understandings of experts. Instead, working men and women located the current turmoil in a cyclical temporality of class and anti-colonial struggle, illuminating intertwined dimensions of the contemporary structural adjustment of capital/labor relations in southern Europe. On the one hand, they pointed to the transition from inclusive forms of capital hegemony based on Fordist-Keynesian models of "embedded capitalism" (Harvey 2007) to selective forms of capital hegemony wherein financial and other processes of accumulation by dispossession (Harvey 2005) and usurious exploitation (privatizations, tax collection, national recapitalization of private banks and sovereign debt, etc.) have turned a part of the working people into "disposable subjects" (Smith 2011). Our interlocutors' emphasis on the cyclical nature of this extractive regime of accumulation encourages us to think of these transformations in terms of the re-actualization and reinforcement of historical forms of capital hegemony rather than as a linear process of change. Our ethnographic studies further show how these reconfigurations occur at particular points in the global topography of capital (Katz 2001), with the extraction of value operating at interlocked scales: between classes at the national-local level, and from the global south to the global north at an international level.

Different scales of dispossession were perceived through the lens of embodied historical experience and memories of social conflict— through particular glocal materializations of the shifting structures of global accumulation—with the emphasis on class or international divisions of labor intertwining with particular configurations of capital/labor relations. In Chalkida, the structural power (Wolf 1989) of neo-colonial forces operating through austerity materialized in industrial relocations and projects to control national resources. In Vélez-Málaga, power structures were personified in well-known *local* families that control much of the land and other means of production, livelihood and wealth, and dominate the networks of corruption linking economic and political elites which have transformed the state into an instrument for the private accumulation of wealth and power. They constituted the visible face of local-national-international chains of accumulation[27] and, together with local politicians, embodied larger fields of organizational power such as the European Union. Likewise, the dependence of subtropical agriculture on international markets, particularly the European Common Market,[28] forged ties of (forced) compliance and submission between working people and these larger-scale structures of economic power.

The reflexive experiences of "crisis" examined in this chapter also reworked particular histories and memories of contention.[29] In the Greek case, the grassroots understanding of austerity as a neocolonial regime can be traced to the formation of the modern Greek nation-state. Even as nationalist discourse was "imported" from the West and its adoption by different social groups was complex (Mouzelis 2007), the German occupation (1941–44) and the Civil War (1945–49) were formative in defining various conflicts in terms of national resistance and of national (on the Right) or patriotic (on the Left) defense of the national project (Marantzidis and Antoniou 2004). The tensions and changes of mind within the Greek Communist Party during the German occupation and Civil War over its alliance with left-wing Slavic Macedonian partisans who were simultaneously fighting for self-determination and unification with the People's Republic of Macedonia in Yugoslavia is a case in point of the strength of national arguments on both sides straining relations between those who could—and sometimes managed to—be ideological allies (Rossos 1997). At the same time, the Civil War and its revolutionary intent to transform Greece into a people's republic cannot be separated from various international interventions (German, British, American, Soviet, Yugoslav) supporting contending projects while seeking to advance their own geopolitical interests (Casanovas 2000). As a result, in several recent episodes in Greek history, local social conflicts and struggles were at least partially nationalized. The nationalization of working people's struggles often co-opted class-based claims that were present in these struggles, thereby obscuring questions of class. As in the past, the present iteration of crisis has followed a similar path and has created a national language of contention.

In Vélez-Málaga, the power regime between classes was structured by the personalization of relations of production and the open dramatization of social inequality and privilege. The explicit nature of subjugation seems to have travelled across generations, embodied in particular memories of suffering, humiliation and violence and articulated through a language of opposition used by the poor where they are *inter pares*.[30] The traumatic experiences and memories—as well as explicit amnesia—of the Spanish Revolution and the Civil War (1936–39) have reworked the conflict between the rich and the poor, while socialist, communist and anarchist languages of contention materialized in particular conflicts between the poor and their local *lords* (*amos*). In both of our field sites, "the phantoms of the past" (Marx 2003 [1852])—embodied historical experiences of social conflict and struggle—informed peoples' judgments and structures of feeling about the ongoing crisis of social reproduction (Knight and Stewart 2016) and their explanatory models of crisis.

The counter-narratives of crisis we found in the field differed radically from scholarly and expert narratives that frame the "crisis" as a state of "exception," searching for the causes of "what went wrong?" and looking for solutions to re-establish the teleology of progress (Roitman 2013). First, the counter-narratives resisted the story of a sudden "failure" of a "working system" and focused on continuities: our interlocutors explained their position of subalternity either in terms of class or of colonial domination, suggesting that it has always been the same. Second, they did not search for new explanations of "what went wrong?" but revisited the old causes tied to objectives of domination, extraction and exploitation, to which they added annihilation out of awareness of their present superfluous role in the accumulation of capital. Third, the crisis was understood as a rhetorical mask concealing the intensification of old relations of exploitation and the extraction of human, natural and financial resources. In this sense, the crisis was perceived to be a lie. Finally, counter-narratives framed the crisis as a breakdown of expectations of inter-generational social and material improvement, foreclosing a future which can no longer be imagined— or is seen in the past—expressing a circular or reversed temporality, a non-modern temporality of *a crisis without a future*. Although history, class and scale informed these counter-narratives of crisis, what was absent was a sense of possible change towards a "better" future, a rendering of their experiences which then questions the modern understanding of history (Koselleck 2001; Bodei 1997). For our interlocutors in Spain and Greece, the question of "what went wrong?" was not an issue. For them, the issue was "where has our future gone?" and how this collapsed temporality could enable their life projects.

Notes

1. We use the terms working and dispossessed people interchangeably; see Sarkis and Matos in this volume.
2. Sarkis pursued fieldwork in Spain, in two centers of the municipality of Vélez-Málaga, the city of Vélez-Málaga and the village of Almayate. Agriculture was traditionally prominent in the household economies of the area. Since the 1990s, the boom in construction and tourism has been concentrated in the locality of Torre del Mar, which was not the focus of Sarkis' fieldwork. With one of the highest rates of formal unemployment in the country (30 percent), the municipality is the main center of the agro-export industry of subtropical crops in Europe. Amaraniakis conducted fieldwork in Chalkida, a mid-sized city 80 km north of Athens and the capital of the island of Evia in central Greece. Due to its location and access to natural resources, industry used to be the driving force of its economy and has shaped the social habitus. Crisis came to Chalkida through industrial decline, which became more acute after 2008. Urban residents had maintained strong ties with food-producing areas in the countryside, re-signified in the time of crisis.
3. The concept "glocal" points to the interlocking of different scales in the configuration of particular geo-historical places. The local is not a dimension

articulated against the global, but a specific concretion of global dynamics (Gupta and Ferguson 1992; Roseberry 1989; Wolf 1982).
4. We understand austerity policies as forms of organizational power (Wolf 1989) readjusting capital/labor relations on a world scale. They follow structural adjustment polices in Latin America, Asia and Africa since the 1980s (Hadjimichallis and Hudson 2014).
5. The president of Evia's trade union stated that in Chalkida and in the wider region of the island of Evia, the real unemployment reached nearly 40 percent, while 60 percent of local businesses closed between 2010 and 2014. See http://www.ert.gr/eidiseis/ellada/sto-40-i-anergia-stin-evvia-o-proedros-tou-ergatikou-kentrou-s-basinas-milai-sto-ert-gr/ (last accessed April 2019). He also stated that "black uninsured labor" is at around 60 percent."
6. In 2008, agriculture employed 22 percent of workers in the municipality (nationally, the rate was 6.4 percent). In 2009, agriculture and fishing continued to generate 36 percent of all new jobs (OALDIM 2010). In 2015, only 5 percent of people searching for employment previously worked in agriculture; 75 percent previously worked in services and construction (Observatorio Argos 2015).
7. Direct and indirect taxation on lower incomes in Greece increased by 337 percent between 2010 and 2014 (Giannitsis and Zografakis 2015). According to the OECD, Spain is among the European countries where the gap between taxation on labor (including self-employed *autónomos*) and capital has most increased since 2007. Taxes on corporate profits were 12.4 percent of total tax receipts in 2007 and 6.2 percent in 2013. Greece followed the same path: from 7.9 percent in 2007 to 3.9 percent in 2013 www.lavanguardia.com/economia/20151203/30567153099/crisis-ciudadanos-mas-impuestos-empresas-menos.html (last accessed April 2019). In Spain, the poorest 20 percent paid higher taxes than any other bracket (except the richest 10 percent) elpais.com/economia/2018/12/04/actualidad/1543943723_079886.html (last accessed April 2019).
8. Over the past seven years, Greek salaried people and pensioners lost between 30 percent and 50 percent of their annual income, while the ILO estimates a 20 percent drop in real salaries in Spain.
9. "Being lost" and "being doomed" has particularly strong connotations for the younger generation (Tsekeris et al. 2015). Graffiti at the southeastern entrance to the city of Vélez-Málaga proclaimed: "We are the fucked generation" (in English).
10. Stamatis' informants used the following terms: "*eimaste protektorato, ypocheirio ton Europeon kai ton Americanon*" (we are a protectorate, subordinate to the European and the Americans).
11. The cost of bailing out the Spanish financial system was between 64,000,000,000 and 100,000,000,000 euros. www.eldiario.es/economia/rescate-financiero-entidades-grandes-recuperara_0_882262517.html ; www.elconfidencial.com/empresas/2014-03-30/cinco-anos-y-100-000-millones-despues-historia-del-rescate-de-la-banca-espanola_109053/ (last accessed April 2019). That the Troika imposed punitive terms on Greece was recognized even by EU officials www.tanea.gr/2013/09/24/economy/

timwritikoi-oi-oroi-daneismoy-tis-elladas-stin-arxi-tis-krisis-eipe-o-klaoys-regklingk/ (last accessed April 2019).

12. The home ownership tax, introduced as a special measure in 2010, became permanent in the following years. It came to be known as *haratsi*, including in mainstream media. *Haraç* was a tribute Christians had to pay to practice their religion under Ottoman rule. Stamatis' interlocutors estimated that each child born in Greece automatically inherits a debt of 30,000 euros as a future taxpayer.

13. Diana Sarkis became close to Marcela during her fieldwork, living with her when arriving at Almayate in May 2015 and spending weekends in her house after moving to the city of Vélez in September 2015. "Those from above/those from below" (*los de arriba y los de abajo*) and "the big/the small" (*el grande y el chico*) were further common ways to express the opposition between the rich and poor in Vélez-Málaga.

14. The Larios family took control of the Torre del Mar sugar factory in 1852 (Guzmán and Santiago 2009). In 1865, Queen Isabel II recognized "the economic merits of the family" with the title of marquis.

15. Younger generations tended to use the terms "those from above" and "the powerful" to refer to people whom those over 50 called "the rich." Likewise, "modest people" (*gente humilde*) and "the people" (*la gente*) tended to substitute for "the poor," where the adjective *humilde* (modest) points to both a material position and a moral quality of being. This shift implies a moralization of social dynamics, with language focusing on the comparative social worth of people beyond their income or political power. This transformation intertwines with the dynamics of *desclasamiento*—the historical shift from working people's dualistic model of systemic inequality towards understanding themselves as "middle-class" (Narotzky 2016).

16. People often used the concept of "middle class" ironically, with expressions such as "they believed that they were middle class" or "it seemed that everyone was part of the middle class" (*se creían que, parecía que*). In some cases, they described as mere illusion the idea that working people had achieved moral and material entitlements following the *transition* to democracy.

17. A 70-year-old man emphasized that the main difference between the current and previous crises is the breakdown in the belief that history is progressing: "Life was harder before. However, we hung on because we were suffering for a future. In my view, what has changed more in the last times are expectations. We see the future as worse than the present."

18. Since 2008, European directives on bottom-trawling have reduced the fleet in the province of Málaga to half of its previous size www.diariosur.es/malaga/mitad-barcos-anos-20180322233920-nt.html (last accessed April 2019).

19. "*Ahora estamos volviendo como antes. Las criaturas no tienen ningún futuro. Ahora es más que explotación. Somos víctimas.... Los pobres ya no servimos a nadie.*"

20. The *Memorando de Entendimiento sobre Condiciones de Política Sectorial Financiera* was signed by Spain and the Troika on 20 July 2012. Spain received a 100,000,000,000 euro "support package" to re-capitalize private banks so that they could repay their debts to German and other international banks. The

memorandum stated that its repayment was assumed as national debt, while Spain accepted economic polices dictated by creditors (i.e. fiscal stabilization polices determining cuts to public spending and tax rates on labor). http://www.mineco.gob.es/stfls/mineco/prensa/ficheros/noticias/2012/120720_MOU_espanyol_2_rubrica_MECC_VVV.pdf (last accessed 14 April 2019).
21. http://www.hcia.gr/en/statistical-elements/sales/.
22. Factory workers often used this expression to describe themselves.
23. primeminister.gr/2012/12/17/9904 (last accessed April 2019).
24. http://www.kathimerini.gr/484488/article/oikonomia/epixeirhseis/giati-apofasisame-na-kleisoyme-to-ergostasio-ths-aget-xalkidas (last accessed April 2019) (cf. Mylonas 2014)
25. Recent statistics place Greece first among European economies in self-employment rates (Williams and Vorley 2015; Antonopoulos and Hall 2014).
26. Kwame Nkrumah (1965) defined neocolonialism as a form of economic dependence that imposes indirect political control.

    As a recently retired cement factory worker elaborated a few days after the Greek referendum in 2015, "Greeks have never been an independent nation-state. From the very beginning, there were three political parties trying to rule Greece: the French, the English and the Russian. You see, we are in a very strategic location, we are at the crossroads of three continents and for that, everyone wants to control us."
27. The Larios family continues to dominate much of the irrigated land around the Vélez River (La Vega) as well as big plots planted with subtropical fruits in the mountains. Following the demise of the sugar cane industry in the 1990s, they invested in real-estate, shopping malls and financial societies. The Montosa family represented for my interlocutors the power of *local* globalized capital to shape the fate of Velenian working people. Frutas Montosa—a *family enterprise* of processing and importing/exporting subtropical crops, known locally as "the giant of avocados"—had a 2016 turnover of over 100,000,000 euros.
28. In 2016, 75 percent of the Velez production of avocadoes and mangoes were exported to the European Union http://www.laopiniondemalaga.es/axarquia/2014/03/20/malaga-reserva-tropical-europa/662534.html (last accessed April 2019).
29. We use the term "memories of contention" to refer to historically embodied experiences of conflict and social struggle that in particular periods in the past functioned as languages of contention (Roseberry 1994) and which, in fragmentary ways, are part of contemporary common sense.
30. See Martínez-Alier (1968) for a very similar case in the province of Córdoba.

References

Antonopoulos, G. and S. Hall. 2014. "The Death of the Legitimate Merchant? Small to Medium-Size Enterprises and Shady Decisions in Greece During the Financial Crisis." In P.C. van Duyne, G.A. Antonopoulos, J. Harvey and A. Mark-

ovska, eds. *Corruption, Greed and Crime Money: Sleaze and Shady Economics in Europe and Beyond*. Nijmegen: Wolf Legal.
Apostolidou, A. 2018. "Greek Depression: Uses of Mental Health Discourse from the Economy to the Psyche." In D. Dalakoglou & G. Angelopoulos (eds). *Critical Times in Greece: Anthropological Engagements with the Crisis*. New York: Routledge: 119–31.
Bodei, R. 1997. *Se la Storia ha un senso*. Bergamo: Moretti & Vitali Editori.
Bourdieu, P. 2005. "Principles of an Economic Anthropology." In N.J. Smelser and R. Swedberg, eds. *The Handbook of Economic Sociology (2nd Edition)*. Princeton: Princeton University Press.
Casanovas, J. 2000. "Civil Wars, Revolutions and Counterrevolutions in Finland, Spain, and Greece (1918-1949): A Comparative Analysis." *International Journal of Politics, Culture and Society* 13(3): 515–35.
Collier, G.A. 1997. *Los socialistas de la Andalucía Rural. Los revolucionarios ignorados de la Segunda República*. Sevilla: Anthropos.
Collins, J. and V. Mayer. 2010. *Both Hands Tied: Welfare Reform and the Race to the Bottom of the Low-Wage Labor Market*. Chicago: University of Chicago Press.
Costa, J. 1982 [1846-1911]. *Oligarquía y caciquismo como la forma actual de gobierno en España: urgencia y modo de cambiarla*. Zaragoza: Guara.
Crehan, K. 2011. "Gramsci's Concept of Common Sense: A Useful Concept for Anthropologists?" *Journal of Modern Italian Studies* 16(2): 273–87.
Dedoussopoulos, A., Aranitou, V., Koutentakis, F. and Maropoulou, M. 2013. "Assessing the Impact of the Memoranda on Greek Labour Market and Labour Relations." Working Paper No. 53, International Labour Office, Geneva.
Engdahl, W. 2013. "The New Mediterranean Oil and Gas Bonanza." *Global Research*. www.globalresearch.ca/the-new-mediterranean-oil-and-gas-bonanza/29609
Federici, S. 2013. *Revolución en punto cero. Trabajo doméstico, reproducción y luchas feministas*. Madrid: Traficantes de sueños.
Frigolé, J. 2005. "Semblazas del caciquismo y del cacique." In M.P. Feliú, ed. *Entre las gracias y el molino satánico. Lecturas de Antropología Económica*. Madrid: UNED.
Giannitsis, T. and S. Zografakis. 2015. "Greece: Solidarity and Adjustment to Times of Crisis." *IMK Study 38*. Macroeconomic Policy Institute, Hans-Böckler Foundation.
Giannitsis, T. and S. Zografakis. 2018. "Crisis Management in Greece." *IMK Study 58*. Macroeconomic Policy Institute, Hans-Böckler Foundation.
Gkintidis, D. 2018. "Free Money, Spoiled Recipients: The Capitalist Crisis as a Moral Question Among Greek Technocrats." In D. Dalakoglou and G. Agelopoulos, eds. *Critical Times in Greece: Anthropological Engagements with the Crisis*. New York: Routledge: 32-44.
Gramsci, A. 1977[1891–1937]. *Antología*. Mexico City: Siglo XXI.
Gramsci, A. 1997. *El materialismo histórico y la filosofía de Benedetto Croce*. Buenos Aires: Nueva Visión.
Gramsci, A. 2010. *Cartas desde la cárcel*. Madrid: Veintisiete Letras.
Gupta, A. and J. Ferguson. 1992. "Beyond Culture: Space, Identity, and the Politics of Difference." *Cultural Anthropology* 7(1): 277–99.

Guzmán, A. and A. Santiago. 2009. "La fábrica de azúcar de Torre del Mar, elemento de un paisaje histórico." *Revista del Patrimonio Histórico del Instituto Andaluz del Patrimonio Histórico* 71: 42–81.
Hadjimichalis, C. and R. Hudson. 2014. "Contemporary Crisis Across Europe and the Crisis of Regional Development Theories." *Regional Studies* 48: 208–18.
Hadjimichalis, C. 2017. *Crises Spaces. Structures, Struggles and Solidarity in Southern Europe*. London: Routledge.
Hall, S. and D. Massey. 2010. "Interpreting the Crisis." *Soundings* 44: 57–71.
Harvey, D. 2005. *The New Imperialism*. Oxford: Oxford University Press.
Harvey, D. 2007. *A Brief History of Neoliberalism*. Oxford: Oxford University Press.
Hertzfeld, M. 2002. "The Absent Presence: Discourses of Crypto-Colonialism." *South Atlantic Quarterly* 101: 899–926.
Hertzfeld, M. 2016. "The Hypocrisy of European Moralism: Greece and the Politics of Cultural Aggression, Part 2." *Anthropology Today* 32(2): 10–12.
Kasmir, S. and A. Carbonella. 2014. "Introduction." In *Blood and Fire: Towards a Global Anthropology of Labor*. Oxford: Berghahn.
Katz, C. 2001. "On the Grounds of Globalization: A Topography for Feminist Political Engagement." *Signs: Journal of Women in Culture and Society* 26(4): 1213–34.
Knight, D. 2014. "A Critical Perspective on Economy, Modernity and Temporality in Contemporary Greece through the Prism of Energy Practice." *GreeSE Working Paper Series 81*, London School of Economics and Political Science.
Knight, D. 2015. *History, Time, and Economic Crisis in Central Greece*. New York: Palgrave Macmillan.
Knight, D. and C. Stewart. 2016. "Ethnographies of Austerity: Temporality, Crisis and Affect in Southern Europe." *History and Anthropology* 27(1): 1-18.
Koselleck, R. 2001. *Los estratos del tiempo: estudios sobre la historia*. Barcelona: Paidós.
Li, T.M. 2010. "To Make Live or Let Die? Rural Dispossession and the Protection of Surplus Populations." *Antipode* 41: 66–93.
Marantzidis, N. and G. Antoniou. 2004. "The Axis Occupation and Civil War: Changing Trends in Greek Historiography, 1941–2002." *Journal of Peace Research* 41(2): 223–31.
Martínez-Alier, J. 1968. *La estabilidad del Latifundismo. Análisis de la interdependencia entre relaciones de producción y consciencia social en la agricultura latifundista de la campiña de Córdoba*. Paris: Ruedo Ibérico.
Martínez Matute, M. and J.L. Pérez. 2017. "La evolución del empleo de las Administraciones Públicas en la última década." *Boletín Económico* 4: 1–12.
Marx, K. 2003 [1852]. *El Dieciocho de Brumario de Luis Bonaparte*. Madrid: Fundación Federico Engels.
Mouzelis, N. 2007. "Nationalism: Restructuring Gellner's Theory." In S. Malesevic and M. Haugaard, eds. *Ernest Gellner and Contemporary Social Thought*. Cambridge: Cambridge University Press.
Mylonas, Y. 2014. "Crisis, Austerity and Opposition in Mainstream Media Discourses of Greece. *Critical Discourse Studies* 11(3): 305–21.
Ministerio de Economía, Industria y Competitividad del Gobienro de España. 2018. *Estadísticas PYME. Evolución e indicadores 16*. www.ipyme.org (last accessed June 2019).

Narotzky, S. 2012. "Europe in Crisis: Grassroots Economies and the Anthropological Turn." *Etnografica* 16: 627–38.
Narotzky, S. 2016. "Between Inequality and Injustice: Dignity as a Motive for Mobilization During the Crisis." *History and Anthropology* 27(1): 74–92.
Narotzky, S. and N. Besnier. 2014. "Introduction: Crisis, Value, and Hope: Rethinking the Economy." *Current Anthropology* 55(S9): S4–S16.
Narotzky, S. and G. Smith. 2010. *Luchas Inmediatas. Gente, poder y espacio en el España rural*. Valencia: Universitat de València.
Nkrumah, K. 1965. *Neocolonialism, the Last Stage of Imperialism*. London: Thomas Nelson & Sons.
OALDIM (Organismo autónomo local de desarrollo integral del municipio de Vélez-Málaga). 2010. *Estudio de necesidades de formación para el empleo en el municipio de Vélez-Málaga*. Fondo Social Europeo del Ministerio de Política Territorial.
Observatorio Argos. 2015. *El mercado de trabajo en el sector agrario andaluz 2014*. Servicio Andaluz de Empleo, Consejería de Empleo, Empresa y Comercio, Junta de Andalucía.
Parker, S. 2004. *The Economics of Self-Employment and Entrepreneurship*. Cambridge: Cambridge University Press.
Peck, J. and A. Tickell. 2002. "Neoliberalizing Space." *Antipode* 34: 380–404.
Raudon, S. and C. Shore. 2018. The Eurozone Crisis, Greece and European Integration: Anthropological Perspectives on Austerity in the EU. *Anthropological Journal of European Cultures* 27(1): 64–83. DOI: 10.3167/ajec.2018.270111.
Roitman, J. 2013. *Anti-Crisis*. Durham: Duke University Press.
Roseberry, W. 1989. *Anthropologies and Histories: Essays in Culture, History, and Political Economy*. New Brunswick: Rutgers University Press.
Roseberry, W. 1994. "Hegemony and the Language of Contention." In G. Joseph and D. Nugent, eds. *Everyday Forms of State Formation. Revolution and the Negotiation of Rule in Modern Mexico*. Durham: Duke University Press.
Rossos, A. 1997. "Incompatible Allies: Greek Communism and Macedonian Nationalism in the Civil War in Greece, 1943-1949." *Journal of Modern History* 69(1): 42–76.
Sapkus, S. 2001. "Poder, cultura y oposición. Discutiendo algunas perspectivas sobre los procesos de dominación y Resistencia." *Razón y Revolución* 7.
Sutton, D. 2018. "The Concealed and the Revealed: Looking into the Hidden Bounty of The Land in Crisis Times." In D. Dalakoglou and G. Agelopoulos, eds. *Critical Times in Greece: Anthropological Engagements with the Crisis*. New York: Routledge.
Smith, G.A. 2011. "Selective Hegemony and Beyond—Populations with no Productive Function: A Framework for Enquiry." *Identities* 18(1): 2–38.
Tsekeris, C. & Kaberis, N. & Pinguli, M. 2015. *The Self in Crisis: The Experience of Personal and Social Suffering in Contemporary Greece*. GreeSE: LSE Hellenic Observatory Papers on Greece and Southeast Europe. June 2015.
Tsoucalas, C. 1986a. "Labour and Labourers in the Capital: Opacities, Questions and Hypotheses." *Greek Review of Social Research* 60: 3–71. (in Greek).
Tsoucalas, C. 1986b. *State, Society, Work in Postwar Greece*. Athens: Themelio. (in Greek).

Tsoulfidis, L. and M. Zouboulakis. 2016. "Greek Sovereign Defaults in Retrospect and Prospect." *South-Eastern Europe Journal of Economics* 14(2): 141–57.

Wettstein, F. 2009. *Multinational Corporations and Global Justice: Human Rights Obligations of a Quasi-Governmental Institution*. Stanford: Stanford University Press.

Williams, N. and T. Vorley. 2015. The Impact of Institutional Change on Entrepreneurship in a Crisis-Hit Economy: The Case of Greece. *Entrepreneurship & Regional Development* 27(1-2): 28–49.

Wolf, E.R. 1982. *Europe and the People without History*. Berkeley: University of California Press.

Wolf, E.R 1989. "Distinguished Lecture: Facing Power: Old Insights, New Questions." 88th meeting of the American Anthropological Association, 19 November, Washington.

Yus, R. and M.A. Torres. 2010. *Urbanismo difuso en suelo rústico. Deterioro ambiental y corrupción en la provincia de Málaga (El caso de la Axarquía)*. Vélez-Málaga: Gabinete de Estudios de la Naturaleza de la Axarquía.

Notes on Contributors

Stamatis Amarianakis is currently finalizing his PhD thesis on "Authoritative Models and Grassroots Responses to Crisis: Reconfigurations of Everyday Life in Chalkida, a Postindustrial Greek City" within the ERC Grassroots Economics Project at the University of Barcelona. His research focuses on households' and individuals' responses to the recent Greek crisis. He is interested in political economy, social solidarity and conflict, and has recently published "Grassroots Meanings of Informality: Resistance, Subsistence and Survival in the Greek Crisis Context" (ANUAC 2017).

Patricia Homs is Adjunct Professor in the Department of Social Anthropology at the University of Barcelona (UB), Spain. She has been a member of the research team in the Grassroots Economics ERC project. Her research interests include cooperatives, social and solidarity economies and entrepreneurship, especially as these relate to agrofood systems. She has been a member of Reciprocity Studies Group (University of Barcelona) since 2012 and of L'Aresta Agroecological Cooperative since 2015. Her recent publications include "(Des)encuentros entre las instituciones y la economía social y solidaria en Cataluña," *Revista de Antropología Social* (2019) and (with S. Narotzky) "Within and Beyond the Market System: Organic Food Cooperatives in Catalonia" in *Food Values in Europe* (Bloomsbury, 2019).

Carmen Leidereiter was awarded a doctorate at the University of Amsterdam in 2019 and has been a doctoral researcher in the ERC-Grassroots Economics Project at the University of Barcelona since 2014. She has undertaken extensive ethnographic fieldwork in Northern and Southern Portugal and is currently working on a monograph on *Permanent Crisis, Dispossession and Embodiment*. Her work focuses on labor–capital restructuring, the affective politics of embodiment and valuation and grassroots economies. Her most recent publication is "Floods that Burn: Spatialization of Class and Environmental Suffering in Austere Times," *Environment and Planning D: Space and Society* (2020).

Giacomo Loperfido is currently an invited fellow at the University of Barcelona. He holds a PhD in Social Anthropology from École des Hautes Études en Sciences Sociales (EHESS), and the Università degli Studi di Bergamo. Before joining the GRECO project, he undertook research in South Africa, Italy and Norway on issues of political violence and radicalism, cultural enclaves and social and economic disintegration in the wider context of a global-systemic crisis bringing about the decomposition of larger political and institutional orders. With Antonio Pusceddu he has recently published "Unevenness and Deservingness: Regional Differentiation in Contemporary Italy," *Dialectical Anthropology* (2019).

Patrícia Matos is an economic anthropologist trained in Lisbon and London. She was part of the ERC Grassroots Economics Project research team and is currently a post-doctoral researcher at CRIA/ISCTE—Institute University of Lisbon. Her research interests include neoliberalism, precarity and labor, gender and the body politics of austerity, welfare, needs and the moralities of distribution. Her forthcoming monograph *Disciplined Agency: Neoliberal Precarity, Generational Dispossession and Call Centre Labour In Portugal* will be published by Manchester University Press in 2020.

Susana Narotzky is Professor of Social Anthropology, University of Barcelona, Spain. She was awarded a European Research Council Advanced Grant to study the effects of austerity on Southern European livelihoods (*Grassroots Economics* [GRECO]). Her work is inspired by theories of critical political economy, moral economies, feminist economics and value regimes. Recent writing addresses the themes of making a living in futures without employment, political mobilization, social reproduction and class. Her most recent publications include "Austerity Lives in Southern Europe: Experience, Knowledge, Evidence and Social Facts," *American Anthropologist* (2019).

Jaime Palomera is a researcher at the Institute of Government and Public Policy (Universitat Autònoma de Barcelona). He writes about real estate and financial bubbles, the housing problem and responses to urban inequality. He has undertaken ethnographic research in several impoverished neighborhoods of Catalonia (Spain) and is actively involved in the fight for housing justice. He was an ERC postdoctoral researcher in the Grassroots Economics Project between 2013 and 2018.

Antonio Maria Pusceddu, PhD, is a researcher at the Centre for Anthropological Research (CRIA), ISCTE—Lisbon University Institute. He has carried out extensive fieldwork in Greece and Albania on borders, ethnicity and mobility. Drawing on his latest field research in southern Italy (as part of the Grassroots Economics Project), he is working on a book manuscript on labor, crisis and social reproduction. He is currently developing a new comparative research project, funded by the Portuguese Foundation for Science and Technology (FCT), on popular ecologies in southern Europe.

Diana Sarkis is an Assistant Professor in Economic Anthropology at the University of Barcelona, and a member of the International Research Network "Thimar" on agriculture, environment and labor in the Arab World. She has carried out extensive fieldwork in Syria (for her PhD) and Spain (within the ERC Grassroots Economics Project). Her work addresses labor/ capital relations in the context of structural adjustment, structures of feeling, forms of agency and frameworks of analysis. Recent publications include "'Amnarja' la wara' (We Are Going Backwards): Economic Reform and the Politics of Labour in Agrarian Syria," *Journal of Peasant Studies* (2020); and "'Muerta a trabajar': Consideraciones feministas sobre la crisis (de la reproducción social) en Vélez-Málaga (Spain)," *Revista Andaluza de Antropología* (2018).

Theodora Vetta is a Juan de la Cierva Fellow at the University of Barcelona. She has carried out extensive fieldwork in Serbia and Greece as part of her doctoral (EHESS, Paris) and postdoctoral research (ERC Grassroots Economics Project). Her work focuses on democratization conflicts, debt and labor under austerity regimes. Her recent publications include the monograph *Democracy Struggles: NGOs and the politics of Aid in Serbia* (Berghahn, 2018). She is currently working on a new project on energy transition and privatization, funded by the Greek Scholarship Foundation.

Index

Agency: 18, 61, 122, 125–6, 193, 200, 208–9 (see also Mobilization)
Autonomy (see Dependence; Dignity; Worth)
Austerity (see also Dispossession; Livelihood)
    Discourse of: 14–15, 81, 82, 89, 104, 113, 115, 120, 214
    Grassroots understandings of: 192–3, 196, 200, 206, 215, 218–30
    Macrosocial effects of: 6, 13, 15, 16, 26, 32, 33, 75, 79, 88, 106, 115–17, 125, 192, 194, 203, 206–7
    Policies of: 11, 25, 46, 80, 113, 115–17, 127, 162, 207, 210, 211, 224, 231

Bailouts: 5, 9, 10, 25, 28, 113, 211, 219 (see also Troika)
Bankruptcy: 14, 40, 77, 113, 177, 179–80
Body (see also Exhaustion; Gender; Health; Labor)
    Embodied experiences of austerity: 192–211
    Embodied metaphors: 16, 197, 198

Capitalism (see also Third Italy)
    Illiberal/monopoly: 3–7, 28 (see also Privilege)
    Neoliberal/competitive: 3, 5, 6, 8, 10, 11, 14, 51, 94, 98, 101, 102, 110, 107, 115, 127, 132, 134, 140, 144, 146, 150, 158–9, 162–4, 208, 219, 224, 225, 227 (see also Entrepreneurship)
    Rentier: 6, 12, 85, 131–42 (see also Homeownership)
    And social responsibility: 102, 106
    Uneven development of: 3, 4–6, 26, 150
Care: 12, 26, 66, 121, 124, 125, 127, 131, 143, 144, 145, 146, 152, 153, 165, 193, 197, 198, 206, 207 (see also Caregivers; Family; Generations)
Caregivers: 58–9, 64–6, 68, 69–70, 114–20, 135, 148, 201–3 (see also Care; Generations)
Cantieri di Cittadinanza: 51, 55, 58, 64–7
Caritas: 201, 223
Charity: 15, 68, 114, 118, 120–3
Citizenship
    Devaluation of: 65–7, 114, 127
    Exclusionary: 1, 7, 14
    Rights of: 7, 11, 13, 15, 45, 51, 55, 67, 68, 147
Civil war: 7, 228, 229
Class war (see also Crisis; Discourse)
    Waged by elites: 13–4, 218–23, 227
    Waged by northern countries: 13–14, 215, 223–9
Collective agency (see Future; Mobilization)
Cooperatives: 11, 12, 92, 94–9, 101–7 (see also Social and solidarity economy)
Credit: 9, 12, 40, 80, 81, 122, 131, 132, 138–40, 149, 154, 175, 178–81, 184–6, 216, 221, 222, 224
Crisis (see also Austerity; Class war; Dispossession; Social reproduction; Temporality; Unemployment)
    Discourses of: 10, 25–6, 75, 78–9, 89, 105, 151, 214–33

Index

Financial crisis of 2008: 9, 11, 16, 55, 127, 135, 186, 211
Cultural stereotypes (see Stereotypes)

Debt
  Household/private: 9, 10, 17, 40, 64, 116, 138–40, 149, 175, 179–80, 182, 186, 188, 204, 208, 221, 226, 232
  Sovereign: 9, 10, 15, 80, 81, 113, 116, 151, 166, 210, 211, 214, 226, 228, 232–3 (see also Austerity; Deficit)
Deficit: 9, 11, 14, 80, 81, 116, 144, 160, 166, 226 (see also Maastricht Treaty)
Deindustrialization: 4, 53, 127, 150–1, 216
Dependence: 6, 12, 16, 40, 45, 52, 53, 61, 63, 67, 120, 122, 127, 144, 147, 156, 157, 164, 175 (see also Interdependence)
Depoliticization: 7, 13–15, 100, 105, 116
Deregulation: 4, 5, 8, 9, 14, 98, 224 (see also Industrial restructuring)
Deservingness: 13, 15, 18, 39, 42, 43, 62, 115, 121, 124, 125, 134 (see also Meritocracy)
Dictatorship: 7, 74, 117, 158
Dignity: 13, 16, 17, 43, 55, 61, 118, 125, 155, 192, 199, 206, 217, 224 (see also Mobilization; Worth)
Discourse
  Elite/expert: 2, 11, 14, 15, 92, 97, 113, 133, 146, 150, 157, 162, 164, 214, 215, 218, 227, 228–9
  Media: 10, 11, 14, 15, 26
  Popular/grassroots: 2, 13–14, 92, 97–100, 143, 197, 198, 214–33 (see also Class war)
Dispossession: 4, 13, 15, 26, 107, 114, 115, 125, 127, 140, 146, 159, 192, 193, 206, 207, 210, 219, 220, 223, 225, 228

Downward mobility: 1, 15, 83, 132, 144, 160 (see also Future; Generations)

Education: 13, 16, 17, 33, 35, 39, 57, 69, 94, 107, 133–4, 144, 157, 192, 193, 222
Embodiment (see Body)
Emigration (see Migration)
Emotional labor (see Care)
Employment: 51, 54, 57, 61, 69, 73, 76, 93, 97, 101, 153 (see also Labor; Livelihood; Unemployment)
  For collective utility: 50–3, 54, 65–6 (see also Subsidized employment)
  Public sector: 30–35, 41, 44–6, 50
  Self-employment: 92–4, 97, 100, 225, 233 (see also Entrepreneurship)
  Stable/unstable: 1, 11, 30, 65, 67, 68, 75, 86, 88, 101, 107, 118, 145, 148, 151, 153, 154, 217 (see also Precariousness; Privilege)
Entrepreneurship: 107, 140
  And identity: 11, 12, 98–100, 173–88
  Promotion of: 3, 11–12, 92–4, 96, 97, 107, 115, 120, 127, 150, 156, 175, 176, 225
  And social economy: 92–112
Estarter: 96, 99, 107
European Central Bank: 9, 10, 25, 113 (see also Troika)
European Economic Community: 6–7, 8, 148, 219
European Commission: 1, 9, 28, 93, 157, 159 (see also Troika)
European convergence: 1, 8, 15, 28, 166, 214
European Employment Strategy: 93
European Monetary Union: 1, 9
Exhaustion: 118, 192–7, 200, 202, 203, 205, 206

Exploitation: 6, 15, 16, 29, 37, 65, 66, 101, 107, 178, 186, 199, 200, 206, 207, 210, 220, 223, 225, 228, 230

Familism (see Southern European welfare model; Stereotypes)
Family (see also Care; Generations; Informal employment; Kinship; Labor; Reciprocity; Southern European welfare model)
  Assets/property: 12, 40, 85, 124, 131–42, 184
  Businesses: 12, 30, 132–42, 163, 164, 166, 177, 178, 184, 186, 187, 233
  Conflict within: 85, 178, 217
  Support networks: 7, 12, 13, 132–3, 139, 150, 160
Feminism: 53, 127, 146, 164, 197, 207–10
Financial crisis (see Crisis)
Financialization: 3, 4, 16, 26, 28, 115, 131, 179, 224
Food: 13, 64, 86, 114, 137, 149
  Food banks: 116, 118, 120, 123, 201
  Food insecurity: 74, 118, 192, 200, 201
Future
  Prospects: 17, 18, 26, 42, 51, 67, 84, 86, 89, 118, 125, 137, 143, 145, 148, 152, 156, 159–65, 194, 197, 198, 217, 222–3, 230, 232 (see also Downward mobility; Generations; Temporality)
  Possibility for systemic change: 7, 126, 159, 200, 210 (see also Mobilization)

Gender: 18, 33, 43, 44, 52, 63, 67, 125, 145, 148, 152, 153, 193, 194, 195, 199, 207, 208, 209, 215, 217 (see also Body; Care; Caregivers; Family; Feminism; Southern European welfare model; Stereotypes; Unemployment)

Generations
  Care between: 152–7, 162–4, 193, 194, 196, 216
  Tensions between: 143–67
  Transfer of resources between: 16, 122, 147, 152, 153, 157, 159, 163, 164, 200, 216–17 (see also Pensions)

Health: 16, 31, 33, 34, 95, 126, 147, 154, 192, 200, 216, 217 (see also Exhaustion; Stress)
Healthcare: 13, 16, 43, 104, 117, 157, 200, 220, 222
Hegemony: 15, 92, 103, 104, 114, 115, 150, 208, 210, 214–16, 227, 228
Homeownership: 12, 17, 85, 138–41, 143, 153, 154, 184

Illegality (see Legality/illegality)
Immigrants: 7, 14, 69, 93, 137, 139
Industrial restructuring: 3, 8, 15–16, 25, 26, 28, 30, 44, 53, 56, 148–53, 180, 197, 214, 224 (see also Structural adjustment)
Inequality: 1, 6, 15, 16, 63, 66, 77, 96, 116, 126, 133, 186, 208, 209, 211, 229, 232 (see also Worth)
Informal (see also Family)
  Economy: 57, 89, 119, 120, 122, 165, 178
  Employment/livelihood: 5, 37, 57, 58, 60–7, 70, 74–89, 123, 147, 148, 150, 157, 202, 205, 216, 223
InOltre Helpdesk: 174, 175, 177
Interdependence: 115, 117, 120, 125, 126, 164, 216, 226 (see also Dependence)
Internal devaluation (see Labor, Dispossession)
Internal migration (see Migration)

Kinship: 3, 7, 11, 30, 33, 37, 42, 45, 117, 131, 132, 135–8, 140, 141, 152, 154, 178, 210 (see also Family; Reciprocity)

Labor
- Accidents: 29, 31, 40
- Aristocracy: 6, 33, 38–9, 45 (see also Privilege; Subcontracting; Unions)
- And capital: 6, 8, 13, 61, 106, 113, 148, 163, 186–7, 197, 207, 210, 215, 223–8, 231
- Day labor: 76, 83, 194, 197, 199, 218, 220, 221, 222
- Devaluation of: 3, 4, 5, 10, 11, 26, 33, 45, 52, 66, 98, 113, 116, 144, 163, 184, 198, 203, 206–11, 220
- Family: 84, 174, 176, 178, 185, 187
- Legislation: 8, 34, 50, 53–5, 61, 66, 107, 149, 160, 161, 165
- Movements (see Mobilization)
- Physical: 18, 31, 206 (see also Working class)
- Surplus: 5, 36, 52, 53, 75, 237

Labor unions (see Unions)
Lavori Socialmente Utili: 50–1, 54, 55
Legality and illegality: 4, 5, 7, 10, 12, 64, 73–89, 187, 216, 223
Livelihood (see Dispossession; Employment; Informal; Labor; Precariousness)

Maastricht Treaty: 1, 9, 132, 160, 166
Marzano Law: 180, 187
Media (see Discourse)
Memorandum of Understanding: 10, 32, 79, 223, 224 (see also Bailouts; Troika)
Meritocracy: 34, 39, 45, 46, 133, 162 (see also Deservingness)
Micro-privilege (see Privilege)
Migration: 8, 9, 16, 41, 83, 117, 137, 149, 155, 216
Mobilization: 7, 13, 14, 15, 26, 30, 43, 50, 55, 61, 62, 67, 68, 107, 160, 210
Morality: 3, 114, 115, 121, 125, 126, 163, 164, 193
Moral economy: 15, 144, 145–7, 152–4, 157, 162–5, 199, 219

Mutual help (see Solidarity)

Needs: 13, 15, 55, 68, 87, 88, 97, 104, 113–26, 126, 127, 159, 193
- Language of: 113–15, 120–1, 124, 125, 127
Neoliberalism (see Capitalism)
New Regionalism (see Southern European welfare model; Third Italy)

Outsourcing (see Subcontracting)

Pacchetto Treu: 53–4
Pensions: 13, 16, 28, 32, 40, 46, 58, 122, 123, 136, 143–5, 147–54, 156–67, 225
Pensioners: 12, 14, 125, 140, 160–4, 218, 231
Platform economy: 4, 6, 84, 97
Precariousness: 11, 14, 26, 29, 30, 35, 38, 39, 61, 65, 66, 92, 101, 132, 138, 143, 144, 148–53, 157, 164, 165, 194, 200, 208, 216, 217, 220, 222
Privatization: 10, 25–8, 33, 38, 39, 43–6, 53, 80, 157, 194, 207, 220, 222, 228 (see also Structural adjustment)
Privilege: 6, 7, 12, 13, 28, 33, 40, 41, 46, 60, 143, 148, 160, 162, 164, 215, 239

Reciprocity: 17, 95, 98, 119, 131, 132, 135, 137, 138, 139, 140, 141, 145, 160, 162, 173, 174, 178, 183
Refugees: 27, 41, 45
Regulation: 2, 4–6, 7–11, 12, 14, 17, 52, 53, 60, 63, 66, 76–82, 89, 149, 185, 186 (see also Deregulation; Scale)
Resilience: 14, 94, 101
Resistance: 7, 10, 18, 85–9, 101, 107, 159, 206, 208, 209, 210, 224, 228

Restructuring (see Industrial restructuring; Structural adjustment)

Scale: 2, 3, 6, 14, 44, 51, 66, 87, 92, 93, 116, 143, 147, 186, 215, 227, 242–3
  Of political economy: 3, 4, 124, 182, 223, 226, 228
  Of regulation: 7–11, 210
Second World War: 27, 227, 228, 229
Self-worth (see Worth)
Social and solidarity economy: 92–107 (see also Cooperatives, Solidarity Economy Network of Catalonia)
Social justice: 14, 92–5, 101 (see also Dignity; Worth)
Social reproduction: 10, 13, 18, 32, 52, 66, 102, 103, 120, 131, 140, 143–50, 158–64, 183, 184, 185, 194, 207, 210, 217
  Breakdown of: 3, 13, 14, 79, 116, 160, 165, 193–7, 200, 215–18, 229
Social security: 158, 166, 192, 201
  Benefits: 51, 58, 69, 114, 122, 193
  Contributions: 10, 84, 136, 157, 202
Solidarity: 13, 26, 40, 43, 62, 101, 103, 132, 133, 140–5, 151, 152, 158–65, 183, 186, 205, 219 (see also Cooperatives; Social and solidarity economy; XES Solidarity Economy Network)
Solidarity Economy Network of Catalonia (XES): 95, 96,
Southern European welfare model: 3, 131, 173–5, 184, 186, 207
Stereotypes: 1, 127, 150, 173, 186, 208, 214
Stress: 14, 51, 85, 117, 118, 194, 196, 200, 202 (see also Exhaustion; Health; Suicide)
Structural adjustment: 1, 15, 113, 124, 144, 149, 156, 157, 163, 200, 207, 210, 211, 220, 227, 231 (see also Labor; Industrial restructuring)
Structural violence (see Violence)
Subcontracting: 5, 12, 26, 29–30, 37, 40, 46, 59, 66, 75, 148, 165, 175, 179–80, 186
Subsidies: 5, 7, 11, 12, 96, 107, 114, 147, 149, 153, 163, 164
Subsidized employment: 50–61, 63, 66–7, 70
Suicide: 117, 174, 177, 182, 185, 187 (see also InOltre Helpdesk)
Sustainability:
  As a value: 92, 93, 95, 99, 101, 104, 143, 164
  Of debt, pensions and public services: 113, 115, 143–5, 156–7, 159, 161, 164 (see also Austerity)

Taxation
  Burden of: 10, 37, 74, 80–1, 84, 88, 113, 126, 136, 160, 194, 211–16, 219, 220, 225, 226, 231
  Corporate tax evasion: 4, 5, 13
  Petty tax evasion: 7, 10, 13, 77–81 (see also Resistance)
Temporality: 51, 54, 55, 60, 63, 65–9, 84, 88, 118, 222, 223, 227, 230 (see also Future)
Third Italy: 173–8, 183–7
Third sector: 13, 98, 106, 114, 131
Third Way: 183
Time (see Temporality)
Troika: 9, 25, 32, 211, 223, 227, 231, 232

Unemployment: 1, 4, 8, 11, 16, 26, 31, 36, 52–6, 66–9, 75, 92, 114, 116, 117, 127, 134, 145, 148, 151, 154, 155, 157, 165, 166, 180, 210, 214, 216, 217
  Benefits: 35, 36, 37, 53, 68, 97, 148, 153, 201
  Gendered: 57, 69, 143, 166, 194
  Structural: 54, 56, 93, 97, 98, 113, 120, 210, 225, 230, 231
  Youth and young adult: 11, 132, 149, 155, 165

Unions: 6, 14, 33, 38, 40, 43–5, 55, 59, 62–5, 148, 159–61, 164, 223–4

Valuation: 3, 13, 15–18, 53, 115, 121, 124, 199, 209 (see also Labor; Needs)

Violence: 6, 116, 193, 208, 215, 219, 229
   Structural: 194, 195, 200, 224

Working class: 1, 30, 76, 114–17, 132, 165, 203, 217, 220
   Pride: 134, 193, 199, 206, 219

Workfare: 11, 50–6, 65–7, 68, 127

Worth: 13, 15–17, 51–3, 59, 62–7, 88, 114, 115, 120, 122, 124, 126, 134, 147, 163, 164, 193, 200, 213, 206, 207, 209, 217, 232 (see also Dignity)

Thanks to our Patreon Subscribers:

Abdul Alkalimat
Andrew Perry

Who have shown their generosity and comradeship in difficult times.

Check out the other perks you get by subscribing to our Patreon – visit patreon.com/plutopress. Subscriptions start from £3 a month.

The Pluto Press Newsletter

Hello friend of Pluto!

Want to stay on top of the best radical books we publish?

Then sign up to be the first to hear about our new books, as well as special events, podcasts and videos.

You'll also get 50% off your first order with us when you sign up.

Come and join us!

Go to bit.ly/PlutoNewsletter